Transparency and Apperception

Transparency and Apperception: Exploring the Kantian Roots of a Contemporary Debate explores the links between the idea that belief is transparent and Kant's claims about apperception.

Transparency is the idea that a person can answer questions about whether she, for instance, believes something by considering, not her own psychological states, but the objects and properties the belief is about. This marks a sharp contrast between a first-person and third-person perspective on one's current mental states. This idea has deep roots in Kant's doctrine of apperception, the claim that the human mind is essentially self-conscious, and Kant held that it underlies the responsibility that a person has for certain of their own mental states. Nevertheless, the idea of transparency and its roots in apperception remain obscure and give rise to difficult methodological and exegetical questions. The contributions in this work address these questions and will be required reading for anyone working on this intersection of the philosophy of mind and language, and epistemology.

The chapters in this book were originally published in a special issue of the *Canadian Journal of Philosophy*.

Boris Hennig, **David Hunter** and **Thomas Land** are faculty members in the Philosophy Department at Ryerson University in Toronto, Canada.

Transparency and Apperception

Exploring the Kantian Roots of a Contemporary Debate

Edited by
Boris Hennig, David Hunter and Thomas Land

LONDON AND NEW YORK

First published 2020
by Routledge
2 Park Square, Milton Park, Abingdon, Oxon, OX14 4RN

and by Routledge
52 Vanderbilt Avenue, New York, NY 10017

Routledge is an imprint of the Taylor & Francis Group, an informa business

© 2020 Canadian Journal of Philosophy

Chapter 3 © 2019 Wolfgang Barz. Originally published as Open Access.

With the exception of Chapter 3, no part of this book may be reprinted or reproduced or utilised in any form or by any electronic, mechanical, or other means, now known or hereafter invented, including photocopying and recording, or in any information storage or retrieval system, without permission in writing from the publishers. For details on the rights for Chapters 3, please see the chapter's Open Access footnote.

Trademark notice: Product or corporate names may be trademarks or registered trademarks, and are used only for identification and explanation without intent to infringe.

British Library Cataloguing in Publication Data
A catalogue record for this book is available from the British Library

ISBN13: 978-0-367-47865-0
ISBN13: 978-0-367-51302-3 (pbk)

Typeset in Myraid Pro
by Newgen Publishing UK

Publisher's Note
The publisher accepts responsibility for any inconsistencies that may have arisen during the conversion of this book from journal articles to book chapters, namely the inclusion of journal terminology.

Disclaimer
Every effort has been made to contact copyright holders for their permission to reprint material in this book. The publishers would be grateful to hear from any copyright holder who is not here acknowledged and will undertake to rectify any errors or omissions in future editions of this book.

Contents

	Citation Information	vi
	Notes on Contributors	viii
1	Assertion and transparent self-knowledge *Eric Marcus and John Schwenkler*	1
2	Kant and the transparency of the mind *Alexandra M. Newton*	18
3	The puzzle of transparency and how to solve it *Wolfgang Barz*	44
4	Spontaneity and Self-Consciousness in the *Groundwork* and the B-*Critique* *Yoon Choi*	64
5	'I do not cognize myself through being conscious of myself as thinking': Self-knowledge and the irreducibility of self-objectification in Kant *Thomas Khurana*	84
6	Kant's "I think" and the agential approach to self-knowledge *Houston Smit*	108
7	Transparency and reflection *Matthew Boyle*	140
	Index	168

Citation Information

The chapters in this book were originally published in the *Canadian Journal of Philosophy*, volume 49, issue 7 (November 2019). When citing this material, please use the original page numbering for each article, as follows:

Chapter 1
Assertion and transparent self-knowledge
Eric Marcus and John Schwenkler
Canadian Journal of Philosophy, volume 49, issue 7 (November 2019), pp. 873–889

Chapter 2
Kant and the transparency of the mind
Alexandra M. Newton
Canadian Journal of Philosophy, volume 49, issue 7 (November 2019), pp. 890–915

Chapter 3
The puzzle of transparency and how to solve it
Wolfgang Barz
Canadian Journal of Philosophy, volume 49, issue 7 (November 2019), pp. 916–935

Chapter 4
Spontaneity and Self-Consciousness in the Groundwork *and the B-*Critique
Yoon Choi
Canadian Journal of Philosophy, volume 49, issue 7 (November 2019), pp. 936–955

Chapter 5

'I do not cognize myself through being conscious of myself as thinking': Self-knowledge and the irreducibility of self-objectification in Kant
Thomas Khurana
Canadian Journal of Philosophy, volume 49, issue 7 (November 2019), pp. 956–979

Chapter 6

Kant's "I think" and the agential approach to self-knowledge
Houston Smit
Canadian Journal of Philosophy, volume 49, issue 7 (November 2019), pp. 980–1011

Chapter 7

Transparency and reflection
Matthew Boyle
Canadian Journal of Philosophy, volume 49, issue 7 (November 2019), pp. 1012–1039

For any permission-related enquiries please visit:
www.tandfonline.com/page/help/permissions

Notes on Contributors

Wolfgang Barz, Department of Philosophy, Goethe University, Frankfurt, Germany

Matthew Boyle, Department of Philosophy, University of Chicago, Chicago, IL, USA

Yoon Choi, Department of Philosophy, Marquette University, Milwaukee, WI, USA

Thomas Khurana, Philosophy Department, University of Essex, Colchester, UK

Eric Marcus, Philosophy Department, Auburn University, Birmingham, AL, USA

Alexandra M. Newton, Department of Philosophy, University of California–Riverside, Riverside, CA, USA

John Schwenkler, Philosophy Department, Florida State University, Tallahassee, FL, USA

Houston Smit, Department of Philosophy, University of Arizona, Tucson, AZ, USA

Assertion and transparent self-knowledge

Eric Marcus and John Schwenkler

ABSTRACT
We argue that honesty in assertion requires non-empirical knowledge that what one asserts is what one believes. Our argument proceeds from the thought that to assert honestly, one must follow and not merely conform to the norm 'Assert that p only if you believe that p'. Furthermore, careful consideration of cases shows that the sort of doxastic self-knowledge required for following this norm cannot be acquired on the basis of observation, inference, or any other form of detection of one's own doxastic states. It is, as we put it, transparent rather than empirical self-knowledge.

1. Belief is a psychological state or attitude, and thus for a person to know what she believes is for her to know herself to be in a certain state, or to have a certain attitude toward how things are. Doxastic self-knowledge is therefore knowledge of psychological reality. And it is natural to conclude from this that this knowledge must be justified through an empirical process, i.e. 'a process in which one observes or detects one's own mental states' (Gertler 2011, 255). According to this natural line of thought, just as I can only come to know what you believe by watching your deliberate actions, observing how you respond automatically to certain stimuli, and keeping track of what you assert, so in order for me to know what *I* believe my doxastic states must somehow be made manifest to me.

Our aim in this paper is to challenge this last assumption. We refer to the position in question as the *empirical* conception of doxastic self-knowledge, since according to it knowledge of one's beliefs, if it is to be knowledge at all, must be a kind of empirical knowledge, or knowledge that is grounded in evidence.[1] On the empirical conception, what accounts for the special character of doxastic self-knowledge is not that this knowledge is non-empirical, but rather the *kind* of empirical grounding it possesses. In particular, self-knowledge is thought to be different from knowledge of other minds because only in one's own case does one have direct or 'first-personal' access to thoughts, feelings, and urges that are manifested only ambiguously in one's overt behavior. The distinctively first-personal character of this evidence, plus the fact that it is (allegedly) abundant and (again, allegedly) less subject to misinterpretation, is supposed to put a person in a position to know her own beliefs in a way that no one else can. Even if this knowledge is not exhaustive or infallible, the empirical conception is supposed to account for how a person usually knows *more* about her beliefs that anyone else can, and how this self-knowledge is usually *more secure* than anyone else's knowledge of her beliefs will be. Nevertheless, according to the empirical conception, knowledge of one's own beliefs is similar to knowledge of the beliefs of others insofar as both are justified through evidence. It is, on the empirical conception, the difference in the *character* and *extent* of the evidence available to the believer herself that is the ground of first-person authority.[2]

Our paper will argue against this position by exploring the connection between self-knowledge and assertion. The empirical conception is false, we will argue, because it cannot account for the way that a person is ordinarily able to express her beliefs by asserting their content. Honest assertion is *speaking one's mind*. And this requires knowledge that one is in the state of mind that one speaks from. But speaking one's mind is not speaking *about* one's mind, and so evidence *that* one believes something cannot put one in a position honestly to assert *what* one believes. Rather, it is a condition of honest assertion that a person's grasp of the belief she asserts be grounded non-empirically, i.e. not in *any* sort of evidence at all.

2. Contemporary discussions of assertion often focus on the knowledge norm:

(KA) Assert that p only if you know that p.

Simplifying somewhat, there are two ways of failing to conform to (KA). One is by asserting something you merely believe but do not know, which is epistemically irresponsible.[3] The other is by asserting something that you don't even believe, which is dishonest.[4] Philosophers discussing the norms of assertion have typically focused on the requirement of epistemic responsibility – for example, they have considered whether acceptable assertion really does require knowledge, or simply justification, and so on (see, e.g., Williamson 2000; Weiner 2005; and Kvanvig 2009). Our concern, however, is not with this, but solely with what is required for assertion to be honest, and thus with conditions of satisfying the following norm:

(BA) Assert that p only if you believe that p.

We grant for the sake of argument that as with most (if not all) norms it might sometimes be best, all things considered, to violate (BA). If this is true it does not show that (BA) is not a norm governing honesty, but only that it might sometimes be best to be dishonest, i.e. to assert something that one does not believe – as if, say, the Nazi at the door asks whether there are any Jews in your attic. Thus we put (BA) forward only as an articulation of the norm governing assertion where the requirement to be honest is not trumped by other considerations.[5] The rule is not intended as a guide to acceptable assertion in general. It captures *part* of our ordinary concept of *one* important feature that assertion often aims at, namely honesty.

It is because assertion is an action, something that a person *does* rather than something that merely happens, that norms for assertion take the form of *rules* that one who asserts can choose whether or not to follow. This is why (BA) is formulated in the imperative mood: it tells a person what *to do* in order to avoid asserting dishonestly. And this is the first step toward seeing the connection between honesty and doxastic self-knowledge. For in order to hold oneself to the rule (BA) – to *obey* this imperative, to *follow* the rule as opposed to merely conforming to it – one who asserts must understand whether or not the conditions it specifies are satisfied. And this shows that honest assertion requires a grasp of one's own beliefs: a person who was 'self-blind' to her doxastic attitudes would be in no position to follow (BA), since she could not tell whether she believed what she was asserting.

We can give further support to this preliminary conclusion by reflecting on a hypothetical case. Begin by imagining a man to whom it is vitally important that he believe that he has lived an enviable life. However, 'deep down' the man does not believe this, but rather believes that he spent much of his childhood living in fear of his father's anger and disapproval. This belief overwhelms him with shame, and it is precisely this shame that makes it so important for the man to believe that his life has been wonderful. He has for a long time managed to avoid thinking about the horror of his childhood, repressing his uncomfortable beliefs in a way that suits the false self-conception to which he clings – a conception according to which, contrary to fact, he is really very happy with his childhood.[6] Yet this repression has not changed the man's actual beliefs about his childhood; it is only a way of keeping himself from bringing them to mind. When he reflects on questions that bear on the quality of his life-experience – even the question of whether he had a happy childhood – his answers reflect his distorted self-conception, rather than his repressed beliefs. So although this man believes that he had an unhappy childhood, this belief lies outside his ken.

So far described, the situation of the man we have just imagined constitutes the **Basic Case** whose details we will vary in several ways as our argument proceeds. In our first variant on that case, suppose that this man finds himself listening to a friend bemoan her very unhappy childhood. This testimony might have brought to mind the man's belief that his own child-hood was unhappy as well, but instead it prompts him to tell himself how very happy he is with the way his life has gone. Despite this, in an effort to appear sympathetic to his friend the man says to her: 'I too had an unhappy childhood'. Call this the case of the **Would-Be Liar**. The essential thing to see is that in speaking as he does, the Would-Be Liar *asserts what he believes* – since as we described the Basic Case this person does in fact believe that he had an unhappy childhood. Clearly, however, the Would-Be Liar does not speak honestly when he asserts this, since his purpose in speaking is to mislead his friend as to what his own life was like. The Would-Be Liar has not *followed* the rule (BA), despite having acted in conformity with it. This example shows that an assertion is not honest just because what the speaker asserts is what she in fact believes. In order to speak honestly, one's assertion and one's belief must not correspond merely by accident.

The case of the Would-Be Liar brings into focus the question that we will consider in more detail below: What is required, beyond merely having a belief in what one asserts, for an assertion to be honest? In particular, what sort of *grasp* of one's belief does honest assertion require?

3. It is tempting to suggest that the reason it is not honest for the Would-Be Liar to say that he had an unhappy childhood, even though he does in fact believe this, is simply that he is ignorant of his belief – that is, the problem is simply that he does not *believe* that he has this belief. Let us suppose that this is so far correct: the Would-Be Liar does not have such a second-order belief. And now let us ask: Would *believing that he believes* that his child-hood was unhappy be enough for the Would-Be Liar to assert honestly that this was so?

Not necessarily. Consider the **Lucky Spiritualist**, who as in the Basic Case has a repressed belief that he had an unhappy childhood. The Lucky Spiritualist visits his psychic, who tells the Spiritualist that he (the Spiritualist) believes his childhood was unhappy. And now suppose that *solely for this reason*, the Spiritualist ascribes this belief to himself. Unlike the Would-Be Liar, the Lucky Spiritualist believes that he believes that he had an unhappy childhood. Despite this, it seems clear that if the Lucky Spiritualist were to tell someone that his childhood was unhappy, this still would not be an honest assertion. For the most that the psychic's testi-mony could put the Spiritualist in a position to assert honestly (if irre-sponsibly) is exactly what she tells him, namely that he *believes* that he had an unhappy childhood. This is because the psychic tells the Spiritualist nothing about his childhood itself, but only about his state of mind towards it – whereas it is his *childhood* that the man would be describing if he said that his childhood was unhappy. Because of this, even though the Spiritualist meets the condition just stipulated – he not only believes, but also believes that he believes, that he had an unhappy childhood – he still cannot honestly assert this.

Nor will it close the gap if we suppose that the man's belief about his belief is grounded in something more reliable than the testimony of a psychic. Consider the **Faithful Patient**, who is otherwise just like the Lucky Spiritualist, but is told not by his psychic but by his highly skilled therapist that he (the Patient) believes that he had an unhappy childhood. Suppose the Faithful Patient ascribes this belief to himself on the strength of the therapist's testimony. We can imagine that the therapist possesses excellent evidence about the Patient's belief as it is manifested in his unguarded behaviors, so that in virtue of this diagnosis the Faithful Patient *knows* that he believes that his childhood was unhappy. Nevertheless the Faithful Patient cannot, just on the strength of this testimony, honestly assert what he knows himself to believe, viz., *that his childhood was unhappy*. For no matter the quality of the evidence provided by the therapist's diagnosis of the Patient's beliefs about his childhood, if the Patient knows of those beliefs only in *this* way he is not in a position to assert honestly *that things are* as he believes them to be. There is, then, more to the norm of honesty than the requirement that one assert only something that one knows oneself to believe.

4. At this point it is worth offering a preliminary diagnosis of why it is that the Lucky Spiritualist or Faithful Patient cannot honestly assert that he had an unhappy childhood. To do this, let us draw on a pair of cases described by Jonathan Dancy (2000, 125), which he in turn credits to John Hyman. First there is Zoe, who calls the zookeeper because she believes there is an elephant in her bathtub. Zoe's action makes sense if we see it as the action of someone who believes that an elephant is in her bathtub and then acts, as we will put it, *from the point of view* of this belief – or through its lens, so to speak. Zoe calls the zookeeper in light of what she believes, namely that there is an elephant in her bathtub. And it is this (putative) fact that she takes to justify her action – an action that is an attempt to do something that will get rid of the elephant.

In contrast to Zoe's case consider also that of Silas, who believes that there is an elephant in his bathtub and therefore places a call, not to the zookeeper, but rather to his trusted psychiatrist. Silas differs from Zoe in that the position of the supposed elephant is not at issue in what he does – for it is rather his *belief* about the elephant that he is trying to get rid of. To make sense of Silas we need to appeal to his psychotic belief but not, as with Zoe, as an attitude that characterizes the *point of view from which* he acts. We can mark this difference by saying that Silas calls the psychiatrist *in light of* his belief rather than from its point of view, or through the lens on the world that it provides. Whereas Zoe will justify her action by appeal to the believed fact that there is an elephant in the bathtub, Silas will justify his by the believed fact that he believes this.

The relevance of these cases to those of the Lucky Spiritualist and Faithful Patient should be clear. Like Silas, neither the Lucky Spiritualist and Faithful Patient can reasonably act *from the point of view* of his belief that he had an unhappy childhood. Yet this is just the kind of act that honest assertion is: in asserting that *p* one says something *about the world*, just as in calling the zookeeper Zoe is attempting to do something about the elephant. As we described their situations, the most that the Lucky Spiritualist or Faithful Patient can reasonably do is take steps to do something *about his belief*, in light of the fact *that* he believes this. These steps might include finding out whether the belief itself is true – and then, perhaps, describing that reality in turn. Yet as long as all he goes on is the testimony of a psychic or a therapist about his own attitudes, the man cannot honestly assert that his childhood *was* as he believes it to be, despite the fact that he believes or knows that he believes this.

Our task, then, is to characterize the distinctive form of self-understanding that makes it possible to speak honestly *from the point of view* of a belief, where this involves something more than knowingly saying what one actually believes.

5. Let us ask again: What more is required for honest assertion than the grasp of one's beliefs that is possessed by the Lucky Spiritualist or Faithful Patient – or, for that matter, by someone like Silas? A simple answer is that the Spiritualist and Patient grasp their beliefs only in an alienated or 'third-personal' way, i.e. a way that would put any other person in receipt of the same testimony in the same position as the Spiritualist and Patient them-selves. And clearly a third party who overheard, say, the therapist's testimony about the Faithful Patient's belief could not then assert that the Patient had an unhappy childhood. Does the fact that the Faithful Patient is also a mere 'observer' of his attitude explain why he cannot honestly assert it?

There are two ways of developing this simple answer, one of which we accept while finding the other inadequate. The inadequate diagnosis is the one that proceeds from the assumption that we outlined at the start of this paper, that doxastic self-knowledge must be grounded in evidence. So long as one accepts this assumption it will seem that the trouble with the Faithful Patient is simply that the *evidence* that grounds his second-order belief is insufficiently first-personal – that is, the trouble is that his evidence is of the second- or third-personal kind, whereas properly *first-personal evidence* would do the trick. By contrast, our more radical diagnosis is that a truly first-personal grasp of what one believes is not grounded in evidence at all.

To see why we favor this more radical proposal, consider one last variant on our Basic Case, in which the role of the Faithful Patient's therapist is occupied by the subject himself, and where the process through which he comes to know his beliefs arises directly from subjective access to his own 'internal' thoughts, feelings, urges, and so on. Call this person the **Perceptive Introspector**. The Introspector notices how he becomes curiously distracted when someone asks directly about his childhood, and how he always tends to think instead of how well-prepared for success he emerged as a young adult. He also notices that although he is an enthusiastic film buff, when invited to see films such as the *400 Blows* or *Pather Panchali*, films he knows to be about difficult childhoods, he always finds himself unaccountably yearning to do something else. It strikes him that these and similar reactions reveal that he believes himself to have had an unhappy childhood, while wishing to avoid being conscious of this belief. This knowledge is reached in a way that is available to no one else, since no one else but the Introspector can have direct access to his thoughts, feelings, and inclinations. Despite this, the knowledge still will not put the Introspector in a position to assert that he had an unhappy childhood. For the position of the Perceptive Introspector is really no different from that of Silas, the Faithful Patient, or the Lucky Spiritualist: his relation to his belief about his childhood is such that he cannot honestly speak *from its point of view* – despite the fact that this is a belief he actually holds, and knows himself to hold in a way that no one else could know this. This example reveals that even 'first-personal' evidence about of one's beliefs is not sufficient for honest assertion.

We will turn in §7 to consider whether honest assertion might be grounded in some other sort of first-personal evidence than that which the Perceptive Introspector draws on. Before that, in §6 we consider a different strategy for responding to our argument.

6. Thus far we have argued that neither merely believing something, nor believing that one believes it, nor knowing that one believes it, nor knowing this belief on the basis of specifically first-personal evidence, is enough to make possible the honest assertion of a belief. It might seem, however, that the missing element we have thus far failed to discover lies not in the relation between the speaker and her belief, but rather in the relation between the speaker and world. Indeed, we observed above that assertion, i.e. speaking one's mind, is not (in general[7]) a way of speaking *about* one's mind. When we express our beliefs through assertion, we do this by speaking about the *objects* of our beliefs, and so the grounds on which we do this must include grounds for taking these objects to be as we say them to be. But evidence *that one believes* something does not (in general[8]) provide any grounds for thinking *that things are* as one believes them to be.

This diagnosis suggests a way of rebutting our challenge to the empirical conception of self-knowledge. Perhaps the problem has been with attempting to understand the honesty of assertion simply through (BA), a norm that says nothing about the *truth* of one's beliefs – whereas one who asserts honestly must do so out of a concern that she say what is true. Given this, one might conclude that what makes honest assertion impossible in the cases described above is only that these subjects would violate a norm against asserting falsehoods:

(TA) Assert that *p* only if *p*.

The proposal on behalf of the empirical conception would then be this. Honest assertion requires not only following (BA), which presupposes a grasp of one's beliefs, but also following (TA), which presupposes a grasp of the fact that things are as one believes them. The Faithful Patient and Perceptive Introspector fail to follow (TA) – and it is *this*, rather than their empirical route to doxastic self-knowledge that explains why they cannot assert their beliefs honestly. To speak from the point of view of a belief, as honesty requires, is to speak with the truth of the believed proposition in mind.

We agree that an aim to assert only what is true is among the conditions of honest assertion. We deny, however, that the envisioned appeal to (TA) as a supplement to (BA) offers a way to defend the empirical conception. This is because, as we will argue below, a correct understanding of (TA) as giving a requirement of honest assertion reveals that following (TA), properly understood, *just is* following (BA), properly understood. Furthermore, this internal connection between belief and truth as conditions of honesty cannot be understood except in light of the thesis that, in paradigmatic cases, a person knows her own beliefs in a non-empirical manner.

To begin, notice that as (TA) is a rule, there is once again more to following it than merely conforming to it. A person who just *happens* to assert something that is true – as a variant on the Would-Be Liar perhaps might[9] – has not thereby asserted honestly, since the conformity between her assertion and the truth will have been an accident. Nor, however, is it enough to add that one who asserts honestly must not only speak the truth but also believe what she asserts, since the Would-Be Liar or any of the other characters above, who do believe what they assert, could *happen* also to speak truly without thereby being honest in their assertions. To use a common metaphor, following (TA) means asserting what is true in a way that *aims* at asserting what is true: and this 'aiming' will be part of the self-conscious activity of the speaker, who must *understand herself* to be speaking with an aim of being truthful. The task of articulating (TA) as a condition of honesty thus raises all of the same questions that arose in our discussion (BA). It cannot help us to resolve them. And so the proposal in question is inadequate.

This point can also be reached from the opposite direction. Just as it is possible to conform to (TA) without following it, so it is possible to *try* to follow (TA) but fail to do so. Such a person will aim at the truth in her assertion but fail to hit her target; she will assert *by mistake* something that happens to be false. While there is a failure here, there will not have been any lapse in honesty. And the intelligibility of this form of failure seems to turn on what the speaker believes: a person will *try* to follow (TA) only if what she asserts is something she believes, and this attempt will be a failure if her belief is false. But once again, not just any assertion of something one believes will amount to an honest attempt to follow (TA), as the examples in the previous section make clear: e.g. the Perceptive Introspector will not even have *tried* to follow (TA) if he asserts, merely on the strength of the 'internal' evidence revealing his belief, that he had an unhappy childhood. The truth or falsity of his assertion is irrelevant to that assessment.

We are now in a position to see why the envisioned response to our argument cannot succeed. It is true that the Perceptive Introspector, Faithful Patient, and Lucky Spiritualist all fail to satisfy the condition on truthfulness given in (TA). Each of them asserts what he believes, and does so because he understands himself to believe this, but *does not* aim to assert only what is true. But this reveals not that honest assertion has a truth-requirement *in addition* to the requirement to assert only what one believes. It reveals instead that, properly understood, the truth-requirement (TA) and the belief-requirement (BA) are different ways of formulating the very same condition. A person who is in a position to follow the norm of truth as stated in (TA) must know not only how *things* are, but also how *she* is, in respect of the requirement to be truthful. This is brought out in the fact that a person who asserts dishonestly what turns out to be true won't then conclude that she wasn't being dishonest after all, while one who asserts honestly what happens to be false may retreat to the judgment that she *believed* what she said, and so at least wasn't being dishonest. But we have yet to see how this doxastic self-knowledge can be grounded in evidence, including evidence of a specially 'first-personal' kind. And the introduction of (TA) does not close that gap.

7. We argued in §2 that in order to assert honestly, a speaker must not only believe what she asserts, but must also grasp the fact that she believes this. The argument of §§3–5 questioned whether this grasp could arise from an empirical process, even one whose nature and scope were distinctively first-personal. Our conclusion, which we work out in more detail in §8 below, is that the self-knowledge that grounds the possibility of honest assertion must be non-empirical. But first we will consider a final reply on behalf of the empirical conception.

The reply we will consider begins with the modest idea that it is dishonest to assert a proposition that does not *seem* to one to be true:

(SA) Assert that *p* only if *p* seems true.

The next step in this reply is the observation that since people tend to believe the things that seem true to them, the fact that something seems to one to be true can provide an empirical route to doxastic self-knowledge – knowledge, that is, that one believes this seemingly true thing. And the final step is the observation that it *will not seem* to our subject in the Basic Case, or any of our variants on it, as if he had an unhappy childhood. Thus, it will be proposed, the true lesson of these cases is that honesty requires that the asserted proposition seem to the speaker to be true, and that its seeming-to-be-true be part of the speaker's route to knowledge that she believes it.

The details of this strategy will depend in part on how one explicates the relevant sense of 'seems'. One way is phenomenological:

> (SA-P) Assert that *p* only if *p* phenomenally seems true.

The concept of a phenomenal seeming – that is, a proprietary phenomenology that attends to actively considering and affirming the truth of a proposition – is contentious,[10] but we will not dwell on that here. We note only that this first interpretation of (SA) can be contrasted with another one, where a person understands her belief not through a bit of phenomenology but rather through an *epistemic* status that links her belief to the world:

> (SA-J) Assert that *p* only if you have compelling doxastic justification for believing that *p*.

This latter condition will seem plausible insofar as we observe that people tend to believe the things that they have compelling doxastic justification for believing, which means that satisfying (SA-J) will be evidence that one satisfies the condition in (BA). However, unlike the routes to self-knowledge of the Faithful Patient and Perceptive Introspector, the possession of compelling doxastic justification also links a person to the *truth* of what she believes, perhaps putting her in a position to assert this belief honestly.

Both (SA-P) and (SA-J) are attractive ways to explain the impossibility of honest assertion in our variations on the Basic Case, since as we have granted it will not seem to the Would-Be Liar, Lucky Spiritualist, Faithful Patient, or Perceptive Introspector as if the beliefs they assert are true, nor will they take themselves to be justified in holding those beliefs. Given this, it may seem that (SA-P) or (SA-J), separately or perhaps in combination, identifies the privileged empirical route to self-knowledge that is missing in those cases. But we will argue below that they do not.

Our initial argument for this conclusion is that (SA-P) and (SA-J) do not give *necessary* conditions for honest assertion: that is, it is possible to assert honestly even if the conditions of (SA-P) and (SA-J) are not satisfied. Consider first that, according to (SA-P), one is dishonest if one makes an assertion unaccompanied by a phenomenal seeming-true. Some doubt whether there is any such phenomenal state. But even the non-doubters couldn't plausibly maintain that a phenomenal seeming accompanies *every* occasion of honest assertion. Over the course of just a single conversation, we might make dozens of assertions about matters that we consider settled, and we may not be actively thinking at all about what we are saying. The idea that each such assertion will be dishonest unless accompanied by a subjective appearance of the truth of the asserted proposition is absurd. This shows that it is possible to assert honestly without satisfying the condition in (SA-P).

(SA-J) avoids this difficulty. So long as a subject makes an assertion partly in light of her justification for thinking that *p* is true, she will be following (SA-J). Her justification need not be *phenomenally* present (whatever that might mean); all that matters is that the subject understands it to be there.[11] There is, however, still a problem with this condition, namely that one can assert something honestly *without* taking oneself to be justified in believing this. For it's not particularly unusual that one believes something for which one knows one lacks justification. If one asserts such a belief, then others might find fault with this,[12] but their grounds for doing so could not rightly include one's having been dishonest – after all, what one asserted is exactly what one believed, and one asserted it from the point of view of the belief itself. *Honesty* does not require asserting only what one takes oneself to be doxastically justified in believing. Even if the *knowledge* norm for assertion involves (SA-J), the requirements of honesty do not.

We take these defects with (SA-P) and (SA-J) to be incontrovertible and fatal to the reply under consideration. There is, however, a more general problem with this reply that we think is worth reflecting on. For there may linger in the mind of the reader a thought that, even if (SA-P) and (SA-J) do not work, (SA) itself remains unimpeached. Behind this thought lies the idea that *(a)* the doxastic knowledge necessary for following (BA) is something beyond holding the belief itself, *(b)* the extra factor is a piece of evidence, and *(c)* the evidence in question must point to one's belief 'from the inside', so to speak. Condition *(c)* refers to the 'seeming' that according to (SA) is a requirement of honest assertion. Our objections to (SA-P) and (SA-J) may thus seem not to impugn this intuition as such, but only to show that more needs to be done to articulate the relevant sense of 'seems'.

The work required to achieve this would be considerable. The phenomenological and epistemic routes considered above are hopeless. Moreover, one can make trouble for (SA) itself. For example, even if a philosopher takes herself to have worked out a convincing proof of, say, compatibilism about free will, she might nonetheless find that the proposition 'Free will and determinism are compatible' *seems false* – especially if she has not recently rehearsed the proof for herself. Nonetheless, it is hard to see how there would be anything *dishonest* in asserting that proposition, if in fact she believes it in the face of the recalcitrant seeming. If this is correct, then it is possible to assert something honestly even if it seems to one to be false. But let us put these worries aside and focus on the very idea that the way things seem to a person could be the privileged source of evidence through which she attains non-alienated, distinctively first-personal knowledge of her belief.

The deeper problem with the appeal to (SA) as a defense of the empirical conception is that there is no good reason why, *if* honest assertion is a matter saying what one knows oneself to believe and the evidence constituted by seeming-truth is good enough to confer this knowledge, then evidence of *other* kinds – i.e., the kinds operative in the cases of the Perceptive Introspector and the Faithful Patient – wouldn't be good enough as well. This concern is especially pressing when we recognize the extent to which how things seem to a person is *not* an infallible indication of what she believes, as the Basic Case and our variants on it all bring out. If we accept that there are cases where a belief is better known 'third-personally' than from the inside, then as long as the role of seeming-truth in doxastic self-knowledge is understood in empirical terms there is no reason why it should be impossible honestly to assert a belief that one knows of only through these other kinds of evidence. The distinction between the right and wrong sorts of empirical process is entirely ad hoc, and raises the suspicion that this requirement is a strained attempt to accommodate a very different truth using the wrong set of resources.[13]

We conclude that (SA) will not help in defending the empirical conception against our arguments. It is time to propose an alternative.

8. We have argued that the empirical conception of doxastic self-knowledge makes it impossible to understand the first-personal grasp of one's beliefs that is required for honest assertion. This is not only because there is no credible account of the empirical process that could permit such a grasp, but also because the idea that *some* empirical processes can ground the required self-knowledge, while other processes that are otherwise equally reliable will not do in this respect, is unmotivated. The conclusion we draw from this is that when honest assertion is possible it must arise from a grasp of one's beliefs that is not grounded in evidence of *any* sort. Following Moran (2001) and others, we can state this conclusion by saying that ordinary self-knowledge of one's beliefs, i.e. the sort of assertion that allows one to assert those beliefs honestly, is *transparent* to belief itself.

The idea that doxastic self-knowledge is transparent finds a classic formulation in a familiar passage from Gareth Evans's *Varieties of Reference*:

> ... in making a self-ascription of belief, one's eyes are, so to speak, or occasionally literally, directed outward – upon the world. If someone asks me 'Do you think there is going to be a third world war?', I must attend, in answering him, to precisely the same outward phenomena as I would attend to if I were answering the question 'Will there be a third world war? (Evans (1982, 225)

Against the empirical conception, we propose that it is only when doxastic self-knowledge is *transparent to belief* in the way described by Evans that a person can assert her belief honestly. Only to the extent that a person knows her belief transparently can she follow the rule (BA) by expressing this belief in honest assertion, speaking *from its point of view* just as Zoe calls the zookeeper because she believes that there's a pink elephant in the bathtub. One who speaks in this way is not merely asserting what she believes (as does Would-Be Liar does), is not merely asserting what she believes or knows herself to believe (as do the Lucky Spiritualist, Faithful Patient and Perceptive Introspector). She is asserting that *p* in light of the (putative) fact that *p*. She speaks honestly, because she is speaking *from the point of the view* of the belief she expresses.

Still one might wonder: How is it so much as possible that a person could have non-empirical knowledge of her beliefs? The argument of this paper does not depend on any specific answer to this question, but it does rule out a misinterpretation of the notion of transparency that has gained some currency in the literature.[14] According to this misinterpretation, transparent self-knowledge arises from a process of the following form:

Step 1: Consider whether *p* is true.
Step 2: If it is, then conclude that one believes that *p*.

For the reasons we explained in §7, we agree with many would-be critics of the transparency method that it is incredible that such a process should be the ground of doxastic self-knowledge. That is, if this process is understood so that the judgment (or appearance of truth, or proposition judged) generated in Step 1 functions as *evidence* justifying the doxastic self-ascription in Step 2, the proposal in question is just a version of the view that we have been arguing against. It is not an account of *non-empirical* self-knowledge.

However, as long as the empirical conception of doxastic self-knowledge is taken for granted, it will seem inevitable that the method of transparency should be construed in this way – as a process by which beliefs about one's own beliefs are justified. But what is Evans offering, if not an account in which a believer's view 'on the world' feeds into a process that results in well-grounded doxastic self-ascriptions? We propose that the key to avoiding this misinterpretation is to see that, for the person who knows her belief transparently, the judgments '*p*' and 'I believe that *p*' *are not separable* in the way that the empirical conception assumes they must be. To say that these judgments are not separable is to say that, for the self-knowing believer, the questions they address – respectively, whether *p* and whether she believes that *p* – do not concern distinct matters, such that her answer to one could be the *basis* of her answer to the other.[15]

There are at least two ways that this inseparability can be understood. **Constitutivist** theories hold that we can have non-empirical knowledge of our beliefs because to take oneself to believe something is, at least in the right conditions, also to believe it.[16] As long as the self-ascription through which belief is supposed to be constituted is not grounded empirically, such a view would avoid our objections to the empirical conception. We note, however, an important barrier to making good sense of Constitutivist proposals: they seem to require seeing doxastic self-attribution as entirely groundless, as the product of a brute disposition or something along these lines.[17] This avoids the pitfalls of the empirical conception but is hardly a credible interpretation of Evans's insight, nor do we find it to possess much independent plausibility of its own.

An alternative to Constitutivism is the **Self-Conscious Conception** of doxastic self-knowledge. This conception reverses the Constitutivist's order of explanation, holding that it is in the nature of belief to be self-conscious, and that because of this a person does not need to rely on introspection or any other empirical process as a source of knowledge of her beliefs. The thought is not that (as for the Constitutivist) the thinker simply finds herself believing that she believes that p and, in virtue of this fact, believes that p. Rather, according to the Self-Conscious Conception a person is ordinarily in a position to grasp what she believes simply in virtue of believing it, as it is part of what it is to view a proposition with the belief-attitude that one thereby knows oneself to so view it. Developing this approach in detail requires explaining how it could be in the nature of a psychological attitude like belief to be non-empirically self-known – a task beyond the scope of this paper.[18]

Nothing in what we have argued here bears directly on the question of which of these accounts (or perhaps some other) of transparent self-knowledge is the right one. Our central contention is that *some* explanation of how there can be non-empirical knowledge of belief is required for an adequate account of honest assertion. Full development of this position is work for another occasion.[19]

Notes

1. What we call the *empirical* conception is equivalent to what Gertler (Gertler 2011) calls *empiricism* about self-knowledge. We prefer our terminology because we deny that what Gertler calls 'rationalism' is the only alternative to it. We wish to emphasize that in rejecting the empirical conception we do not deny that *what is known* (viz., the thinker's belief) in an instance of doxastic self-knowledge is an empirical fact. Rather, our claim is that the *process by which* such facts are known is not empirical in the sense just spelled out.
2. As is often the case with widespread assumptions, the thesis that doxastic self-knowledge is a kind of empirical knowledge is not usually formulated or defended as such in the philosophical literature. But looking closely one can see how this empirical conception is shared ground among a range of otherwise differing accounts of first-person authority. Gilbert Ryle's behaviorist view in *The Concept of Mind* (1949) and D.M. Armstrong's account of introspection in *Belief, Truth and Knowledge* (1973) are cases in point: while

TRANSPARENCY AND APPERCEPTION

Armstrong grounds self-knowledge in a dedicated faculty through which beliefs and other mental items are brought to consciousness, and Ryle denies that there is any such faculty, both assume that there is *some* way in which self-knowledge results from tracking sources of information (or, as Ryle puts it, 'data') about one's states of mind. More recently, Peter Carruthers joins Ryle in rejecting any appeal to a faculty of direct introspection, but on his *interpretive* account of self-knowledge the reliability of self-attributions is due in part to the fact that 'we almost always have a great deal more evidence available to us when we interpret ourselves than when we interpret others' (2010, 105). And Quassim Cassam has recently advanced an account on which self-knowledge is a species of *inferential* knowledge: 'In the most straightforward case,' he writes, 'you know that you have [an attitude] A insofar as you have access to evidence that you have A and you infer from your evidence that you have A' (2014, 138). Despite their differences, all of these accounts conceive of doxastic self-knowledge as justified by an empirical process in the sense we have defined.

3. Goldberg describes such an act as 'reckless'. See Goldberg (2015, ch. 6.)
4. Things will be more complicated if knowledge does not require belief (see, e.g., Schwitzgebel and Myers-Shulz [2013]). Still it seems that on such a view there will be some attitude short of knowledge – if not belief, then perhaps something like acceptance in a context – that suffices for honest assertion, and our arguments below will apply in turn to such a requirement.
5. On the defeasibility of norms of assertion, see Kvanvig (2009).
6. Whether this 'managing' involves intentional action, subpersonal mechanisms, or some combination of the two need not concern us here.
7. The obvious exception is when one asserts certain sorts of things about oneself.
8. Here the exception will be any case where there is a special reason to believe that one's beliefs are correct.
9. We have in mind a simple case where someone deliberately asserts the opposite of something she falsely believes. What she says will be true, and so her assertion will be in accordance with (TA), but she will not have *followed* that rule, and will not have asserted honestly. We take no stand on whether such an assertion counts as a lie.
10. For doubts about this idea, see Robinson (2005) and Soteriou (2007) .
11. Two obvious questions that we will not belabor: On what basis must the subject understand herself to be doxastically justified? And on what basis must she understand herself to believe as she does on the strength of this justification?.
12. Though they might not be right to – for the belief might be 'properly basic'.
13. A further problem with this reply is that even if there is some intuitive pull to the thought that honest assertion requires the seeming-truth of the asserted proposition, there is none at all to the idea that this requirement is due to the way that seeming-truth provides a special sort of *evidence* for what one believes. If the proposal in question were correct (as we have argued it is not), it would be correct only in spite of the fact that it flies in the face of the phenomenology of doxastic self-knowledge.
14. For misinterpretation (or creative reconstruction) along these lines, see Fernandez (2003); Byrne (2011); Gertler 2011, 188–190); Cassam (2014, 3–5 and *passim*).

15. Cf. Moran (2001, § 2.6).
16. Recent Constitutivist proposals include Heal (2001), Schwitzgebel (2011), and Coliva (2011).
17. Among contemporary Constitutivists, Schwitzgebel (2011) is notable in embracing this consequence.
18. See Boyle (2011) and Marcus (2016) for work in this vein.
19. Versions of this paper were presented at the 2016 Orange Beach Epistemology Workshop and a 2018 workshop on Transparency and Apperception at Ryerson University. Thanks to David Barnett, Nick Byrd, Trent Dougherty, John Greco, Boris Hennig, Ulf Hlobil, David Hunter, Anna-Sarah Malmgren, Mark McCullagh, Alexandra Newton, Ram Neta, Sarah Paul, Ted Poston, Jeremy Redmond, Sergio Tenenbaum, Marshall Thompson, and Jonathan Vogel for valuable feedback.

References

Armstrong, D. M. 1973. *Belief, Truth and Knowledge*. Cambridge: Cambridge University Press.

Boyle, M. 2011. "Transparent Self-Knowledge." *Aristotelian Society Supplementary Volume* 85 (1): 223–241. doi:10.1111/j.1467-8349.2011.00204.x.

Byrne, A. 2011. "Transparency, Belief, Intention." *Aristotelian Society Supplementary Volume* 85 (1): 201–221. doi:10.1111/j.1467-8349.2011.00203.x.

Carruthers, P. 2010. "Introspection: Divided and Partly Eliminated." *Philosophy and Phenomenological Research* 80 (1): 76–111. doi:10.1111/phpr.2009.80.issue-1.

Cassam, Q. 2014. *Self-Knowledge for Humans*. Oxford: Oxford University Press.

Coliva, A. 2011. "One Variety of Self-Knowledge: Constitutivism as Constructivism." In *The Self and Self-Knowledge*, edited by A. Coliva. Oxford: Oxford University Press.

Dancy, J. 2000. *Practical Reality*. Oxford: Oxford University Press.

Evans, G. 1982. *Varieties of Reference*. Oxford: Oxford University Press.

Fernandez, J. 2003. "Privileged Access Naturalized." *The Philosophical Quarterly* 53 (212): 352–372. doi:10.1111/phiq.2003.53.issue-212.

Gertler, B. 2011. *Self-knowledge*. London: Routledge.

Goldberg, S. 2015. *Assertion: On the Philosophical Significance of Assertoric Speech*. Oxford: Oxford University Press.

Heal, J. 2001. "On First-Person Authority." *Proceedings of the Aristotelian Society* 102 (1): 1–19. doi:10.1111/1467-9264.00105.

Kvanvig, J. L. 2009. "Norms of Assertion." In *Assertion: New Philosophical Essays*, edited by H. Kappelan and J. Brown. Oxford: Oxford University Press.

Marcus, E. 2016. "To Believe Is to Know You Believe." *dialectica* 70 (3): 375–405. doi:10.1111/1746-8361.12144.

Moran, R. 2001. *Authority and Estrangement: An Essay on Self-Knowledge*. Princeton: Princeton University Press.

Robinson, W. 2005. "Thoughts without Distinctive Non-Imagistic Phenomenology." *Philosophy and Phenomenological Research* 70 (3): 534–561. doi:10.1111/j.1933-1592.2005.tb00414.x.

Ryle, G. 1949. *The Concept of Mind*. New York: Barnes and Noble.

Schwitzgebel, E. 2011. "Knowing Your Own Beliefs." *Canadian Journal of Philosophy* 35: 41–62.

Schwitzgebel, E., and B. Myers-Schulz. 2013. "Knowing that *P* without Believing that *P*." *Noûs* 47 (2): 371–384. doi:10.1111/nous.12022.

Soteriou, M. 2007. "Content and the Stream of Consciousness." *Philosophical Perspectives* 21 (1): 543–568. doi:10.1111/phpe.2007.21.issue-1.

Weiner, M. 2005. "Must We Know What We Say?" *The Philosophical Review* 114: 227–251. doi:10.1215/00318108-114-2-227.

Williamson, T. 2000. *Knowledge and Its Limits*. Oxford: Oxford University Press.

Kant and the transparency of the mind

Alexandra M. Newton (iD)

ABSTRACT
It has become standard to treat Kant's characterization of pure apperception as involving the claim that questions about what I think are transparent to questions about the world. By contrast, empirical apperception is thought to be non-transparent, since it involves a kind of inner observation of my mental states. I propose a reading that reverses this: pure apperception is non-transparent, because conscious only of itself, whereas empirical apperception is transparent to the world. The reading I offer, unlike the standard one, can accommodate Kant's claim that the I of pure apperception is the same as the I of empirical apperception.

When I am asked whether I think there will be a third world war (when asked about my thoughts), I do not answer this question by looking inwards, at the contents of my mind, but by directing my attention outwards, at current events that might portend the advent of another world war. This phenomenon, which has come to be known as the *transparency* of questions about the mind (about what I think or judge) to questions about the world (about what is the case), is often thought to be central to Kant's reflections on self-consciousness in theoretical judgment. When he introduces transparency, Gareth Evans, for instance, says 'I believe we may have here an interpretation of Kant's remark about the transcendental "I think"' (Evans 1982, 228). Kant says that the 'I think' that expresses transcendental apperception (or self-consciousness) is a 'wholly empty representation' (A345-6/B404). It is empty, according to transparency views, because we see *through* ourselves to the world; we do not make ourselves an object of attention, but are conscious of our thoughts and judgments by directing our attention outwards, at the world we think about. These claims are usually taken to be restricted to what Kant calls 'transcendental' or 'pure apperception' (A107, B132). 'Empirical apperception' or inner sense, by contrast, involves directing my attention inwards, and passively observing an inner, temporally ordered stream of consciousness.[1]

Kant famously maintains that the I of pure apperception is 'identical' with the I of empirical apperception 'as the same subject' (B155). There are not two I's here, but one. As he notes in the *Anthropology*, this gives rise to a puzzle: the '"I" appears to us to be double (which would be contradictory): 1) the "I" as subject of thinking (in logic), which means pure apperception (the merely reflecting "I"), and of which there is nothing more to say except that it is a very simple idea; 2) the "I" as object of perception, therefore of inner sense, which contains a manifold of determinations that make an inner experience possible' (7:134n.). As transparency accounts of pure apperception under- stand the puzzle, it is this: how can the I that always recedes behind con- sciousness be the same as the empirical I that appears as an object of consciousness? To put it in terms used by Wittgenstein, how can the I that is the 'limit of the world' also be an I that 'belongs to the world' (Wittgenstein 2001 *Tractatus*, 5.632)? Or in Sartre's terms, how is the I that is nothing (i.e. is not posited as an object of consciousness) the same as the I that is something (i.e. is posited as an object of consciousness)? As we shall see in the first section of this paper, transparency readings of Kantian pure apperception have no way of answering these questions.

In the second section I will argue that the identity of the pure and empirical I's can be made intelligible only if we revise the accounts of pure and empirical apperception that are presupposed by transparency views and standardly assumed in the literature on Kant. First, with regard to pure apperception, we must call into question the subject-object (or force-content) distinction that is dogmatically assumed by transparency views. I will argue that the object is not originally distinct from the act of thinking in transcendental apperception. So thinking does not go outside of itself in thinking its object. Second, I will question the view that empirical apperception is a kind of inner observation of my mental states. In a reversal of the standard reading, it will emerge that transparency plays no role in transcendental apperception but is central to Kant's account of empirical apperception. The *empirical self* is fleeting and impossible to grasp as a persisting object; we are conscious of our representations in inner sense only by directing our attention outwards, at persisting objects of outer sense. Rather than thinking of the empirical self as an object of reference, a particular given to consciousness as something particular, I will argue that the empirical I is the universal I of pure apperception in its act of self-particularization.[2] This will enable us to appreciate how the I of pure apperception is non-accidentally the same as the I of empirical apperception.

1. Transparency accounts of pure apperception

There are two broad approaches to the transparency of pure apperception – one of which I will call 'Evansian' after Gareth Evans, the other 'Sartrean'. The Evansian approach assumes that there are particular beings in the objective, spatio-temporal order that are able to refer to objects, including to themselves. We can ask *how it is* that they are able to refer to themselves when they self-ascribe mental states in such thoughts as <I think p > .[3] Transparency characterizes the peculiar 'procedure' that they employ in such self-ascriptions, distinct from the methods they use to become aware of properties ascribed to objects other than themselves (or to objects that just happen to be themselves) (Evans 1982, 225).[4] On the Sartrean approach, by contrast, the transparent I does not refer to itself or identify itself with a being in the world, but distinguishes itself from all beings in the world. Transparency thus is not a method used in self-ascriptions of mental states, but characterizes self-consciousness *without* self-reference. Whereas on the Evansian approach, the transparent I presupposes an empirical I that is in the world, the Sartrean approach reverses this: the empirical ego, as an object of what he calls 'thetic consciousness', presupposes the transparent I (the I of non-thetic self-consciousness).

It is not my intention in this paper to settle exegetical questions about Evans's or Sartre's own accounts of self-consciousness. My main purpose is to discuss their appeals to Kant, and to assess whether their transparency approaches to Kantian pure apperception are compatible with the sameness of the transcendental and empirical I's.

The Evansian approach, which has come to dominate much of the literature on Kant, assumes a distinction between two standpoints: one, external, from which I think of an objective world (Evans calls this the 'fundamental level of thought' (Evans 1982, 105f., 152, 210)); the other, internal, from which a being within this world thinks of herself first-personally, or from a first-person perspective.[5]

Evans notes that in thinking about myself *from within*, I ascribe thoughts to myself in a manner very different from the way that I ascribe properties to outer objects. It is not by observing myself thinking <p>, or by using criteria for identifying myself as the one who thinks <p>, that I know I think p. It makes no sense to be aware of the thought <p> without being aware that I am the one thinking it; I don't have to identify myself as the thinker of this thought in order to know that it is mine. I am aware of <p> as mine by directing my attention solely at p itself. The thinker of <p> can thus be said to be transparent to the world: for in consciousness of thinking p, it is not conscious of itself as an object of thought at all, but recedes *behind* what it thinks. It is in this context that Evans says 'I believe we may have here an interpretation of Kant's remark about the transcendental "I think"' (Evans

1982, 228). The transparent or transcendental I is not an object of reference and so does not enter the content of my thoughts, but is, as Evans says, 'purely formal' (Evans 1982, 226).

However, Evans thinks that this formal self-consciousness is not sufficient to 'constitute a full understanding of the content of the judgment "I believe that p"', since the content of that judgment involves the use of I as a referring expression (Evans 1982, 226). To think that transparency is sufficient to secure the referential significance of 'I' would be to make the Cartesian mistake of inferring from thinking alone to an object or substance that thinks. Evans follows Strawson in reading Kant's core insight (against the rationalists) to be that self-conscious thought is inseparable from a conception of oneself as an embodied being located within an objective world: transcendental apperception is inseparable from empirical apperception or inner sense. For if we could not situate ourselves within an objective world-order that is there independently of our perspective from within it, we would not have a capacity to refer to ourselves in self-ascriptions of thoughts or beliefs.[6] It is in the self-locating thought of empirical apperception, through which I become conscious of my spatio-temporal position, that Evans thinks I identify myself with a being in the world. Empirical apperception thus establishes self-reference.[7]

Notice that the transparency method for ascribing particular thoughts to myself will only work if the I that thinks <p> is conscious of itself as the same as the I in the self-ascription <I think p > . This is often overlooked, as though the puzzle of transparency that Evans's account raises could be that of how I can go from a mind-independent fact about the world, <p>, to a fact about my mind, <I think p > .[8] The real puzzle does not concern the relation between these thought-contents (whether inferential or not), but rather between the I that disappears – the *transcendental* I that thinks <p> – and the I that appears or that becomes the object of self-ascription – the *empirical* I of <I think p > . How am I conscious that the I of <I think p> is the *same* as the I that thinks <p>? Evans tries to avoid this difficulty by assuming an empirical I and by thinking of the transcendental, transparent I as a merely abstract aspect of it.[9] The transcendental I of <I think>, he says, is embedded in, or conceivable only against the 'background' of, the use of I in self-locating thought (Evans 1982, 226). For instance, in thinking <I think p>, I am ascribing the thought <p> to myself, as an empirical being in the world, distinct from others. The point of the transparency method is that I can do this in abstraction from any consideration of that which distinguishes my thinking <p> from your thinking <p > . I can do it simply by focusing my attention on p. It is thus by abstracting from the empirical foundation of I-thoughts that I form the idea of an entirely empty or formal I, a 'consciousness in general' that is *impersonal* and universal.

But once we take this abstractive approach, it emerges that the transcendental I is not transparent as the account purports it to be. To borrow Sartre's words from a different context, the empirical I cuts through the transcendental I like an 'opaque blade' (Sartre TE, 40).[10] For the subject of thinking – properly understood – now just is the empirical subject, and its acts of thinking, which were operative in thinking <p>, are psychological acts ascribed to this individual subject as its properties. Thus, these mental acts were already there, cutting through my consciousness of p, even though I was abstracting away from them. The subject therefore always thinks the outer world through its subjective, limited perspective, from a place within it. It thinks *what is* from the perspective of how things *seem to be* to it. One cannot think of the objective world (what is) as an abstraction out of the subjective world (what seems to be). If the objective world is thought of as an abstraction, as, for instance, what all 'seemings' share in common, it is not truly objective. Likewise, if the I that thinks the world is an abstraction out of the empirical I, it is not truly transparent to the objective world. Evans wants to be able to say that the objective world-order is already there, independent of perspectives of subjects within it. But by placing the subject within an objective context, he has placed it in a jail from which the subject cannot free itself by simply trying to 'abstract away' from the fetters of its confinement. The subject is not in a position, from within the confinement of its subjective perspective, to distinguish how things *seem to be* to it from how they objectively *are*.

In readings of Kant, this approach to transcendental apperception would have the disastrous consequence that transcendental idealism is a subjective idealism. The first *Critique* adopts the first-person standpoint of the thinker in determining ways in which it thinks about or gains cognitive access to the world. But on this reading, the transcendental structure of the world would be the formal structures discovered from within an externally limited, subjective perspective of a being in the world. One might *say* that subjects within the world have objective knowledge of the world around themselves – but one cannot *entitle* oneself to that claim if one has already confined the subject to a perspective from within it.[11]

The Sartrean approach is more Kantian in that it does not dogmatically assume a distinction between external and internal viewpoints, or between the objective world-order and the first-person perspective of a being within that world-order, but allows philosophical reflection to begin from within a standpoint that transcends this distinction and first makes it possible.[12] Sartre notices that thought about an objective world-order is inseparable from self-consciousness in thinking it. All consciousness is consciousness of something other than itself (it is characterized by *intentionality*); in Sartre's words, it is thetic, for it posits an object beyond itself. But it is also (non-thetically) conscious of itself *as of* something other, and thus of itself as distinct from the object of consciousness.[13] But in non-thetic consciousness of itself it is not conscious of itself as having any given characteristics, or of being limited in any way. Rather, consciousness is conscious of itself as *nothing* in contrast to the *'something'* it thetically posits or is conscious *of*: consciousness is, as Sartre puts it, 'all-lightness, all transparency' (*toute légèreté, toute translucidité*) (Sartre TE 1960, 42; altered translation; BN, 1956, 78).[14] So self-consciousness is completely transparent to the world because to be self-conscious is to be conscious of escaping ourselves (going outside ourselves, transcending ourselves) in being intentionally directed at outer objects or at states of affairs.[15] Indeed, transparency is a poor metaphor for characterizing the subject on this view, insofar as it leaves in place the idea of a medium through which we look outwards, at the world.[16] When we go outside, there is nothing, not even a medium, left inside (there is no opaque blade that cuts through its consciousness of the world).[17] Everything, on the Sartrean view, including mental states, is external to the non-thetic 'I', because everything *transcends* our consciousness of it: 'everything is finally outside, everything, even ourselves. Outside, in the world, among others' (Sartre 1970, 5).

The I of non-thetic self-consciousness, according to the Sartrean approach, is not a thing (spatio-temporal object) that I am conscious of in a special way. Non-thetic self-consciousness is not a peculiar kind of thought *about* myself (with a special Fregean sense), but is the entirely empty form of all thinking (indeed, of all consciousness) in general. Insofar, then, as the 'I think' is an expression of non-thetic self-consciousness, <I think p> means just the same as <p>: the <I think> does not add any additional content to that which I think, namely, to <p> – the <I think> expresses *nothing*. Thus, the non-thetic <I think p> is not a self-ascription in Evans's sense, but accompanies any thought in general (not just thoughts about myself).[18] Contrary to the Evansian approach, Sartre maintains that 'consciousness ... can be limited only by itself' (Sartre TE 1960, 39). So the limits of the empirical ego are *inside* consciousness; only within consciousness can we draw a distinction among the objects of thought, between an ego that is a being in the world and others outside it, or between the way things appear to me, as a particular in the world, and the way they are outside that perspective.[19]

In the *Transcendence of the Ego* Sartre suggests that this nothingness of consciousness in relation to its object is the proper way to understand Kant's thesis that the 'I think' is an empty representation. Insofar as general and transcendental logic are concerned with mere empty forms of thinking and judging, they must be concerned with the merely 'logical conditions' that are 'necessary for the existence of an empirical consciousness', i.e. conditions for intentional relations to objects (Sartre, TE 33). These are not psychological conditions or given characteristics of the subject; the 'transcendental field', as Sartre says, is 'impersonal; or if you like, pre-personal, without an I' (Sartre, TE 36). On Sartre's reading, they can be understood as the formal structures of intentionality, i.e. ways in which consciousness (or thinking) is directed at the world (or being).

Notice that Sartre does not face the difficulty of explaining how the I that thinks is the same as the I that perceives or the I that runs, since all acts of consciousness – whether in thinking, perceiving, or (practical) intention, are intentional acts, and thus have the same 'nothingness' – the same *non-thetic I* – at their core. But on Sartre's view the non-thetic I cannot become an object of experience: the I that is *nothing* is not the same as the posited ego that appears and is *something*. Sartre says that the latter is a transcendent object just like any other object of consciousness, and so is distinct from consciousness of it: the transparent I can always say 'I am not what I am' (Sartre BN, 260). Indeed, Sartre suggests that this ability to step back from, or to negate, the object-ego, constitutes our freedom. The sense in which I can identify myself with the object-ego, as when Sartre says 'I am what I am not', is very different from the sense in which I am *not* identical with it ('I am not what I am', ibid.). In *Being and Nothingness*, he suggests that I identify myself with an object-ego in the way that the craftsman identifies himself with the tool in his employment of it. The tool is not given to him as an alien object, but is the instrument of his engagement with the world (Sartre, BN 303ff.).[20] (This is the kind of self-identification that Korsgaard appeals to when she says that I can identify myself with my vacuum cleaner (Korsgaard 2009, 37)). In the *Transcendence of the Ego*, Sartre puts this by saying that I can become 'intimate' or familiar with an ego-object as my own (Sartre TE, 86). But notice that this still leaves us with two I's: one, which is truly a subject-I and transparent to the world, and another, which provides a familiar dwelling for it within the world. Intimacy is not sameness.

As a reading of Kant, the Sartrean approach thus leaves us without resources to interpret Kant's claim that there is no 'doubling' of I's. According to Kant, there are not two I's here, but one. It is *I* who am affected in sensory perception, not merely a body that I occupy. Indeed, my actions would be unintelligible as *mine* if I could not say that I *am* this individual, particular self that exists in the world, but could only say that I *am intimate with* this individual. For surely it is *I*, not a person I occupy, who acts in the world.[21]

We have seen with Sartre, against Evans, that the transcendental I cannot be a mere abstraction out of the empirical I and be fully transparent; on the contrary, the empirical I only comes into view for a transcendental I, and thus presupposes the latter. But the Sartrean approach makes it seem that any attempt to *identify* the transcendental and empirical I's as the *same* I would be a confusion. For, on this approach, the transcendental I is the empty subject of an act of intentionality, which is universal and formal, while the empirical I is one of the many particular objects that it can become conscious of. In what sense of *identity*, then, can Kant claim without confusion that they are identical? I shall return to this question in Section 3.

2. Kant on transcendental apperception

First, we would be well advised to turn to Kant's own reflections on transcendental apperception in the first *Critique*, since the above accounts may have been led astray by assuming that transparency plays any role in it. My remarks here will be brief, as my main goal is to articulate the relation between transcendental and empirical apperception (in the next section). We saw that transparency accounts of pure apperception characterize thinking primarily through *intentionality*: to think is to be conscious *of* something distinct from the thinking of it. I am conscious that I think <p> by going outside myself and focusing my attention on p. Since, by thus going outside, I leave nothing inside myself, the I could be said to be transparent to the world.

However, Kant's fundamental conception of thought doesn't involve thinking of thought as an act of intentionality. This is especially evident in his general logic, where thinking is understood as a (formal) act or function of synthesis, in abstraction from the relation it bears to any object. But even in transcendental or material logic (as expounded in the B-edition of the first *Critique*), which I will focus on here, Kant does not originally think of the relation that thought bears to its object as one of intentionality. It is not in the *pure* self-consciousness of judging, but in the *empirical* awareness of a temporally extended act of judging, that Kant discusses judgment's intentional relation to an object that is 'outside' of it. One should not confuse the relation that judgment originally bears to an object at the transcendental level (of pure apperception) with the intentional relation that representations in inner sense bear to the objects of outer sense at the empirical level, or so I shall argue. In the former relation, the act of judging does not go 'outside' itself, but remains entirely immanent to itself.

In the B-edition Transcendental Deduction, Kant glosses the 'relation of representations to an object' as their 'objective validity' (B137). Objective validity is what is expressed by the 'copula **is**' in a judgment (B141f.). A judgment thus 'relates to an object' insofar as it is objectively valid. Kant later clarifies that if a judgment is objectively valid, we can infer that it is true (A125, A788/B816, cf. A131/B170, A202/B247). For a judgment is objectively valid only if it accords with the laws of the understanding (both logical and transcendental), and no lawful exercise of the understanding (as a capacity for knowledge) can be false (A293-4/B350). The relation to the object therefore must include 'the agreement of cognition with its object', which is Kant's nominal definition of truth (A58/B82).[22]

When a judgment is objectively valid, the representations within it are related to 'the original apperception and its **necessary unity**' (B142); i.e. it is not accidental or haphazard that I combine representations in this manner, rather I combine them from a consciousness that they belong together necessarily, not just for me, but for any subject of judgment. Judgment thus involves a consciousness of itself as not just true, but non-accidentally true, i.e., as knowledge. When Kant says that false cognition 'does not agree with the object *to which it is related*' (A58/B83, my emphasis), this does not mean that a cognition relates to an object (or is objectively valid) *insofar* as it is false, but that it relates to an object insofar as it is true: 'in every erroneous judgment there must always lie something true' (JL 9:54). For instance, the false judgment that the table is brown may contain the truth that the object is a table, and thus may still contain relation to an object (objective validity).[23]

Some interpreters have rejected this interpretation of 'objective validity', since Kant says that all judgments have objective validity (B142); it would thus have the absurd consequence that all judgments are true.[24] However, it should come as no surprise that the analytic of transcendental logic ('analytic of truth') considers all judgments to be true, if we read it as taking a first-person standpoint on judgment. Within the self-consciousness of an act of judging, as an act of the capacity to know and thus to judge truly, I cannot think of my judgment as false or even as possibly false. For to judge is to make a claim about the way things are; it is to think of one's judgment as true.[25] I cannot judge <S is P> and, in that same act, think that <S is P is false> or even <S is P may be false>. It is only when I step back and consider *whether* I should make a judgment, or when I reflect on how I have judged in the *past*, and thus take an external perspective on judging, that I can think of a judgment as possibly false.[26]

Indeed, the reason Kant takes this first-person standpoint on judgment is that there is no external or *sideways-on* perspective on the truth of cognition at all: this is what Kant suggests by identifying the objective validity of a cognition with 'objective unity of the *apperception* of the concepts contained therein' (my emphasis; B140f.). Agreement with the object is not a relation that acts of judging bear to an external object, a relation that can somehow be viewed from outside of apperceptive acts of judging: for 'I can compare the object with my cognition [...] only by cognizing it' (JL 9:50; cf. A57-58/B82-83). My judgments of the object can only be corrected by other *judgments* of it. The relation of *agreement* with the object is thus *internal* to the relation of acts of judging (cognizing) amongst themselves, and so is internal to the apperception or self-consciousness of such acts.[27]

There are two ways to read this internality: either truth is internal to apperceptive acts of judging because the primary bearers of truth are the *contents* of these acts, or because the primary bearers of truth are the *acts* of judging themselves. Along the lines of the first interpretation, John McDowell has suggested that for Kant, as for Wittgenstein, truth is internal to the act of judging because when I judge truly, my mind does not stop anywhere short of the world. What I judge – the content of my judgment – is identical with what is the case. Thus, there is 'no gap between thought, as such, and the world', understood as 'everything that is the case', and hence no need for an external relation of correspondence between what is inside of my judgment (its content) and an object external to it (McDowell 1994, 27). Rather, there is an identity of what I judge and what is the case in the world.[28] Although this eliminates the 'sideways-on' conception of truth as an external relation between contents inside the mind and objects outside of it, it still retains a distinction between the *act* of judging (force) and the *content* judged. The truth-bearers, on McDowell's reading, are the *contents* of judging, not the acts of judging them. Acts of judging can be said to be true in the sense of correct only insofar as the contents of judgments are true, i.e., are identical with states of affairs. This is in line with transparency views of transcendental apperception, since it is by focusing on something distinct from acts of the mind – namely on their true contents – that I become conscious of these acts as my own.

However, there is scant textual evidence that Kant, like his Fregean successors, distinguishes the act of judging from the content judged.[29] Moreover, when Kant says that objective validity is expressed by the 'copula **is**' in a judgment, this means that it is expressed by an *act* of judging (B142). For unlike the Fregean conception of judging as an act external to the content judged, Kant views the act of judging as an act of *synthesis* of representations *internal* to what is judged – precisely that act of synthesis that is logically expressed by the copula 'is'. The primary truth-bearers are acts of judging (of synthesis), not act-independent contents of judgment, since truth in the primary sense is objective validity, and it is the *act* of judging (internal to what is judged) that is true in the sense of valid or correct.

To be conscious of the truth of my judgment thus is not to direct one's mind towards an act-independent fact in the world, rather it is to be conscious of the act of combining representations in one necessary unity of consciousness, one judgment. A judgment <S is P> is true when the predicate <P> agrees with the object thought through the subject-concept <S> – i.e., when there is a necessary agreement among the representations combined within a judgment, in accordance with the logical and transcendental principles of possible experience. Agreement with the object is thus internal to agreement of the representations in a judgment amongst themselves, in the act of their synthesis.

Thus far we have focused on Kant's claim, from the first half of the B-deduction, that cognition's 'relation to an object' consists in its objective validity. Contrary to interpretations that read 'objective validity' as intentionality or objective purport, I have argued that objective validity is the non-accidental truth expressed by the copula 'is' in judgment, and that consciousness of being ('is') in the sense of being true (veritative being) and consciousness of thinking (or judging, synthesis) are the same.[30] Such acts of thinking (as objectively valid acts of synthesis) are only possible under conditions of a manifold given from elsewhere, but this does not entail that consciousness of the truth of the thought is consciousness of something given from elsewhere. To be conscious of truth is not to reach out beyond the act of thinking or judging to an independent object that it is true of, rather truth (objective validity) is internal to the act itself (i.e. to the copula). Thus, to be conscious that my cognition 'relates to an object' in the sense of being 'objectively valid' just is to be self-conscious in the act of judging.

Now, the I of <I think> in such acts is formal or empty, but not because it is nothing *in contrast* with *something* (the truths) thought about; rather, it is empty because it is consciousness of truth in general (or of an 'object in general'), which is not actually, but is only potentially, all particular truths (about particular objects).[31] The formal concept <I think> is the logical concept of the functions of thinking in judging (functions of logical synthesis) that are the bearers of truth.[32] To relate this concept to objects is not to go outside it, but to fill it with transcendental and empirical content.[33] For contentful knowledge of objects does not require directing our attention away from logical functions and towards an external object, but becoming conscious of these same logical functions in their role of determining a sensible manifold, i.e. in their role of making particular, empirical truths (experience), and the objects of these truths (objects of experience), possible (KrV A158/B197).

Moreover, consciousness of the objective unity of various representations through <I think> is an impersonal, universal, and merely formal act of self-consciousness (see Engstrom 2013). It is not, as such, consciousness of a particular agent or thing that performs an act of combining, as this would restrict the truth (in the above sense) to what holds merely *for me*. As Kant emphasizes in the *Paralogisms* chapter, the <I think> expresses the formal logical unity of consciousness of subject and predicate concepts, i.e., the copula unifying the thought <S is P> – it does not add a substance or underlying subject to the thought itself (B406f.). The thought <S is P> and the thought <I think S is P> thus are the same thought; the latter does not bring attention to myself as an individual distinct from others. The <I think> merely expresses the logical, objective unity of the thought (objective synthetic unity of apperception), which is common to, or identical in, the elements in the thought, both in me, and in any other rational thinker (this sameness or identity Kant calls an 'analytic unity' of apperception). For I am conscious, in judging, that the judgment holds not just for me, but for any rational subject.[34] The logical or transcendental 'I' thus is not an expression used to refer to a particular individual, but is the common 'consciousness in general' that is shared by all possible (identical) acts of knowing, and thus by all truths (B143).

Although transparency views are right to emphasize that I am conscious of my judgments in transcendental apperception in an impersonal manner, merely through consciousness of what is true, this does not mean that I am conscious of something outside of the act of judging itself – an act-independent content, for instance, or a mind-independent world-fact. Indeed, *nothing* at all – nothing, at least, that is anything 'for me' – is outside the transcendental I, understood as the 'original-synthetic unity' of all my representations in one consciousness (B132). The transcendental I is conscious only of *itself* and its own activity, and thus is non-transparent to any world-facts distinct from or external to itself and its activity.[35]

3. Empirical apperception

What the above elucidation of Kant's account shares with transparency views of self-consciousness is that in transcendental apperception of my thoughts and judgments, I am not conscious of any given character of myself, as the individual subject of thought.[36] I am conscious of thinking <S is P> just *in* thinking S is P, without at all thinking about myself as the individual thinking it. Indeed, I can also become conscious of what *others* think (nameless others) by abstracting entirely from the differences between them and myself, and focusing only on what I understand them to say. The experience of disagreement or error may direct our attention at these empirical differences, but within a setting where we are jointly determining what to think and we refrain from errors, it does not matter who says what: reason (consciousness in general) is determining what it thinks. It is not the transcendental subject, but empirical subjects – both myself and others – that are transparent, since reason (the transcendental I) 'sees through' them to itself alone in becoming conscious of what it thinks.[37]

Contrary to logical and transcendental apperception, empirical apperception introduces an 'inner' realm of subjectivity distinct from the 'outer' realm of objects given to me in space (the form of 'outer sense'). For Kant says that inner sense provides us with an 'intuition of our self and our inner state' (A33/B49; cf. A22/B37), while outer sense provides intuitions of outer objects. Whereas all being is immanent to the transcendental I, inner sense distinguishes my thoughts and perceptions, *my* being, from the being both of outer objects and of other subjects. As Plato and many classical philosophers noticed, the further we descend into our particular, empirical selves, the more distanced we become from what is. We should not cherish the false hope that we will establish contact with what truly is through our senses: truth is to be found 'only in judgments' (A293, B350).

Since we have identified being (what is) or truth with what is judgeable, we are now in a position to understand the division, within the concept of being (the object in general), between my being and the being of outer objects, as a division internal to judgment. Like all divisions in thought, this division is only possible under sensible conditions of a manifold given from elsewhere. But it is nevertheless an act of dividing (separating), an act of thinking; hence the members of the division are not external to that act. Kant calls the empirical I an 'object' of experience because it is an object of thought (empirical judgment), like any other. Thought does not encounter particular objects of thought and the distinctions among them but is itself the source of these distinctions, insofar as it thinks not only the objects but also their differences. That is, the <I think> *specifies itself* into the thoughts <I think x> and <I think y > . As an object of thought, I am contained in this way under the universal, formal concept <I think>, just like any other object of thought.

In what sense, then, is the transcendental I identical only with *me*? How is my empirical I, which is *not* identical with the being of the outer object which it thinks, identical with the transcendental I, which *is* identical with the being of what it thinks? To understand this we must distinguish two senses of identity or sameness. First, there is the sameness of the I with anything it thinks. Just as anything that falls under a concept F must be 'homogeneous with' or at least partially the *same* as that concept F (since 'the concept must contain that which is represented in the object'), anything that is an object of <I think> – i.e., anything that is an object of thought at all – must contain the <I think> within it and thus be the same as it (A137/B176). Kant does not call this sameness with the <I think> *homogeneity*, but instead calls it an 'analytic unity of apperception', because the <I think> is not a *genus* common to a determinate sphere of objects, distinct from other *genera*. Rather, as we have seen, the <I think> is indeterminate or without limit in its extension: there is nothing outside of its realm (indeed, even a 'table of nothing' is *inside* its realm – cf. A292/B348). My empirical I, like all other empirical I's and all other objects of thought, is in this sense the *same* as the transcendental I.[38]

But in the second sense of sameness or identity, only my empirical I is the same as the transcendental I. The key to understanding *this* identity is to see that my empirical I is not just *thought* by the transcendental I, but is also self-consciously *affected* by it. The empirical I becomes an object of thought through an act of self-affection – which is how the transcendental I situates *itself* within its own thought of an objective world. Whereas outer objects are given to me from elsewhere (in outer sense), only I am capable of being given to myself by myself (in inner sense). Rather than encountering myself as an already given particular existing in the world, I particularize myself, and, in inner sense, am able to become conscious of myself as an appearance in the world, in relation to others.

This approach can help us understand why Kant argues, in the Refutation of Idealism, that I do not have direct access to myself as an inner object that I encounter, but that I am conscious of myself in inner sense only through my active engagement with objects of outer experience. Very briefly, the argument proceeds as follows. I am conscious of my own representations only in their temporally determined relations to one another. But according to the First Analogy, 'all determination of time presupposes something permanent in perception' – that is, it presupposes a substance (B275). This abiding substance cannot be 'something in me', since Kant shares Hume's insight (against the rationalists) that we do not experience ourselves as permanent in time; there is no intuition of ourselves as substances – everything in inner sense is 'in constant flux' (B291). Hence, the permanent substance underlying inner time-determinations must be an outer appearance: 'the determination of my existence in time is possible only through the existence of actual things which I perceive outside of me' (B275-6). I am temporally conscious of my own representations only by directing my attention outwards, at the objects of outer sense: 'The consciousness of my own existence is at the same time an immediate consciousness of the existence of other things outside me' (B276).

Thus, although inner sense is a kind of self-affection, it does not involve being affected by myself *qua* outer object (qua something *other*).[39] The objects of outer perception must be given to me, i.e. I must receive sensations or impressions from them by being affected by them, and there is no way to know that the object that affects me is the same as the subject affected (although the critical philosopher leaves this sameness an open possibility). As Wittgenstein suggests, although it makes sense to say, after a car crash: 'Here is a limb, but is it mine?', it does not make sense to say: 'These are representations, but are they mine?' (Wittgenstein 1958, 67f.). My access to my inner states is not like access to outer things, or to a body that just happens to be mine, but is first-personal self-awareness: I am aware of my representations *qua* non-accidentally *mine* – for instance, I'm aware of temporally extended acts of thinking as non-accidentally the same as the non-temporal, logical act of thinking.

Kant can acknowledge this first-personal character of empirical apperception because whereas sensations make up the materials of outer sense, 'the representations of outer sense make up the proper material with which we occupy our mind' (B67). That is, there aren't any special materials of inner sense. It's not that first, we are affected by the object in representations of outer sense, and then, in a separate act, we are affected again, now by the representations of these objects. In addition to outer sensations, there aren't any inner sensations.[40] I don't need to receive impressions from my inner states (perceptions, thoughts, etc.) in order to be aware of them as such. I can become conscious of intuiting and perceiving simply *by* intuiting and perceiving. In the case of thought, I am empirically aware of my thoughts by thinking them, not by stepping back from them and observing myself think them.[41] And in perceiving a line, I am aware of perceiving it by 'drawing it in thought', not by stepping back and observing myself as I draw it.[42] It's just that these activities through which I am empirically self-aware are temporally extended, which is on Kant's view the same as saying that they're acts of self-affection.[43]

In order to make sense of temporally extended acts of the mind ('motion [*Bewegung*]' of the mind, *kinesis*: B155), Kant thinks that we need to think of these acts as performed under the condition of an object affecting me (or having affected me) in outer sense. Temporal relations cannot arise *ex nihilo*, or from logical relations alone; that is, time is not a form of mere *spontaneity*, but of *receptivity*: temporal intuition rests on affection by objects outside of me. Therefore, I am conscious of my inner states in inner sense only by directing my attention outwards, at objects of outer sense.

We are now in a position to ask whether the transparency of *empirical* apperception is Evansian or Sartrean. That is, in directing my attention at objects of outer sense, am I a particular spatio-temporal perspective on the object, distinct from other perspectives (Evansian), or is my empirical I entirely empty – am I nothing at all, not even a particular perspective alongside others (Sartrean)? Sartre says 'all consciousness is positional in that it transcends itself in order to reach an object, and it exhausts itself in this same positing. All that there is of intention in my actual consciousness is directed toward the outside' (Sartre BN 1956, 11). This seems to be precisely the case for temporal consciousness: it is always escaping itself, constantly going from one moment to the next, and from one object to the next. I can say of myself (originally) only *that* I am, but not that I am anything in particular (B157n.).

On a Sartrean approach to Kantian inner sense, empirical self-awareness would be an awareness of its own 'emptiness'. But contrary to Sartre, we can now characterize this emptiness (or nothingness) as the emptiness of the *empirical* I and distinguish it from the emptiness of the *transcendental* I. Whereas the transcendental I is the emptiness of 'consciousness in general' that remains within itself, even in its acts of self-division and self-specification, the empirical I is the emptiness of temporal consciousness, which is constantly escaping itself. In transcendental apperception, I am not conscious of myself as distinct from others, or even from the objects of thought, whereas in empirical apperception I constantly distinguish myself (as existence) from anything that I am conscious of. Whereas the 'nothing' of transcendental apperception is the emptiness of universality, since the transcendental I can be shared by any thinker, the 'nothing' of empirical apperception is the emptiness of radical singularity, since the empirical I cannot be shared by any other thinker.[44] Transcendental apperception is empty as the capacity to (spontaneously) *determine* any object, whereas empirical apperception is the emptiness of the passive capacity *to be determined* by any such acts of determination.

The Evansian approach to the transparency of empirical apperception, by contrast, would identify my empirical I with a particular, determined spatio-temporal perspective in the world. In an influential paper, Markos Valaris adopts this approach in his interpretation of Kantian inner sense: it provides us, he argues, with an awareness that 'representations disclose a part of the objective world *as seen from the subject's point of view*'; and, since the subject 'is aware of its own perspective on things, then by the same token, it is aware of itself as having a determinate location in the same space and time as the things it perceives' (Valaris 2008, 6). The problem with this approach is that it is not clear why I should not be able to imagine *others* occupying the same spatio-temporal location or perspective that I occupy. Since I *cannot* imagine others sharing my empirical I, the empirical I cannot be simply identified with a spatio-temporal perspective. Rather, there must be an original Sartrean awareness of myself in inner sense as radically singular and irreplaceable, underlying my awareness of the perspective on the world *that I occupy*. This radically singular self-awareness is precisely the kind of self-awareness that original consciousness of my existence in time provides: for to be aware of myself as existing in time is not *ipso facto* to be aware of the shareable, particular position in the objective time-order that I occupy. The empirical I is originally aware of itself as having no position, but as constantly fleeing any position, as time itself does. *My being in time escapes* all objectification.[45]

The Sartrean approach to the transparency of the empirical I is suggested by some of Kant's remarks about awareness of myself as *existing*. Kant says that the category of existence applies to outer objects, presumably because we can subsume them under this concept: we can think of them as particular things that exist. This requires a distinction between the existences (the objects) and the existence of these existences (the category). Outer objects are particulars that have being, implying a distinction between particular beings and their being.[46] By contrast, when I am conscious of *myself* existing, I do not employ the category of existence ('here existence is not yet a category' B423n.). Presumably this is because I am not given to myself as a particular thing that can be subsumed under this concept. I am aware of existing, but not of being a particular thing that exists. All that I am, *qua* existence, is a realm of possibilities of what I can become; I am nothing determinate, not even a self-determining being, but am sheer *determinability*: 'I cannot determine my existence as that of a self-active being, rather [...] my existence always remains only sensibly determinable, i.e., determinable as the existence of an appearance' (B158n.). We should thus say not that I am a thinking thing that exists, but that '**I exist** thinking' (B420).[47] My existence

> expresses an indeterminate empirical intuition, i.e., a perception [...] but it precedes the experience that is to determine the object of perception through the category in regard to time; and here existence is not yet a category, which is not related to an indeterminately given object, but rather to an object of which one has a concept, and about which one wants to know whether or not it is posited outside this concept (B423n.).

I am conscious of my existence in indeterminate, temporal intuition in a way that precedes the application of the category of existence to outer objects. My existence is not that of an intentional object of thought, but it is the possibility of standing-out (ex-istere), or of the emergence in time of thinking itself.[48] My existence is thus the openness (determinability) of being in time. One wants to know whether there is a thing – an object in the spatial order – that *has* this being (an object 'posited outside this concept'), but one cannot know this at all, since one cannot know that the object given to me in outer sense is non-accidentally I (i.e. is non-accidentally identical with the existing act of thinking).

Thus, the 'I' of empirical apperception is not originally a referring expression used in self-ascriptions, because it does not refer to a given particular being, or even a particular perspective, in the world, but, like Sartre's non-thetic I, is radically singular by distinguishing itself from all particulars. The transition from the universal I of <I think> to the radically singular I of indeterminate intuition in <I exist> is not the transition to a particular being encountered at a location in a spatio-temporal framework.[49] However, it is the transition to an I that *can* be situated as a particular in the world, because I can, through syntheses of the imagination under concepts of the understanding, *determine* my existence in relation to other objects.[50] As a determinate perspective in the objective spatio-temporal order, I am an object of *thought* (or cognition), not just an object of indeterminate empirical intuition. But since this self-determination is down-stream of an originally *indeterminate* intuition of myself, the I that is determined is originally nothing – not even a particular position or perspective alongside others.[51] Like Aristotle says of the passive intellect, the empirical I is nothing at all before it thinks (Aristotle DA, 429a23).

In thinking, the empirical I becomes something, because its existence acquires determination (KrV B157-8n.). I become aware of my thoughts' position in a temporal order by (myself) ordering them in time. The empirical I thus is not already, as an object of (indeterminate) empirical intuition, confined within an objective, spatio-temporal framework (it is not already at a temporal location, already something), as on an Evansian account of the self-conscious subject. Rather, the transcendental I determines its temporal position itself through syntheses of the imagination (syntheses of ordering in time), in accordance with the transcendental principles of objective thought in general. There are not two acts here, but one: the empirical I's being-determined is the same activity as the transcendental I's act of determination. In the same way, being kicked and kicking are not two acts, but a single one, seen either from the side of agency or from the side of the patient. But in the case of kicking, the agent who kicks is distinct from the patient who is being kicked (or they are, per accidens, the same). By contrast, the patient or 'empirical I' is nothing at all before it is determined. Hence, the identity of determining and being determined reveals the (non-accidental) identity of transcendental and empirical I's.

4. Conclusion

On the reading I have developed, we are able to say that the transcendental I is the same as the empirical I, since it is the same act of thinking of which I am conscious non-temporally in transcendental apperception, and temporally in empirical apperception. This sameness can be expressed, not by saying that the empirical I can be subsumed as an already given particular under the universal, transcendental I, but by saying that the empirical I is the self-particularizing and self-concretizing universal I. I am originally not a being, but am thinking or being (truth) itself, insofar as it is capable of emerging in time. Transparency accounts of pure apperception, by contrast, conceive of the transcendental self as originally escaping itself, leaving itself behind, in its engagement with the world. They can only understand the empirical self to be one of the objects it encounters, and thus to be distinct from it.

Although it would exceed the limits of this paper to discuss this in more detail, I think this reading of the relation between transcendental and empirical apperception puts us in a better position to understand our community with other empirical subjects. For now we can say that consciousness in general is common to, or the same across, the first-person singular, the second person, and the third person (in the first sense of 'sameness' articulated above). Reason sees itself in the other, and at the level of pure apperception, when it grasps being in the sense of being-true, sees *through* the other. But it is also, in its descent into a spatio-temporal world, conscious of itself as dividing into a community of empirical subjects and as the 'same as' each of them (in the second sense of sameness distinguished above). Thus we can say not only that there is a plurality of first persons, but that there is a first-person plurality – not only a collection of *I*'s, but a *we*: for the division of consciousness in general into individual, singular consciousnesses is internal to the transcendental I. However, I cannot say more about this here: this is a difficult topic that will have to await further study.

Notes

1. See, for instance, (Evans 1982, Allison 2004, 290f.,; Strawson 1966, 248f.. Boyle 2009) distinguishes 'an active and a passive kind of self-knowledge', suggesting that passive self-knowledge or inner sense is a kind of inner experience (Boyle 2009, 160).
2. I am grateful to Adrian Haddock for helping me formulate my claim in these terms.
3. Following the recommendation of an anonymous reviewer, I use brackets to mention thought-contents.

4. On this approach, I-thoughts have a peculiar, first-personal Fregean 'sense' or mode of presentation [*Art des Gegebenseins*] of the object they refer to. Longuenesse follows this approach when she writes, "'I' and 'A' are different modes of presentation of the entity that is also referred to by the proper name, 'E.A.'. 'A' is sufficiently specified by the description: 'name that refers to whoever is currently saying or thinking 'A is F'; but 'I' needs the further specification – 'word that refers to whoever is currently saying or thinking "I am F" and whose use depends on non-thetic consciousness (of) whoever is saying or thinking "I am F"' (Longuenesse 2017, 65).

5. This is also implied by Strawson's claim that 'the concept of a person is logically prior to that of an individual consciousness' (Strawson 1966, 103). The concept of a person is that of a being in the world, and that of individual consciousness is that of the consciousness possessed by this being in the world. The first-person standpoint is thus parasitic on there being an objective world, and a person within it.

6. The identification of myself with a particular individual in the world is a self-locating thought that I can think only from within a first-person perspective. Thus, in Kantian terminology, Evans's point is that we can become aware of ourselves as elements in an objective spatial order from within inner sense – indeed, Evans is suggesting that there is bodily self-awareness in inner sense. Evans criticizes Kant for thinking that awareness of oneself as in space would require knowing ourselves as others know us – as objects of outer sense: 'The idea that I can identify myself with a person objectively construed is often mis-expressed, e.g. in terms of the idea that I realize that I am an object to others (also an object of outer sense, as Kant says: Critique of Pure Reason, B145). This misleadingly imports an ideal verificationist construal of the point' (Evans 1982, 210).

7. To identify myself with a being in the world is to situate myself within the external, objective context: 'to know what it is for [$\delta t = I$] to be true, for arbitrary δt, is to know what is involved in locating oneself in a spatio-temporal map of the world' (Evans 1982, 211). It is unclear exactly how Evans thinks he can get self-reference just out of self-locating thought (see Sebastian Rödl's criticism of this move in his 2017, 280ff.). Perhaps Evans thinks that insofar as I am conscious of myself as occupying a particular perspective from within the world, and thus as having limits, I am conscious of myself as a particular being, because the limits are here understood as given to con-sciousness – or as simply encountered. But they are not encountered in the same way that I encounter outer objects. They are encountered as *my* limits – as the limits through which I engage with the world (the world would be nothing to me without them). Whereas Evans thinks of the transparent or 'purely formal' I as the limit of the entire world, and thus as lacking a perspective from within it, he thinks of the empirical *object*-I as a perspective that defines the limit of my ego-centric world. So he thinks that I encounter the empirical I as an object of reference, because the empirical I is the perspective that I encounter as a special kind of inner object. At the end of this paper, I will use Kant to criticize the Evansian view that the empirical I is a perspective, and will argue along Sartrean lines that it is nothing at all (not even a perspective).

8. See, for instance, (Byrne 2011, 2018).

TRANSPARENCY AND APPERCEPTION

9. This is also Strawson's strategy: 'If we try to abstract this use, to shake off the connexion with ordinary criteria of personal identity, to arrive at a kind of subject-reference which is wholly and adequately based on nothing but inner experience, what we really do is simply to deprive our use of "I" any referential force whatever. It will simply express, as Kant would say, "consciousness in general"' (Strawson 1966, 166).

10. This is taken from Sartre's criticism of Husserl. See ftn. 19.

11. McDowell notes in his Appendix to Evans's chapter on self-identification that Evans himself became increasingly aware of the dependence of the 'fundamental level of thought' on the subjective viewpoint of the egocentrically located empirical subject. This can make it sound like he began to concede the subjective idealistic consequences of his view: 'Section 6.3 [...] gives the impression that the objective or impersonal mode of thought about space can be understood as a mode of spatial thinking organized around a framework of known objects and places – the "frame of reference". But such a mode of thinking will not be capable of achieving a higher degree of impersonality than that achieved by the subject's thought about the objects and places which constitute the frame; [...] it seems plausible that a subject's right to be counted as thinking about these familiar objects and places turns partly on his conception of the role they have played in his past life – being visited by him, seen by him, etc. [...] In that case, the seemingly objective mode of thinking about space is, after all, contaminated by egocentricity' (Evans 1982, 265).

12. Philosophers such as Richard Moran or Christine Korsgaard, who think of the first-person standpoint as the standpoint of a particular being in the world, and thus as already confined to a region within it, would not be Kantian in this sense (Moran 2001, 63; cf. Korsgaard 2009, 125f.).

13. 'Consciousness is aware of itself insofar as it is consciousness of a transcendent object' (Sartre 1960, 40). 'Every positional consciousness of an object is a non-positional consciousness of itself' (Sartre BN 1956, 40).

14. In *The Transcendence of the Ego*, Sartre puts this by saying that consciousness is 'purely and simply the consciousness of being consciousness of that object. This is the law of its existence. We should add that this consciousness of consciousness [...] is not positional, which is to say that consciousness is not for itself its own object. [...] Now we ask: is there room for an I in such a consciousness? The reply is clear: evidently not' (Sartre 1960, 40–41).

15. Sartre does say that non-thetic self-consciousness is immanent to itself, but it is immanent to itself as an act of transcendence, of going outside (e.g. Sartre 1956, 77).

16. It is a sign of the poverty of language that we have no first-person universal pronoun, and that we always speak of first-person consciousness as a first-person 'standpoint' or 'perspective'. Both of these terms suggest that we are conscious from some place (standpoint) or position (perspective) within the world.

17. This point is helpfully made by Jean-Philippe Narboux in a recent essay on self-consciousness (Narboux, unpublished).

18. Sartre thus would not agree with Moran's claim that from 'within the first-person perspective' (non-thetic consciousness), I acknowledge that the 'fact believed and the fact of one's belief are two different matters' (Moran 2001, 62).

19. Although it is not my intention to interpret Sartre here, I do wish to distinguish the view I am calling Sartrean from other views that bill themselves as Sartrean. Matthew Boyle has argued that non-thetic self-consciousness is transparent to the world because it is entirely directed outwards, at the objects of consciousness. But he thinks that although the mental act of being intentionally directed at the world initially is not an object of consciousness, I am implicitly aware of it as the 'manner' in which I apprehend the object: '[the subject] shows an awareness, implicit but open to reflective articulation, of the specific kind of relation in which she stands to the object of her representation' (Boyle, unpublished, 27). Richard Moran similarly argues that there is an unthematized awareness of being committed to the truth of what I think when I am non-thetically aware of my judgments (Moran 2001, 84). The transition from the outward-looking thought <p> to the inner fact, <I believe p>, according to Moran, would not be legitimate if I did not already implicitly see myself (as an empirical subject) playing a role in the determination of what I believe through the exercise of my rational agency (Moran 2012, 3). Thus, on both Boyle's and Moran's views, the I of non-thetic self-awareness – understood relationally, as my attitude taken towards an object – can become an object of thetic self-awareness (see also Longuenesse 2017, 47). This means that the self of non-thetic self-awareness is not fully transparent in Sartre's sense, for the subject is (even if only implicitly) aware of the manner in which she looks outwards, towards the world. Since she implicitly sees the mode of apprehension, in addition to that which she sees through it, her mind cannot be said to be aware only of what is outside, but is also aware of something inner (a 'manner of apprehending' the object, or an exercise of rational agency). And it is this implicit awareness of something inner – not merely the awareness of something outer – that, on these views, licenses the explicit self-ascription of mental states in *thetic* self-consciousness. Boyle's and Moran's views are empirical variants of the Husserlian view that Sartre rejects, according to which the transcendental I is 'so to speak, behind each consciousness, a necessary structure of consciousness whose rays (*Ichstrahlen*) would light upon each phenomenon presenting itself in the field of attention' (Sartre TE, 37). As Sartre argues, this implicit awareness of the structure through which I am aware of the world would make consciousness 'personal': it would introduce a given character of the subject of awareness into her consciousness of the objective world. (In Husserl, this character is innately given, while in Boyle and Moran it is empirically given.) But this would mean that it destroys the objective character of what she is conscious of: the world would become the world *as it appears to her*, through her manner of apprehending it. In Sartre's words, Husserl's transcendental ego would 'divide consciousness; it would slide into every consciousness like an opaque blade', and would thus be 'the death of consciousness' (Sartre TE, 40).

20. It is important to distinguish these two senses of 'identity', because otherwise these two statements would be contradictory: 'I am what I am not' and 'I am not what I am'. It does not help to insist that I am a contradiction, for which I is it that asserts itself to be a contradiction? We would have to posit a *third* I that both is identical with the posited ego and is not identical with it.

21. In this paper I am primarily concerned with the sameness of the transcendental and empirical I's of theoretical cognition. As Kant explains in the introduction to the third *Critique*, theoretical cognition (and therefore theoretical philosophy) comprises not just perceptions, but also actions (KU 20:200–1, 200n.). So the empirical I of theoretical cognition is both an I that perceives and an I that acts. In practical cognition, peculiar difficulties arise with regard to the relation between the noumenal self (I of moral freedom) and the phenomenal self (the I that acts in nature), which I will set aside for my purposes here.
22. This section is heavily indebted to Stephen Engstrom's reading of Kant's Copernican turn in his article 'Knowledge and its Object' (Engstrom 2017).
23. For a different reading of this passage, according to which false judgments relate to an object *insofar* as they are false, see (Tolley 2011, 204).
24. See (Allison 2004, 87–88; Longuenesse 1998, 82).
25. The core case of judgment is assertion, which presents a thought as 'actual (true)' (A74/ B100). On problematic judgment, see ftn. 25.
26. Kant obviously acknowledges problematic judgments that do not involve an awareness of the (sufficient) grounds of the truth of the judgment – and thus are not assertoric. However, *problematic* judgments are not the same as *merely problematic* judgments, which strictly speaking are not judgments at all, but mere thoughts. Problematic judgments, such as opinions, still count as judgments because they have 'connection with truth which, although it is not complete, is nevertheless more than an arbitrary invention' (A822/B851). Problematic judgments can 'grow up' to become assertoric and apodeictic, i.e., can be 'gradually incorporated into the understanding' (A76/B101). By contrast, *merely* problematic judgments do not make a truth claim, but instead think of a thought as merely logically possible (i.e., involving no contradiction), and thus cannot become assertoric.
27. I am grateful to an anonymous reviewer for helping me clarify this.
28. Jennifer Hornsby has called this an 'identity theory of truth' (Hornsby 1997).
29. 'Synthesis alone is that which properly collects the elements for cognitions and unifies them into a certain content' (A77-8/B103). This can be understood as indicating that content is itself a holding together or synthesis of elements of cognition. This would require further elucidation, but it exceeds the limits of this paper to provide it here. See (Tolley 2011) for a Fregean reading of Kant that distinguishes content and act (force).
30. Notice that being in the sense of 'reality' or 'existence' (categorical being) is not the same as thinking, since I can think what is not real, or what does not exist. It is only being in the sense of truth (objective validity), which is 'higher' than categorical being, that is the same as thinking (judging).
31. To echo Aristotle: 'When thought has become each thing ... its condition is still one of potentiality, ... and thought is then able to think itself' (Aristotle DA, 429b6-9).
32. 'Thinking, taken in itself, is merely the logical function and hence the sheer spontaneity of combining the manifold of a merely possible intuition' (B428).
33. This metaphor of 'filling' empty forms with content can be misleading, since as discursive forms the logical functions of judging are not to be understood on the model of empty forms of intuition that get filled with matter. Kant distinguishes the way the transcendental I (or capacity for judgment, as an analytic-universal) contains all things from the way time contains all that

happens (as a form of intuition), and from the way God contains all things (as a synthetic-universal) (KU §76). Crucially, there is a sense in which the function of judging itself is still empty, even when it has been filled with 'transcendental content', since it remains a capacity that can be employed in infinitely many other judgments. This emptiness of logical functions of judging (qua capacities) is a way of characterizing the finitude of the discursive intellect.

34. 'Objective validity and necessary universal validity are reciprocal concepts' (P 4:298; see also A104-5).

35. I am grateful to an anonymous reviewer for helping me clarify this point. Notice that on this reading, thought is not initially grasped as the thinking of a being situated within an objective context. Contrary to the Evansian approach to transparency, thinking is not an occurrence in a subject located within an objective, spatio-temporal world, rather the spatio-temporal world, including the time-determinations of the schematism chapter, are internal to thought. Truth therefore will not be understood as truth-at-a-context, rather all contexts will be internal to truth. And most importantly for our topic, self-consciousness will not be consciousness indexed to an individual in the world, rather the singularity of the thinker will be internal to 'consciousness in general', the I of pure apperception.

36. I am borrowing from Sebastian Rödl's language in his new book, *Self-Consciousness and Objectivity* (Rödl 2018, 1ff.).

37. In other words, as I argued in the last section, the transcendental I (reason) thinks only itself. An anonymous reviewer has expressed skepticism about my construal of reason or apperception here as 'fundamentally generic or intersubjective rather than individual'. But if the primary truth-bearers are acts of judging (not act-independent contents), and if truths can be shared with others in communication, then surely self-conscious acts can be shared. This means that the *I* is shared, since the transcendental I is just the unity of such acts of judging. We should not dogmatically assume that reason and its exercises are powers or attributes attached to individual subjects. Instead, if the argument for the priority of transcendental over empirical apperception is valid, we should think of individual subjects as first made possible by the (universally shared) capacity for knowledge (i.e., by reason, or the transcendental I).

38. A species is only partially homogeneous with a genus. For instance, an ostrich is an animal, but it is *more* besides that. By contrast, all species are fully the same as the <I think>, since there isn't anything more (anything additional, not contained in the <I think>) that they can be. All species determinations of genera are therefore entirely internal to <I think>. So although the <I think> is not a particular concept (or genus), but the form of all concepts in general, one can nevertheless think of particular concepts as specifications of it.

39. According to Allison, inner sense does not 'relat[e] representations to objects' but instead 'makes these representations themselves into (subjective) objects, which it cognizes as the contents of mental states' (Allison 2004, 278–9). This would make my inner states into objects given to me; but Kant appears to be saying that representations cannot be made into objects. We can only become conscious of them through the acts of representing outer objects.

40. Valaris emphasizes this aspect of inner sense in his interpretation, to which I am heavily indebted (Valaris 2008).

41. Contrary to Boyle, who restricts the 'objects of inner sense' to 'sensations, appetites, and other kinds of mental "affection"' (Boyle 2009, 160), I think it is clear that Kant thinks we can become empirically aware not just of our passive states, but also of our acts of thinking and judging: 'I can say that I as intelligence and thinking subject cognize my self as an object that is thought, insofar as I am also given to myself in intuition' (B155).

42. In inner sense, Kant says that 'I merely represent the spontaneity of my thought, i.e., of the determining, and my existence always remains only sensibly determinable, i.e., determinable as the existence of an appearance' (B158n.).

43. In *Self-Consciousness*, Sebastian Rödl argues that all knowledge is *either* 'receptive knowledge' *or* 'spontaneous knowledge', and that first-personal self-knowledge is spontaneous knowledge. But if my reading of self-affection is accurate, it is both receptive *and* first-personal or spontaneous (see, for instance Rödl 2007, 144f.).

44. Strictly speaking the transcendental I appears to be 'nothing' in a sense that precedes the 'concept of an object in general', which Kant says underlies the distinction between 'something' and 'nothing', and thus precedes both a table of something and the 'table of nothing' (A290/B346). As a logical sort of 'nothing', the transcendental I is the concept of the 'original-synthetic unity of apperception' that precedes the 'objective unity of apperception' and thus precedes the concept of an object (B131ff.). The 'nothingness' of the empirical I, like that of the logical I, also does not belong on the 'table of nothing' at A292/B348, because the empirical I, as an object of indeterminate empirical intuition, is not an object of determinate empirical intuition, and so does not fall under the 'concept of an object in general'. I am thankful to Addison Ellis for pressing me to think about these different senses of 'nothing'.

45. As I will clarify in the following, this is not to deny Valaris's point that I can become aware of my particular perspective in space and time, and can thus situate myself in the world as an appearance alongside other appearances, through syntheses of the imagination in inner sense. I only mean to deny that this can be an exhaustive account of inner sense.

46. There is also a sense in which the object is the same as its being, since objects are homogeneous with the concepts they can be subsumed under (as argued above). But the sameness of the object and its concept in that sense is merely formal. Since this formal object is the same across different material objects (identity in difference), there is still a distinction between what is the same (formal object: being) and what is different (material objects: beings).

47. This contrasts with Longuenesse's reading, according to which I refers to a thing that exists even at the level of transcendental apperception: 'We just learn to use "I" to refer to ourselves insofar as, necessarily, in thinking we ascribe thinking to ourselves, the individual currently engaged in the act of thinking, and aware of thinking by perceiving the fact that we think' (Longuenesse 2017, 89). See also Kitcher, who interprets empirical apperception as a kind of self-ascription of mental states (Kitcher 2011, 124).

48. This is an allusion to Heidegger's analysis of the etymology of existence ('ek-sistence') as a standing-out (Heidegger 1998, 147f.).

49. I am grateful to Sebastian Rödl for pointing out to me the distinction between 'particular' and 'singular' in this context.

50. Valaris helpfully shows how even my spatial perspective is something that I become aware of in inner sense, since the juxtaposition of things in space is an act of imaginative synthesis (placing one thing alongside another) and hence available to empirical self-awareness (Valaris 2008, 8f.).
51. Kant indicates that these acts of self-determination presuppose an indeterminate intuition of my existence in the following passage: 'The **I think** expresses the act of determining my existence. The existence is thereby already given, but the way in which I am to determine it, i.e., the manifold that I am to posit in myself as belonging to it, is not thereby given' (B157n.).

Acknowledgments

I have presented previous versions of this paper at three events. The first was a conference on *Introspection, Self-Consciousness, and Self-Knowledge* at the University of Nebraska, Lincoln, in May 2015. The second was a conference on *Transparency and Self-Consciousness* at Ryerson University in Toronto in May 2018. And the third was a colloquium talk at the University of Leipzig, Germany in June 2018. Thanks to all the audiences at these events for their challenging questions and astute comments. Special thanks to Irad Kimhi, Sebastian Rödl, Matthew Boyle, Adrian Haddock, David Sussman, and Stephen Engstrom for helpful conversations directly related to the topic of this paper. I also thank two anonymous reviewers for their extensive and detailed comments, many of which led me to rewrite the latter half of this paper.

ORCID

Alexandra M. Newton http://orcid.org/0000-0002-7491-9728

References

Allison, H. 2004. *Kant's Transcendental Idealism*. New Haven: Yale University Press.
Aristotle,. 1984. "De Anima" (DA). Translated by J. A. Smith. In *The Complete Works of Ar\istotle*. 1 Vol. edited by J. Barnes. Princeton: Princeton University Press.
Boyle, M. 2009. "Two Kinds of Self-Knowledge." *Philosophy and Phenomenological Research* 78 (1): 133–164. doi:10.1111/phpr.2008.78.issue-1.
Boyle, M. unpublished. "Transparency and Reflection."

Byrne, A. 2011. "Transparency, Belief, and Intention." *Proceedings of the Aristotelian Society Supplementary Volume* 85 (1): 201–221. doi:10.1111/j.1467-8349.2011.00203.x.

Byrne, A. 2018. *Transparency and Knowledge*. Oxford: Oxford University Press.

Engstrom, S. 2013. "Unity of Apperception." *Studi Kantiani*, Fabrizio Serra Editore, 26: 37–54.

Engstrom, S. 2017. "Knowledge and Its Object." In *Kant's Critique of Pure Reason: A Critical Guide*, edited by J. O'Shea, 28–45. Cambridge: Cambridge University Press.

Evans, G. 1982. Varieties of Reference. Edited by J. McDowell. Oxford: Oxford University Press.

Heidegger, M. 1998. "On the Essence of Truth." In *Pathmarks*, edited by W. McNeill, 136–154. Cambridge: Cambridge University Press.

Hornsby, J. 1997. "Truth: The Identity Theory." In: *Proceedings of the Aristotelian Society* 97: 1–24, Aristotelian Society was held at Birkbeck College, London.

Kant, I. 1992. Jäsche Logic (JL). In: Lectures on Logic. Translated and edited by J. M. Young. Cambridge: Cambridge University Press.

Kant, I. 1998. *Critique of Pure Reason* (KrV). Translated and edited by Guyer, Paul and Wood, Allen W. Cambridge: Cambridge University Press.

Kitcher, P. 2011. *Kant's Thinker*. Oxford: Oxford University Press.

Korsgaard, C. M. 2009. *Self-Constitution. Agency, Identity, Integrity*. Oxford: Oxford University Press.

Longuenesse, B. 1998. *Kant and the Capacity to Judge*. Princeton: Princeton University Press.

Longuenesse, B. 2017. *I, Me, Mine. Back to Kant, and Back Again*. Oxford: Oxford University Press.

McDowell, J. 1994. *Mind and World*. Cambridge, MA: Harvard University Press.

Moran, R. 2001. *Authority and Estrangement. An Essay on Self-Knowledge*. Princeton: Princeton University Press.

Moran, R. 2012. "Self-Knowledge, 'Transparency', and the Forms of Activity." In *Introspection and Consciousness*, edited by D. Smithies and D. Stoljar, 211–238. Oxford: Oxford University Press.

Narboux, J.-P. unpublished. "Is Self-Consciousness Consciousness of One's Self?"

Rödl, S. 2007. *Self-Consciousness*. Cambridge, MA: Harvard University Press.

Rödl, S. 2017. "The First Person and Self-Knowledge in Analytic Philosophy." In *Self-Knowledge. A History*, edited by U. Renz. Oxford: Oxford University Press: 280–294.

Rödl, S. 2018. *Self-Consciousness and Objectivity. An Introduction to Absolute Idealism*. Cambridge, MA: Harvard University Press.

Sartre, J.-P. 1956. *Being and Nothingness (BN)*. Translated by H. E. Barnes. Gallimard. New York: Washington Square Press.

Sartre, J.-P. 1960. *The Transcendence of the Ego. An Existentialist Theory of Consciousness (TE)*. Translated by F. Williams and R. Kirkpatrick. New York: Hill and Wang.

Sartre, J.-P. 1970. "Intentionality: A Fundamental Idea of Husserl's Phenomenology." *Journal of the British Society for Phenomenology* 1 (2): 4–5. doi:10.1080/00071773.1970.11006118.

Strawson, P. 1966. *The Bounds of Sense. An Essay on Kant's Critique of Pure Reason*. London: Routledge.

Tolley, C. 2011. "Kant on the Content of Cognition." *European Journal of Philosophy* 22 (2): 200–228. doi:10.1111/j.1468-0378.2011.00483.x.

Valaris, M. 2008. "Inner Sense, Self-Affection, and Temporal Consciousness in Kant's Critique of Pure Reason." *Philosophers' Imprint* 8 (4): 1–18.

Wittgenstein, L. 1958. *Blue and Brown Books*. New York: Blackwell Publishers.

Wittgenstein, L. 2001. *Tractatus Logico-Philosophicus (Tractatus)*. New York: Routledge.

δ OPEN ACCESS

The puzzle of transparency and how to solve it

Wolfgang Barz

ABSTRACT
According to the transparency approach, achievement of self-knowledge is a two-stage process: first, the subject arrives at the judgment '*p*'; second, the subject proceeds to the judgment 'I believe that *p*.' The puzzle of transparency is to understand why the transition from the first to the second judgment is rationally permissible. After revisiting the debate between Byrne and Boyle on this matter, I present a novel solution according to which the transition is rationally permissible in virtue of a justifying argument that begins from a premise referring to the mental utterance that is emitted in the course of judging '*p*.'

The puzzle of transparency is a by-product of the transparency approach to self-knowledge according to which one comes to know one's own mental states, not by peering inward, but by focusing on the aspects of the external world that one is aware of in virtue of having the mental states in question. Roughly stated, the puzzle is this: how should the focus on external states of affairs (such as the location of Toronto) bring about knowledge about my mental states (such as my belief that Toronto is located in Ontario)? Naturally, this only puzzles people who think that the transparency approach is by and large correct. If you think that the transparency approach is wrong-headed anyway, then there is no puzzle for you. Nonetheless, the puzzle is of interest even to opponents of the transparency approach since, if there were no satisfying solution to the puzzle, then this would be a point against the transparency approach. Thus, even opponents of the transparency approach may find the following beneficial.

The notion of transparency is notoriously ambiguous: different philosophers associate different ideas with it. To forestall possible misunderstanding, then, it is essential to rule out those meanings of 'transparency' which are not relevant in this context. I conduct this task in Section 1. Furthermore,

---

© 2019 The Author(s). Published by Informa UK Limited, trading as Taylor & Francis Group.
This is an Open Access article distributed under the terms of the Creative Commons Attribution-NonCommercial-NoDerivatives License (http://creativecommons.org/licenses/by-nc-nd/4.0/), which permits non-commercial re-use, distribution, and reproduction in any medium, provided the original work is properly cited, and is not altered, transformed, or built upon in any way.

I tentatively defend the transparency approach against a widespread objection. In Section 2, I present the puzzle of transparency and explain what is so puzzling about it. In Section 3, I outline a solution proposed by Byrne (2005) and revisit Boyle's (2011) criticism of it. Finally, in Section 4, I present my solution to the puzzle which is, in a sense, a syncretic proposal that tries to reconcile the opposing views of Byrne and Boyle.

1. Some preliminary remarks on the notion of transparency

First, let me emphasize that by 'transparency' I will not refer to the traditional, sometimes called 'Cartesian,' claim that if a person is in a certain mental state, then this person is in a position to know that she is in that state. This is the idea that Ryle (1949) once dubbed 'self-intimation' and Williamson (2000) today calls 'luminosity.' However, self-intimation and luminosity have nothing to do with the idea of transparency, at least as used here. In this paper, the notion of transparency refers to the idea that, typically, a person comes to know that she is in a particular mental state, not by peering inward at her mental state itself, but by focusing instead on certain aspects of the external world. Let us call transparency in this sense – the sense that is relevant here – self-ascriptive transparency.

Self-ascriptive transparency should be distinguished from both phenomenal transparency and transparency of doxastic deliberation. Phenomenal transparency is the claim that, when I try to attend to the phenomenal properties of one of my perceptual experiences, I end up attending to some features of mind-independent objects. Phenomenal transparency is most prominently emphasized by Tye (1995). Tye says, for example, that, if I try to attend to the phenomenal color of my visual experience of a ripe tomato, I end up attending, not to some feature of my experience, but to the red surface of the ripe tomato. Notice that phenomenal transparency might be related to, but is far more specific than, self-ascriptive transparency – for phenomenal transparency is restricted to situations in which I try to discover the type and content of my own perceptual experiences. In contrast, self-ascriptive transparency is not so restricted but also covers situations in which I try to discover the type and content of other mental states, especially so-called propositional attitudes such as belief and desire.

However, I will not expand on all the different types of propositional attitudes but will focus on belief.[1] The claim of self-ascriptive transparency on which I will concentrate is that we come to know that we believe that p – where p stands for a proposition about the external world – not by peering inward and rummaging through our belief-box, so to speak, but by focusing instead on the external-world-proposition that serves as the content of our belief. In other words, the idea is that I come to know that I have a particular belief, not by focusing on anything mental, but by focusing exclusively on the worldly items my belief is about.

Self-ascriptive transparency in this sense is related, but not quite the same as transparency of doxastic deliberation, as discussed by Shah and Velleman (2005). Whereas transparency of doxastic deliberation is the claim that I can answer the question whether I *should* believe that p by answering the question whether p, self-ascriptive transparency is the claim that I can answer the question whether I, *in fact*, believe that p by answering the question whether p. Thus, there is some similarity here, but the notion of self-ascriptive transparency is not the same as the notion of transparency of doxastic deliberation.

Having differentiated between different meanings of transparency, I will use the term 'transparency' in the following to cover only self-ascriptive transparency. The other types of transparency will play no role in what follows.

One well-known source of the transparency approach to self-knowledge (henceforth 'TA') is an often-cited passage from Evans's *Varieties of Reference* (1982) according to which I answer the question whether I believe that there will be a third world war by answering the question whether there will be a third world war. The essence is that, to achieve doxastic self-knowledge, as it may be called, I do not have to look inside but at the world. Thus, the usual and everyday method of knowing one's own beliefs – which has been traditionally considered a kind of *intro*spection – turns out as a specific variety of *extro*spection.

To be sure, talk of 'extrospection' should not be taken too seriously here. In particular, proponents of TA are not committed to the view that we come to know our own beliefs by sense perception. Instead, TA only implies that, typically, we come to know our own beliefs by *some* outward-oriented mental activity that may, but need not be sense perception. According to Moran (2001), for example, the outward-oriented mental activity consists in *weighing the evidence* for and against a particular proposition. To use Evans' original example for illustration, suppose that I am asked whether I believe that there will be a third world war. According to Moran, I answer this question by weighing the evidence for and against the prospect of a third world war. Suppose, for example, that I may find that the reasons for the proposition *that there will be a third world war* outweigh the reasons against it. Consequently, I will make the judgment that, yes, there will be a third world war. This, in turn, drives me to the conclusion that I, in fact, believe that there will be a third world war. Call this the 'evidence-based account' of the outward-oriented mental activity in which we engage to determine our own beliefs.

The evidence-based account has some serious drawbacks.[2] The objection is that considering the reasons for and against the proposition p will, at least in many cases, create a new belief rather than uncover an already existing one. Suppose, for example, that I never thought about the possibility of a third world war before the question of whether I believe that there will be a third world war was directed at me. Thus, at the time of the question, I did *not* believe that there will be a third world war. However, after deliberating on the issue, I find that the reasons for the prospect of a future world war outweigh the reasons against it. Consequently, I conclude that I *have* the belief in question, though I did not have that belief at the time the question was directed at me. Similarly, the procedure described by the evidence-based account may result in ignoring beliefs that I have. Just think of beliefs that are not in line with the evidence at my disposal, such as religious beliefs, deeply ingrained prejudices, or superstition. By weighing the evidence at one's disposal, one will, hopefully, realize that one should refrain from believing propositions not supported by one's evidence. Accordingly, one will conclude that one *lacks* the beliefs in question, though one actually has them – at least at the time before the process of deliberation started.

In light of these objections, it is often argued that TA is ill-conceived and has to be superseded either by an improved version of the inner sense theory (Gertler), by some kind of expressivism (Finkelstein) or even by a Ryle-inspired inferentialism (Cassam). However, this reaction is a bit over-hasty. Even if Moran's evidence-based account fails, this does not imply that TA goes down the tube. In my view at least, there is a promising alternative to the evidence-based account that remains perfectly in accord with the basic idea of TA. According to this alternative, the outward-oriented mental activity by which we come to know our own beliefs does not consist in weighing the evidence for and against a particular proposition, but just in *understanding* the proposition in question. Nishi Shah and David Velleman nicely summarize the procedure as:

> "posing the question whether p and seeing what one is spontaneously inclined to answer. In this procedure, the question whether p serves as a stimulus applied to oneself for the empirical purpose of eliciting a response ... [T]he procedure requires one to refrain from any reasoning as to whether p, since that reasoning might alter the state of mind that one is trying to assay. Hence, asking oneself whether p must be a brute stimulus in this case rather than an invitation to reasoning" (Shah and Velleman 2005, 506).

To use Evans's example for illustration again, suppose you are asked whether you believe that there will be a third world war. Furthermore, suppose that you believe that there will be a third world war. Now, recall that having a belief to the effect that p implies having the disposition to judge that p whenever the issue arises (and conditions are favorable). So, given that you believe that there will be a third world war, once you understand the proposition that there will be a third world war, your disposition to make the respective judgment is triggered and you spontaneously judge – that is, you judge without reflecting on any evidence – that there will be a third world war. Consequently, you conclude that you believe that there will be a third world war. This account, which may be called 'spontaneous judgment account,'[3] manages without the idea of deliberation or assessment of reasons or weighing evidence. Accordingly, it is immune to the objections that are commonly raised against Moran's evidence-based account. So the failure of Moran's evidence-based account does not engulf TA in the abyss. The spontaneous judgment account is still there as a fallback option.

Indeed, the spontaneous judgment account is not without difficulties either. One might wonder, for example, whether one's spontaneous judgment about a certain matter is a reliable indicator of one's belief.[4] However, I will not enlarge upon this question – for my overall aim in this paper is not to defend a specific variant of TA, but to discuss a puzzle, the puzzle of transparency, which pertains to both the evidence- and the spontaneous judgment account. My aim at this point was only to tentatively defend TA against a widespread but, in my view, unwarranted objection and thereby pave the way for exposing the puzzle of transparency, to which I will turn in the next section.

2. The puzzle of transparency

To get a better understanding of the puzzle, it may be helpful to abstract from the differences between the evidence-based and the spontaneous judgment account and to emphasize their similarities instead. According to both accounts, the achievement of doxastic self-knowledge is a two-stage process. At the first stage, the subject arrives at a judgment in response to a specific outward-oriented question. At the second stage, the subject proceeds from this judgment to a further judgment, this time about her own belief. Let us take a look at those two stages in slow motion. Suppose, for example, that a subject who believes that Toronto is located in Ontario wonders whether she believes that Toronto is located in Ontario. According to both the evidence-based and spontaneous judgment account, the subject can answer this question by answering the outward-directed question whether Toronto is located in Ontario. So, if things go well, then the subject will – be it due to a process of deliberation or not – arrive at the judgment that Toronto is located in Ontario.

However, making the judgment that Toronto is located in Ontario is not the end of the story – for this judgment does not state anything about the attitude the subject has towards the proposition *that Toronto is located in Ontario*. It simply says that Toronto is located in Ontario, which is just a fact about how things stand in the external world. It does not say anything about how things stand *with the subject*; it does not say that the subject *believes* that Toronto is located in Ontario. So, to arrive at a state of self-knowledge, the subject has to move on from the judgment that Toronto is located in Ontario to the judgment that *she herself believes* that Toronto is located in Ontario. Let us call this latter judgment 'second-order judgment,' and the former judgment 'first-order judgment.'

Now, a new question arises: why is it *rational* for the subject to proceed from the first-order judgment that Toronto is located in Ontario to the second-order judgment that she believes that Toronto is located in Ontario? It does not seem obvious that the transition from a judgment about a geographical fact to a judgment about the mental state of a specific person is rationally permissible. On the contrary, it seems that the transition from 'Toronto is located in Ontario' to 'I believe that Toronto is located in Ontario' is utterly bad! To begin with, the proposition *that Toronto is located in Ontario* does not logically imply the proposition *that I believe that Toronto is located in Ontario*. There is not even an empirical supporting relation between the first and the second proposition. To empirically infer from the fact that Toronto is located in Ontario, that there is some specific person in Middle-Europe, namely Wolfgang Barz, who has a particular belief about Toronto's location seems quite bizarre. There is just no empirical connection, no law of nature or such that guarantees or even makes it probable that Wolfgang Barz has a certain belief, given Toronto's location. In other words: There is just no suitable relation between the two propositional contents – the content of the first-order and the content of the second-order judgment – that could explain why the transition from the first- to the second-order judgment is epistemically admissible, good, or something that is rational to do. However, proponents of TA are committed to the view that the transition is admissible, good, and rational. Hence, there is a problem.[5]

Note that the puzzle of transparency is not supposed to be a skeptical challenge to self-knowledge. The motivation behind the problem is not to suggest that it is impossible to know our own beliefs. Rather, the motivation behind the problem is to emphasize that proponents of TA owe us an answer to the question of why the transition from a judgment about the external world to a judgment about one's own mind is rationally permissible. Unless proponents of TA provide an answer to this question, their dialectical position is quite weak – for who wants to accept an account of self-knowledge that portrays us as relying on an irrational belief-forming method? Thus, the problem is not a general skeptical problem on par with, say, Boghossian's (1989) trilemma about self-knowledge. It is a specific problem for proponents of TA.

This becomes especially clear if it is realized that for proponents of inner sense models there is no puzzle at all. When I make the judgment that Toronto is located in Ontario, then, let us suppose, there is a token representation of the proposition *that Toronto is located in Ontario* somewhere in my mind. According to proponents of inner sense models, I can take notice of this representation: I can see it flashing up in my mind, so to speak. This, it could be said, is the reason why the transition from 'Toronto is located in Ontario' to 'I believe that Toronto is located in Ontario' is justified. However, proponents of TA cannot take this line.

50 TRANSPARENCY AND APPERCEPTION

They may agree that, when I make the judgment that Toronto is located in Ontario, then there is a representation of the proposition *that Toronto is located in Ontario* flashing up in my mind. However, according to proponents of TA, we must do without any special faculties of inner sense, self-scanning devices, or self-monitoring capacities. Thus, we lack the capacity to look inside and see which mental representations are flashing up there – mental representations are just hidden from our view. So, the puzzle of transparency might be described as the challenge of explaining why it is rational to proceed from a judgment about the external world to a judgment about one's mind, *given that we lack any capacity to look inside and directly observe our mental representations.*

Now, after having outlined the puzzle, I will turn to its solution. To set the stage for my proposal, I would like first to review a suggestion made by Alex Byrne and then consider Matthew Boyle's criticism of it.

3. Byrne's proposal and Boyle's criticism

At the heart of Byrne's (2005) proposal lies the observation that anyone who proceeds from the judgment that *p* to the judgment that she herself believes that *p* can be described as following an epistemic rule. An epistemic rule is a hypothetical imperative which states that, if some specific condition is satisfied, then you should do this or that. In the case of proceeding from the judgment that *p* to the judgment that I believe that *p* the respective epistemic rule reads:

(BEL) If *p*, judge that you believe that *p*![6]

As Byrne points out, anyone who follows this rule necessarily ends up with a true judgment. To follow BEL the subject must first determine whether the condition mentioned in BEL's antecedent is satisfied. This is done by considering whether *p* is the case (this corresponds to the first stage of achieving doxastic self-knowledge that I distinguished above.) Now, if the subject comes to the conclusion that *p* is the case and that, thereby, the condition mentioned in the antecedent is satisfied, then she is in a state of believing that *p*. Thus, says Byrne, BEL is self-verifying: unless the subject believes that *p* she cannot follow the rule. Following the rule presupposes that the subject believes that *p*. So, following the rule guarantees that the subject will end up with a true second-order judgment.

Byrne is entirely correct regarding the self-verifying character of BEL. However, I doubt whether this provides an answer to the question 'Why is it rational for the subject to proceed from a first- to a second-order judgment?' The fact that BEL is self-verifying implies that proceeding from a first- to a second-order judgment is highly reliable. However, being *highly reliable* is not sufficient for being *rationally permissible*. This is at least suggested by Laurence BonJour's (1980) case of the reliable, but unknowing, clairvoyant, that is, someone who has the power to scry facts reliably without knowing that he possesses this power. The mere fact that the clairvoyant's beliefs are reliably produced does not suffice to make his beliefs rationally permissible. From the clairvoyant's perspective, his beliefs come out of the blue. That his beliefs turn out to be true must seem a sheer accident from the clairvoyant's perspective. It seems that the situation of a subject who follows BEL is similar to the situation of the unknowing clairvoyant: the subject forms her second-order judgment by means of a highly reliable method, but – unless she is aware that the method is highly reliable – she finds herself at a loss how to make sense of the truth of her second-order judgment: as we saw earlier in this paper, there is just no suitable evidential relation between the propositional contents of first- and second-order judgments. Matthew Boyle nicely puts the point: 'a modicum of rational insight will inform me that, even if it is true that P, this by itself has no tendency to show that I believe it.' Thus, Boyle continues, 'Byrne's ... approach ... represents the subject as drawing a mad inference' (Boyle 2011, 230–231). So something is missing from Byrne's account: Byrne does not tell us, why, *from the perspective of the subject who engages in the transparency procedure*, to proceed from first-order to second-order judgments is a rational thing to do.

Perhaps one may be inclined to think that there is an easy way out for Byrne here: just add – besides the condition that the subject forms her second-order judgment in accordance with a self-verifying rule – the further condition that the subject also *realizes* that she acts in accordance with a self-verifying rule. It might be suggested that, once this further condition is met, the subject is in a position to see that proceeding from first- to second-order judgment is rational. Recall that this is the move that BonJour once recommended regarding the clairvoyant: to make the clairvoyant's beliefs rational from the clairvoyant's perspective, just provide him with the knowledge to the effect that his beliefs are formed using a highly reliable method.[7] However, this strategy will not work in the case at hand because to realize that one acts in accordance with BEL, one needs to know that one's second-order judgment is based on one's first-order judgment. This, in turn, implies that one knows that one judges, and hence believes, that p. Thus, the strategy already presupposes the kind of self-knowledge that needs to be explained in the first place.

In response to this dilemma, Matthew Boyle (2011) has suggested an alternative view, the so-called 'reflective approach,' which tries to explain the inherent rationality of the transition from first- to second-order judgment without depicting this transition as an inference. According to Boyle, believing p and knowing oneself to believe p are not two different mental states, but two aspects of the same mental state. When I believe something, says Boyle, then I am tacitly aware of the fact that I believe it. So, when I pass from first- to second-order judgment, I consciously acknowledge what

I already tacitly knew. In light of this account, the transition from first- to second-order judgment is not a kind of inference from one propositional content to another, but an act of reflection, an act of making explicit or articulate a piece of knowledge that there was all along. According to Boyle, this explains why proceeding from first- to second-order judgment is rational from the perspective of the subject.

There is something right and something wrong in Boyle's view. Boyle is right when he claims that Byrne represents the subject as drawing a mad inference and, thus, cannot explain why the transition from first- to second-order judgment is rational from the subject's point of view. However, I find it hard to accept Boyle's view that believing *p* and knowing oneself to believe *p* are aspects of one and the same mental state. I cannot believe that anytime we form a belief about the external world, we are tacitly aware of ourselves as believing the proposition in question. I have no argument, but I think that this persistent virtual self-awareness, as it may be called, is phenomenologically implausible. At least from my experience, there are many situations in which I form a belief about the external world absentmindedly, that is, without any, even tacit, awareness of myself as having the belief in question.[8]

However, I will not harp on about this point because, even if one accepts the view that we are always tacitly aware of our beliefs, it is still unclear how the process of making this tacit self-awareness explicit is supposed to work without violating the requirement to do without any inwardly directed monitoring or detecting capacities. As a proponent of TA, Boyle cannot say that what he calls 'reflection' proceeds by way of observing or taking notice of the content of our tacit self-awareness. Nevertheless, Boyle seems to endorse such a view:

> "The reflective approach explains doxastic transparency ... as a matter ... of shifting one's attention from the world with which one is engaged to one's engagement with it – an engagement of which one was already tacitly cognizant" (2011, 228).

To my ears at least, this sounds pretty much like a rejection of TA. If doxastic self-knowledge is achieved by a shift of attention from the outer to the inner realm, then the idea of transparency gets lost. Thus, to retain the plausible aspects of Boyle's criticism of Byrne without giving up TA, we need to formulate a third alternative: an alternative that does not represent the subject as drawing a mad inference, yet avoiding notions incompatible with TA. This is precisely what I will attempt in the next section.

4. A novel solution to the puzzle

First, I would like to introduce some auxiliary assumptions on which I will rely in what follows. The most important assumption is that making a judgment is the mental analog to making an assertion. Making an assertion contains at least three elements: first, the asserter – the person who makes the assertion; second, the vehicle of assertion, which are the words uttered by the asserter; and third, the assertive force with which the words that the asserter utters are uttered. I assume that these three elements are also present in the case of judgments, especially that there is a mental analog to the vehicle of assertion: mental words and mental sentences that are mentally uttered or thought with assertoric force. It may seem as if the admission of mental words commits me to some demanding empirical hypothesis such as Fodor's language of thought. However, I do not think that I am thus committed because the assumption that there are mental words does not imply that those words are physical structures in the brain. They may be structures of a Cartesian mental substance instead. So the claim that there are mental words as such is neutral concerning the physicalism/dualism-debate in the philosophy of mind and hence should be acceptable for philosophers of all stripes. The picture I would like to suggest, then, is this: when someone makes a judgment to the effect that p, he or she thinks some mental sentence that means that p with assertoric force – where the verb 'to think' refers to the mental analog of the activity of uttering.[9]

Let us return to the question of why the transition from first- to second-order judgment is rational from the perspective of the subject. Suppose again that I make the judgment that Toronto is located in Ontario – either as the result of a process of deliberation or as the spontaneous outcome of understanding the proposition in question. According to the picture I just drew, I think a sentence that means that Toronto is located in Ontario with assertoric force. Now, my strategy to solve the puzzle of transparency is to formulate a justifying argument that is anchored in the mental sentence that is thought when making the judgment that Toronto is located in Ontario. The argument will only employ rather trivial premises that any normal subject can justifiably believe without engaging in inner observation. So, if the argument succeeds, it will explain why the transition from first- to second-order judgment is rational from the first-person perspective without violating the requirement to do without any inwardly directed monitoring or detecting capacities.

If, as I assume, making the judgment that Toronto is located in Ontario consists in mentally uttering a sentence that means that Toronto is located in Ontario, it must be possible for me to refer back to that mental utterance in subsequent thought, just as during a conversation with someone else it is possible for me to refer back to one of his or her utterances. Moreover, since there could be no doubt that I understand my own mental utterance, it must be possible for me to ascribe to it the property of *being a sincere assertion to the effect that Toronto is located in Ontario*. This will be the first premise of the justifying argument that I am about to formulate:

(1) **That** is a sincere assertion to the effect that Toronto is located in Ontario.

Notice that the word 'that' in bold letters does not refer to the proposition *that Toronto is located in Ontario*, but to the mental utterance of the words, 'Toronto is located in Ontario,' that, according to my assumption, takes place when making the judgment that Toronto is located in Ontario.

It might be objected that I could not refer back to an utterance – whether mental or not – unless I focused on its syntactic features such as the shape or sound of the words uttered. However, it should be clear that proponents of TA cannot admit this because it would violate the requirement to do without presupposing any inwardly directed monitoring or detecting capacities. So it seems that premise (1) is not admissible by the standards of TA.

My response is that I do not accept the view that one could not refer back to an utterance unless one focused on its syntactic features: it suffices that one attends to its *meaning*. Imagine that, immediately after I publicly uttered the words 'Toronto is located in Ontario' with assertoric force, you forget about the shape and sound of my words so that you cannot even tell whether I spoke English, German, French or whatever. As long as you grasped the meaning of my words, however, you will still be able to refer back to them – for example, by using a description such as 'the last utterance in our conversation that meant that Toronto is located in Ontario.' To refer back to my utterance, you do not need to focus on or remember its shape or sound; you only have to understand it. The same goes for mental utterances: you do not need to take notice of their syntactic features (whatever they are); you only have to understand them. The activity of understanding the meaning of one's own utterances – whether mental or not – in turn, does not presuppose any act of inner observation or any inwardly directed monitoring or detection. It only presupposes the mastering of language. Thus, premise (1) is admissible in the present context.

It might be objected that I am too quick to draw this conclusion. In order to understand a public utterance, it is necessary to notice it first. If you don't see or hear an utterance, you cannot understand it. Seeing or hearing an utterance amounts to grasping its syntactic features. Now, if mental utterances are analogous to public utterances, then there must be some mental analog to the activity of taking notice of an utterance, call it 'mental noticing.' Mental noticing, in turn, is a kind of inwardly directed monitoring capacity whereby subjects grasp the syntactic features of their current mental utterances. Thus, it seems that my account is doomed to fail from the outset: the postulation of mental utterances brings in its train the acceptance of an inwardly directed monitoring capacity.[10]

My reply is that it might be true that, in order to understand a *third person* public utterance, it is necessary to notice it first. However, it is not true that, in order to understand one of *my own* public utterances, it is necessary to notice it first. In the first person case, understanding and uttering occur within the same act, at least as far as assertions are concerned: to make an assertion is to utter words you already understand; you don't need to notice your words before you can make sense of them. From the first person perspective, the sense is already there. Thus, the postulation of mental utterances is innocent: it does not commit us to the existence of an inwardly directed monitoring capacity.

However, premise (1) is still suspicious in another respect. Recall that premise (1) not only presupposes that I refer back to some utterance; it also presupposes that I ascribe the property of *being a sincere assertion* to it. So the question is: how am I to *know* that the mental utterance to which I refer back is a sincere assertion? It might be said that I do not know that an assertion made by another person is sincere unless I know that the person who makes the assertion believes what she says. Further, it might be said that the same goes for one's own assertions. Thus, it seems that knowing the sincerity of my own assertion requires me to know that I believe that Toronto is located in Ontario. That is to say, premise (1) already presupposes the truth of the claim that the justifying argument (I am about to formulate) is supposed to establish. Thus, it seems that premise (1) is not admissible for reasons of circularity.

However, you need not know that the speaker believes what she says to be justified in believing that she is sincere. It suffices that you are not in possession of evidence to the effect that the speaker is insincere. At least, this is the default rule in normal conversational situations: as long as you do not detect any signs of insincerity on the side of the person opposite, you are justified in believing that she is sincere – you do not need to establish first what the person believes. I see no reason why this rule, when it comes to one's own mental utterances, should cease to be in force. Recall that the hypothetical subject of my example believes that Toronto is located in Ontario. Since, in this case, the subject and the speaker are the same person, there are no possible signs of insincerity that the subject might detect. Consequently, the subject is justified in believing that the speaker – who happens to be herself – is sincere.[11] Thus, premise (1) is admissible. There is no danger of circularity here.

Up to this stage of the argument, the subject is licensed to conclude that there is *someone* who makes a sincere assertion to the effect that Toronto is located in Ontario. However, the subject is not licensed to conclude that *she* is the one.[12] Thus, a further premise is needed:

(2) The person who utters **that** is identical to the person who utters *this*, and I am the person who utters *this*.

Again, the word 'that' in bold letters refers back to the original utterance of the mental sentence 'Toronto is located in Ontario.' In contrast, the word 'this' in italics – as it appears both in the first and the second conjunct – refers to premise (2) itself. Let us take a look at the first conjunct of (2) first. The first conjunct identifies the utterer of the original mental sentence, 'Toronto is located in Ontario,' with the utterer of (2). The question is: how does the subject know that the utterer of the original sentence is identical to the utterer of (2)? At first sight, it might be tempting to suppose that the subject cannot know whether two given utterances have their source in the same person unless the subject has taken a close look at both utterances and carefully compared their features, such as their characteristic sound or tone. However, this line of thought would lead into a blind alley again, because comparing characteristics of mental utterances would presuppose an ability to overhear those utterances and notice their characteristic features with an inner ear. Thus, the unwelcome commitment to inwardly directed monitoring capacities would return.

Fortunately, there is another way of justifying the first conjunct of premise (2) that does without any such unwelcome commitments. I take my cue here from a paper by Enoch and Schechter (2008) in which they address the question of why we are justified in employing basic belief-forming methods such as inference to the best explanation, modus ponens or reliance on perception. Enoch and Schechter argue that we are justified in employing these methods in virtue of the fact that employing them is indispensable for successfully engaging in activities that are central to rationality. Such activities include understanding the world around us, deliberating about what to do, planning for the future, and so on. If, for example, I would refrain from employing any inference to the best explanation, I would not be able to make sense of the external world. That implies that I could not engage in a rationally required project. Thus, the method of inference to the best explanation is essential for being rational. In a sense, then, basic belief-forming methods are justified in virtue of their pragmatic indispensability.

This idea naturally extends to *beliefs*. If a belief is such that holding it is a necessary precondition for being rational, then one is justified in holding it, even in the absence of any positive evidence. The first conjunct of premise (2) expresses such a belief: it attributes of two mental utterances, which are in fact one's own, the property of having common authorship. Consider what happened if one would lack beliefs of this type, that is, if one would not believe of mental utterances, which are in fact one's own, that they have common authorship. In my view, this would amount to a state of mental disorder similar to thought insertion, that is, a state in which the subject feels as if the thoughts that are hers stem from someone else. Being in a state of mental disorder similar to thought insertion is a severe obstacle to engaging in the activity of reasoning. However, not being able to engage in the activity of reasoning would deprive us of the kernel of our rationality. Thus, believing of two mental utterances that come up in one's mind that they have common authorship is indispensable for being rational. The first conjunct of premise (2), then, is justified in virtue of its pragmatic indispensability. The subject does not need to gather any positive evidence.

At this point, a severe difficulty looms.[13] It might be said that the strategy I adopt to justify the first conjunct of premise (2) – the 'Enoch and Schechter strategy' for short – might be used to solve the puzzle of transparency in a simple and straightforward way. It seems plausible to say that transitions from first- to second-order judgments are indispensable for successfully engaging in activities that are central to rationality. If we would not carry out this transition, we would not be able to achieve doxastic self-knowledge. However, we need to achieve doxastic self-knowledge in order to understand ourselves. Thus, the transition in question is pragmatically indispensable for being rational, just as other fundamental belief-forming methods are, such as inference to the best explanation, use of modus ponens or reliance on perception. Now, if the Enoch and Schechter strategy is right when applied to the first conjunct of premise (2), it cannot be wrong when applied to transitions from first- to second-order judgments. So, why not choose the Enoch and Schechter strategy instead of constructing a justifying argument to solve the puzzle? Why not claim that the transition from first- to second-order judgment is justified in virtue of its pragmatic indispensability?

The problem with this proposal is that the Enoch and Schechter strategy amounts to a form of externalism. In order to be justified in the Enoch and Schechter way, employment of the belief-forming method in question has to be indispensable for being rational. However, the subject does not need to *believe* that employment of the belief-forming method is indispensable for being rational. According to Enoch and Schechter, a subject might be justified in employing a belief-forming method even if she does not have access to the fact due to which she is justified.[14] Hence, the Enoch and Schechter strategy is of no help for explaining why the transition from first- to second order judgments is rational *from the subject's point of view*.[15]

This response may provoke a second, more worrisome, concern: why should we think that the method for acquiring doxastic self-knowledge should be subject to a more rigorous standard of rationality than other basic belief-forming methods? If what Enoch and Schechter (2008) argue with respect to inference to the best explanation, use of modus ponens, reliance on perception, and other basic belief-forming methods is correct, and I am right that the Enoch and Schechter strategy is a form of externalism, then it seems that subjects are perfectly justified in using those methods without their being rational from the subject's perspective. Why shouldn't we conclude that the same goes for our method for acquiring doxastic self-knowledge? Why shouldn't we conclude that we are perfectly justified in proceeding from first- to second-order judgments despite the fact that this transition is not rational from the subject's perspective? It seems, then, that I apply double standards: as regards inference to the best explanation, use of modus ponens, reliance on perception, and other basic belief-forming methods I seem to tolerate the view that a belief-forming method may be justifiably employed without being rational from the subject's perspective; however, when it comes to the method for acquiring doxastic self-knowledge I insist on the view that it cannot be justifiably employed unless it is rational from the subject's perspective. This seems to be inconsistent at least.

Let me say in response that, according to TA, the method for acquiring doxastic self-knowledge is not a *basic* belief-forming method on a par with inference to the best explanation, use of modus ponens and reliance on perception. Recall that, according to TA, doxastic self-knowledge does not require some special-purpose epistemic capacity (such as inner observation) that comes in addition to other epistemic capacities. Instead, the method for achieving doxastic self-knowledge is parasitic upon other belief-forming methods such as perception and inference. TA is, in Byrne's terminology, *economical* in that it explains doxastic self-knowledge 'solely in terms of epistemic capacities and abilities that are needed for knowledge of other subject matters.'[16] Thus, even if proponents of TA accept the Enoch and Schechter strategy in regard to basic belief-forming methods, they are not committed to accepting it in regard to the method for achieving self-knowledge – for this latter method is non-basic.

What about the second conjunct of premise (2): 'I am the person who utters *this*' – where the word 'this' refers to the utterance in which the word 'this' appears? The second conjunct of premise (2) is simply true by definition of the first-person pronoun 'I.' Any token of 'I' refers to the person who is the author of the utterance in which that token appears. Because it makes this definition explicit, the second conjunct of premise (2) is an *a priori* truth. Again, there is no need for postulating any inwardly directed monitoring or detecting capacities to explain how the subject can know (or be justified in believing) it.

The rest of the justifying argument falls rather easily from the assumptions already accepted. From (1) and (2) it follows that:

(3) I sincerely assert that Toronto is located in Ontario,

from which, backed by the trivial claim that whenever someone sincerely asserts that *p* she believes that *p*, it follows that I believe that Toronto is located in Ontario, QED.

Note that the justifying argument just outlined does not start from the proposition *that Toronto is located in Ontario*. Instead, it starts from a premise referring to a specific mental utterance. Thus, the proposition *that Toronto is located in Ontario* makes no direct contribution to the argument. However, it makes an indirect contribution: it is vital for the argument that the mental utterance to which the first premise refers expresses the proposition *that Toronto is located in Ontario*. So, even if there is no suitable evidential relation between the proposition expressed by '*p*' and the proposition expressed by 'I believe that *p*,' this does not imply that there is no reasonable way from the judgment '*p*' to the judgment 'I believe that *p*.' The point of my proposal is that the act of judging '*p*' is accompanied by certain beliefs which evidentially support the proposition expressed by 'I believe that *p*.'

According to my proposal, then, the justification involved in the achievement of doxastic self-knowledge is perfectly normal inferential justification. Thus, it might be objected that we typically do not come to know our own beliefs by inference: our judgments about our own beliefs are *spontaneously* formed. However, this objection is based on a misunderstanding concerning the idea of inferential justification. The idea of inferential justification concerns the way a belief is *justified* – it does not concern the way a belief is *formed*. Note, especially, that to be inferentially justified in holding the belief that *p*, one does not need to *infer* that *p* from the premises of which the justifying argument consists. Rather one only needs to *justifiably believe those premises*. It is not even required that those beliefs are occurrent.[17] So, in a sense, inferential justification can go without inference. Therefore, it is not self-contradictory to claim that there are judgments which are both spontaneously formed and inferentially justified. Second-order judgments are a case in point.

Nonetheless, it might be objected that the conditions on doxastic self-knowledge that follow from my proposal are still too strong – for, even if the subject does not need to infer the conclusion 'I believe that Toronto is located in Ontario' by explicitly going through all steps of the justifying argument, the subject needs to *believe* premises (1) and (2) at least. And this might seem highly implausible. Aren't those premises just figments of the philosopher's imagination? I do not think they are. Premise (1), recall, gives expression to our capacity for understanding our own thoughts. Premise (2), in turn, gives expression to our capacity for reasoning, particularly the capacity for treating one's own thoughts as having their source from the same subject and thinking of that subject as oneself. So, even if the wording of premises (1) and (2) may seem odd at first sight, we are all familiar with them. An analogy might bring the point home. Consider your capacity to read aloud the sentence 'The Aguasabon Falls is a must-see attraction in Terrace Bay.' You would not be able to read aloud that sentence unless you believed that **that word** is pronounced [ði:] – where '**that word**' refers to the first word of the sentence above. So, when you read the sentence aloud, you surely believe at that moment that **that word** is pronounced [ði:]. Of course, you do not *think* or *judge* that **that word** is pronounced [ði:] when you read the sentence aloud – you just *believe* it. Moreover, of course, you do not have any awareness of your belief that **that word** is pronounced [ði:] when you read the sentence aloud, nor do you remember having had that belief in the aftermath. The belief, as it were, entirely stays in the background (and disappears once the word 'the' gets out of sight). Nonetheless, it is (or was) there. The same applies to the beliefs that correspond to premises (1) and (2): they are there as long as the first-order judgment is performed, but entirely stay in the background (and vanish once the mental utterance 'Toronto is located in Ontario' dies away).

5. Résumé

The main question of the paper was: 'Why is the transition from first- to second-order judgment rational from the perspective of the subject who performs that transition?' Byrne did not provide an answer; he only told us that the transition is highly reliable. Boyle correctly identified this weakness in Byrne's account, but his counterproposal had some shortcomings. According to Boyle, the transition is rational from the subject's point of view because it involves a shift of attention to some mental fact of which the subject was already tacitly aware. However, the notion of a shift of attention from the external to the mental realm bears the danger of losing the idea of transparency. Therefore, I outlined an alternative. According to this alternative, the transition from first- to second-order judgment is rationally permissible in virtue of a justifying argument that starts out from a premise referring to the mental utterance emitted during the act of judging. Thus, Boyle is right when he claims, *pace* Byrne, that we do not infer that we believe that *p* from the premise that *p*. However, Boyle is wrong when he thinks that we are permanently tacitly aware of our beliefs. Rather, whenever we make a judgment to the effect that *p*, there is a set of background beliefs by virtue of which we are inferentially justified in judging that we believe that *p*. In short: we have no tacit permanent self-awareness of our first-order beliefs, but we do have permanent inferential justification for forming second-order judgments.[18]

Notes

1. I deal with self-knowledge of non-doxastic attitudes such as wishes, desires, and intentions in Barz (2015). For more on self-knowledge of one's visual experiences, see Barz (2014).
2. Cf. Gertler (2011), Cassam (2014), Finkelstein (2012).
3. I owe this label to Andi Müller.
4. See Peacocke (1998, 90) for an example that is often assumed to cast in an unfavorable light the thesis that judgment is sufficient for belief.
5. Cf. Byrne (2005, 95, 2018, 74–98). See also Dretske (2003, 2), Evans (1982, 231), Gallois (1996, 47), Martin (1998, 110) and Moran (2003, 413).
6. My formulation slightly deviates from Byrne's as he uses 'believe' instead of 'judge.' However, in his (2005), footnote 22, Byrne himself admits that using 'judge' would be better.
7. Cf. BonJour (1980, 63).

8. Maybe this is not quite fair to Boyle's view – for Boyle might claim that knowledge is not a form of awareness but a kind of ability. See Marcus (2016) and Campbell (2018) for defenses of Boyle's reflectivism along these lines. However, since my chief objection to Boyle's account does not depend on whether knowledge is a form of awareness or not, I do not pursue the matter any further here. Thanks to David Hunter who drew my attention to this point.

9. Note, again, that the assumption that there are mental words is neutral concerning the question of how mental content is physically encoded. Thus, thinking a mental sentence is *not* the same as 'tokening a string of symbols of the language of thought' in Fodor's sense. Thanks to Peter Kuhn for encouraging me to be clearer on this point.

10. I owe this objection to Henning Lütje.

11. To forestall possible misunderstandings, let me emphasize that the justification in question licenses the subject merely to believe that the author of the utterance – whoever that may be – is sincere. It does *not* license the subject to believe that the author of the utterance is identical to herself. Thus, the argument cannot directly proceed to the conclusion 'I believe that Toronto is in Ontario,' but needs premise (2) for this purpose.

12. One might object that it is conceptually impossible to sincerely assert p without knowing that it is oneself who asserts p. Thus, nobody can sincerely assert that p but, for example, wonder whether it is him or her who asserts p. However, it seems that my description of the case presupposes that it is possible to sincerely assert that Toronto is located in Ontario without knowing that it is oneself who asserts it. Hence, there is a problem. In my opinion, this objection is based on a misunderstanding. Note that I do not describe a point in time of a real subject's mental life here. Instead, I describe the logical stage of the justifying argument I am about to formulate. Compare: from a psychological point of view, it might be impossible to believe 'A is a bachelor' without believing that A is male – for believing the first proposition without the second would show that one does not master the concept 'bachelor.' However, from a logical point of view, the premise 'A is a bachelor' does not license one to conclude that A is male; the further premise 'All bachelors are male' is needed. So, the fact that one is not licensed to conclude (without further ado) from 'A is a bachelor' that A is male does not imply that it is possible to believe that A is a bachelor without believing that A is male. Similarly, in the case at hand, the fact that premise (1) does not license the subject to conclude that she is the one who asserts that Toronto is located in Ontario does not imply that it is possible to sincerely assert that Toronto is located in Ontario without knowing that it is oneself who asserts it. Thanks to Eric Marcus for prompting me to reconsider and improve my thoughts on this matter.

13. I owe this and the following objection to Sarah Paul. I thank her for pressing me on these points.

14. Cf. Enoch and Schechter (2008, 568).

15. This reply might seem perplexing at first sight. One may say: 'Given that the Enoch and Schechter strategy is a form of externalism, why do you adopt it when justifying the first conjunct of premise (2)? Isn't that detrimental to the purpose of explaining why transitions from first- to second-order judgments are rational from the subject's point of view?' Answer: no, it isn't. Assume that the first conjunct of premise (2) is justified in the Enoch and Schechter way and that

the subject does not believe that believing the first conjunct of premise (2) is indispensable for being rational. This does not imply that the subject does not believe the first conjunct of premise (2). On the contrary, it is perfectly possible that the subject does believe the first conjunct of premise (2), though she has no grasp of its justifier. Note that, to be justified in believing B on the basis of E, one needs to be justified in believing E, but one does not need to have cognitive access to E's justifier. Hence, the fact that the justifier of the first conjunct of premise (2) might be inaccessible from the subject's point of view does not mean that the justification of the conclusion 'I believe that Toronto is located in Ontario' is likewise inaccessible. In short: even if the subject does not know why she is justified in believing the premise, she is in a position to know why she is entitled to draw the conclusion. Thus, use of the Enoch and Schechter strategy in connection with the first conjunct of premise (2) is not detrimental to the purpose of explaining why transitions from first- to second-order judgments are rational from the subject's point of view.

16. Byrne (2018, 14). See also Byrne (2005, 92).
17. I consider this to be the received opinion about inferential justification. If the subject were required to actually entertain and accept all propositions that constitute the evidence justifying her belief, then virtually no belief would ever be inferentially justified. Cf. Fumerton (1976, 566).
18. An earlier version of this paper was presented at the workshop 'Transparency and Apperception' organized by Boris Hennig, David Hunter, and Thomas Land at Ryerson University, Toronto, in Mai 2018. Thanks to the audience on that occasion for helpful discussion, especially David Barnett, Boris Hennig, Ulf Hlobil, David Hunter, Thomas Khurana, Thomas Land, Eric Marcus, Sarah Paul, Gurpreet Rattan, Houston Smit, and Jonathan Way. For extremely helpful comments on a previous draft many thanks to Philipp Hey, David Hunter, Peter Kuhn, Andi Müller, Henning Lütje, and Sarah Paul. Finally, special thanks to Mark Davies (who knows why).

References

Barz, W. 2014. "Introspection as a Game of Make-Believe." *Theoria* 80: 350–367. doi:10.1111/theo.2014.80.issue-4.
Barz, W. 2015. "Transparent Introspection of Wishes." *Philosophical Studies* 172: 1993–2023. doi:10.1007/s11098-014-0386-9.
Boghossian, P. 1989. "Content and Self-Knowledge." *Philosophical Topics* 17: 5–26. doi:10.5840/philtopics198917110.
BonJour, L. 1980. "Externalist Theories of Empirical Knowledge." *Midwest Studies in Philosophy* 5: 53–73. doi:10.1111/j.1475-4975.1980.tb00396.x.
Boyle, M. 2011. "Transparent Self-Knowledge." *Proceedings of the Aristotelian Society Supplementary Volume* 85: 223–241. doi:10.1111/j.1467-8349.2011.00204.x.
Byrne, A. 2005. "Introspection." *Philosophical Topics* 33: 79–104. doi:10.5840/philtopics20053312.
Byrne, A. 2018. *Transparency and Self-Knowledge*. Oxford: Oxford University Press.
Campbell, L. 2018. "Self-Knowledge, Belief, Ability (And Agency?)." *Philosophical Explorations* 21: 333–349. doi:10.1080/13869795.2018.1426779.
Cassam, Q. 2014. *Self-Knowledge for Humans*. Oxford: Oxford University Press.

Dretske, F. 2003. "How Do You Know You are Not a Zombie?" In *Privileged Access*, edited by B. Gertler, 1–13. Aldershot: Ashgate.

Enoch, D., and J. Schechter. 2008. "How Are Basic Belief-Forming Methods Justified?" *Philosophy and Phenomenological Research* 76: 547–579. doi:10.1111/phpr.2008.76. issue-3.

Evans, G. 1982. *The Varieties of Reference*. Oxford: Clarendon Press.

Finkelstein, D. 2012. "From Transparency to Expressivism." In *Rethinking Epistemology – Volume 2*, edited by G. Abel and J. Conant, 101–118. Berlin, New York: de Gruyter.

Fumerton, R. A. 1976. "Inferential Justification and Empiricism." *The Journal of Philosophy* 73: 557–569. doi:10.2307/2025616.

Gallois, A. 1996. *The World Without, the Mind Within*. Cambridge: Cambridge University Press.

Gertler, B. 2011. "Self-Knowledge and the Transparency of Belief." In *Self-Knowledge*, edited by A. Hatzimoysis, 125–145. Oxford: Oxford University Press.

Marcus, E. 2016. "To Believe Is to Know that You Believe." *Dialectica* 70: 375–405. doi:10.1111/dltc.v70.3.

Martin, M. 1998. "An Eye Directed Outward." In *Knowing Our Own Minds*, edited by C. Wright, B. Smith, and C. Macdonald, 99–121. Oxford: Oxford University Press.

Moran, R. 2001. *Authority and Estrangement*. Princeton: Princeton University Press.

Moran, R. 2003. "Responses to O'brien and Shoemaker." *European Journal of Philosophy* 11: 402–419. doi: 10.1111/1468-0378.00193.

Peacocke, C. 1998. "Conscious Attitudes, Attention, and Self-Knowledge." In *Knowing Our Own Minds*, edited by C. Wright, B. Smith, and C. Macdonald, 63–98. Oxford: Oxford University Press.

Ryle, G. 1949. *The Concept of Mind*. London: Hutchinson's.

Shah, N., and D. Velleman. 2005. "Doxastic Deliberation." *The Philosophical Review* 114: 497–534. doi:10.1215/00318108-114-4-497.

Tye, M. 1995. *Ten Problems of Consciousness*. Cambridge, MA: MIT Press.

Williamson, T. 2000. *Knowledge and Its Limits*. Oxford: Clarendon Press.

Spontaneity and Self-Consciousness in the *Groundwork* and the B-*Critique*

Yoon Choi

ABSTRACT

According to some influential readings of the *Groundwork of the Metaphysics of Morals*, the view presented there of the kind of spontaneity we are conscious of through theoretical reason and the significance of such self-consciousness is irremediably at odds with the Critical theory, and thus roundly and rightly rejected in the second edition of the *Critique of Pure Reason* and the *Critique of Practical Reason*. This paper argues, on the contrary, that the *Groundwork* can be read as articulating for the first time the account of self-consciousness and spontaneity that Kant goes on to develop in the B-*Critique*, especially the B-Transcendental Deduction.

Abbreviations

Following standard practice, I refer to the 1781/1787 editions of the *Critique of Pure Reason* using the A/B pagination. All other texts are referred to using the abbreviations below, followed by volume and page number from the Academy edition: *Kants Gesammelte Schriften*, ed. Akademie der Wissenschaften (Berlin: Walter de Gruyter, 1900–). Unless otherwise noted, translations of Kant's texts are from *The Cambridge Edition of the Works of Immanuel Kant*, ed. Paul Guyer and Allen Wood (Cambridge: Cambridge University Press, 1992–).

Anth.: *Pragmatic Anthropology*
CJ: *Critique of the Power of Judgment*
CPrR: *Critique of Practical Reason*
G: *Groundwork for the Metaphysics of Morals*
JL: *Jäsche Logic*
MM: *Metaphysics of Morals*
M-D: *Dohna Metaphysics*

M-L1: *L1 Metaphysics*
M-L2: *L2 Metaphysics*
M-Mrong.: *Mrongovius Metaphysics*
M-Vig.: *Vigilantius Metaphysics*
Progress: *What Real Progress has Metaphysics Made in Germany?*
Prol.: *Prolegomena to Any Further Metaphysics*

Introduction

There is a long and ongoing debate about how to understand the central arguments of the *Groundwork of the Metaphysics of Morals* (1785) and the *Critique of Practical Reason* (1788), Immanuel Kant's two foundational works in moral philosophy, in relation to each other.[1] Is a single theory being given two complementary presentations?[2] Or does a significant shift in doctrine, perhaps even a 'great reversal,' as one philosopher put it (Ameriks 2000, 226), occur between the two texts? And if there is a substantive change, is it an improvement?[3] At stake is an issue of special importance: the justification of morality. What kind of justification, if any, can be given of a fundamental moral law? What kind of justification, if any, do we *need* of a fundamental moral law?

This essay focuses on Kant's thought during the same time period, but it foregrounds a different pair of texts: the *Groundwork* and the second edition of the *Critique of Pure Reason* (1787). Kant explicitly claims that this second edition of the *Critique of Pure Reason* (hereafter 'B-*Critique*') and the *Critique of Practical Reason* are in 'precise agreement' (*CPrR* 5.106; also 5.6–5.7). If we accept this, even just as a characterization of how Kant would like to be interpreted, then we would expect that at least some of the differences said to obtain between the 1785 *Groundwork* and the 1788 *Critique of Practical Reason* would be visible between the *Groundwork* and the 1787 *Critique of Pure Reason*, or at least that there would be some degree of ineliminable and disquieting tension between the two texts. But this is not, I will argue, what we find.

One Kant scholar who reaches the opposite conclusion is Karl Ameriks, and a quick summary of his account will provide me with a useful backdrop against which to situate my proposal. In a series of groundbreaking studies, Ameriks lays out the following narrative (2000, 191, 211–219, 2003). As student transcripts of metaphysics lectures delivered by Kant in the mid- to late-1770s reveal, during this period, Kant defends a set of rationalist arguments about the nature of the soul, arguments that purportedly prove that the soul is simple, substantial, single, and absolutely spontaneous – that is, transcendentally free, an uncaused cause. But a few short years later, in the A-*Critique* (1781), Kant rejects all of these arguments as fallacious – all, that is, but one. There is a conspicuous silence about spontaneity. In

66 TRANSPARENCY AND APPERCEPTION

Ameriks's view, this is because Kant still endorses his pre-Critical position on the matter: the soul is absolutely spontaneous and we can know that it is. The central piece of evidence for this, according to Ameriks, is the *Groundwork*. There, Ameriks argue, the pre-Critical argument for our absolute spontaneity is essentially reprised, as Kant infers our absolute spontaneity from some self-conscious capacity of theoretical reason (cf. *G* 4.452 and *M-L1* 28.268–269; Ameriks 2000, 211–219, 2003, 225–247). But such a view would inevitably 'suffer...shipwreck,' as Ameriks puts it (2000, 191), for it lays claim to just the kind of metaphysical knowledge that the *First Critique* puts beyond our grasp. On Ameriks's reading, this failure shapes not just the doctrine of the *Second Critique* but also the revisions Kant makes to the *Critique of Pure Reason* for its second edition. In particular, Ameriks takes Kant to be at pains to develop his theory of self-consciousness in such a manner as to 'systematically block...even the suggestion of any kind of argument to absolute freedom' (2003, 258).

Ameriks's framework is, in my view, deeply illuminating. But whereas Ameriks sees a decisive break between the *Groundwork* and the B-*Critique*, it is possible to read the texts – especially *Groundwork III* and the B-*Transcendental Deduction* – as not just consistent with each other but strongly continuous, developing a single line of thought between them. I will suggest that the concerns about self-consciousness that Ameriks draws attention to in the B-*Critique* thread through *both* texts, and that the B-*Critique* fills in an account of self-consciousness, the shape of which is first outlined in *Groundwork* III. This essay is thus primarily devoted to laying out a reading of the *Groundwork* as prefiguring the B-Transcendental Deduction's account of self-consciousness. This task occupies part I; part II turns more programmatically to the B-Transcendental Deduction, delineating some of the parallels that emerge but also pointing to an important difference that obtains between the two. On the reading I end up with, a central aim of both texts is to argue for the necessity of a kind of self-consciousness that is fundamentally a consciousness of oneself as at once sensibly determined and free. The struggle to articulate this conception of self-consciousness and defend its possibility is central not only to the B-Transcendental Deduction, but also to *Groundwork III*.

Part I: *Groundwork III*

The first edition of the *Critique of Pure Reason* is published in 1781, after a long period of gestation – the so-called 'silent decade'. But just two years after it is published, Kant identifies two sections of it that he is 'not fully satisfied with': the Transcendental Deduction and the Paralogisms (*Prol.* 4.381). These two sections of the text present Kant's theory of the cognitive role of self-consciousness: the Transcendental Deduction identifies the essential role of self-consciousness in making empirical cognition possible, while the Paralogisms reveal that the same self-consciousness generates an illusion of self-knowledge. Kant would indeed re-write these sections of the *Critique of Pure Reason* wholesale for the 1787 edition of the *Critique*, but it would not be surprising if we could see Kant grappling with these issues in the intervening years. I will suggest that they are central to Kant's thought in the 1785 *Groundwork for the Metaphysics of Morals.*

But the main purpose of the *Groundwork* is, of course, not to give an account of self-consciousness, but to undertake the 'search for and establishment [*Festsetzung*] of the supreme principle of morality' (G 4.392; all emphases in original unless otherwise noted). The search, which unfolds over the first two parts of the text, begins with 'common cognition' and, by 'proceeding analytically,' excavates the moral principle underlying such cognition (G 4.392; see also G 4.445). In the course of this 'search,' it emerges that morality confers on humanity a special value as an end-in-itself (G 4.428–4.429); that as moral subjects, human beings possess dignity and command respect (G 4.436); that morality is an exercise in autonomy (G 4.431). But whether we really are such moral subjects as our everyday moral cognition takes us to be – that is left an open question until the third and final part of the *Groundwork*. There Kant turns to 'establishing' the moral principle, and with it, the value of humanity and the reality of human dignity and autonomy. It is this closing argument that I focus on in what follows.

§1. The Problem of Groundwork III

The search for the moral principle ends with a formulation of it as a principle of autonomy. *Groundwork III* picks up here, identifying freedom as the condition of autonomy. Kant defines freedom as the property of a will whereby it 'can be efficient independently of alien causes *determining* it' (G 4.446). This is a merely '*negative*' definition, he notes, but 'there flows from it a *positive* concept of freedom' as the property of a will by which it can be a 'law to itself' (G 4.447). And since this positive concept of freedom just describes a will under the principle of autonomy, and since the principle of autonomy is a formulation of the moral principle, it turns out that the 'free will and a will under moral laws are one and the same' (G 4.447).[4]

It thus appears that to establish the moral principle, we need to establish the reality of our freedom. But what Kant argues next is not that we are free – only that we must think of ourselves as free. The argument begins with the claim that 'reason must regard itself as the author of its principles, independently of alien influences' (G 4.448). Since heteronomy obtains just when a 'foreign impulse…give[s] the law' (G 4.444) (and since Kant takes heteronomy and autonomy to be exclusive and exhaustive), Kant's premise is that reason must regard itself as autonomous (G 4.448).[5] If this is true for reason in general, it is true for practical reason in particular; 'consequently, as practical reason or as the will of a rational being[, reason] must be regarded of itself as free' (*G* 4.448). Indeed, it follows that 'freedom must be presupposed as a property of the will of *all* rational beings' (*G* 4.447; emphasis mine). But Kant goes on to argue that a being that 'cannot act otherwise than under the idea of freedom is actually free, in a practical respect' – where to be free in such a 'practical' manner is to be subject to 'all laws that are inseparably bound up with freedom...just as if [we] had been validly pronounced free' (*G* 4.448). From this it follows that if we must think ourselves free, we must take ourselves to be bound by the laws of freedom; and since, as established earlier, 'freedom must be presupposed' of all rational beings, we must take ourselves and all other rational beings to be bound by the moral law.

But what does *not* follow from this argument is that we really *are* free. In these opening paragraphs, then, Kant renders the problem of *Groundwork III* more acute, rather than resolving it. Kant has shown that reason compels us to regard ourselves as free and thus as subject to the moral law – but he has given us no assurance that our freedom is not illusory. There is thus a justificatory task that remains outstanding, but there is another problem, too. As Kant puts it, were we to be asked why we acknowledge the moral law and the demands it places on us, why we hang our own 'personal worth' on our moral self-assessment, 'we could give...no satisfactory answer' (*G* 4.449–4.450). On the account just given, reason compels us in a way that leaves us fundamentally unintelligible to ourselves.

§2. The Solution to the Problem

What is the solution? Kant notes that 'one resource...still remains':

> whether we do not take a different standpoint when by means of freedom we think ourselves as causes efficient a priori than when we represent ourselves in terms of our actions as effects that we see before our eyes (*G* 4.450).

I will suggest that Kant takes the account just given in §1 – that we must presuppose our freedom, and that with this presupposition comes a commitment to the moral law – not to be wrong or mistaken, but to be importantly incomplete: it leaves out a shift in standpoint that occurs along the way. But what are these two standpoints? Instead of immediately characterizing them, Kant takes a circuitous route that starts from (what turns out to be) one standpoint and ends up in another standpoint. At least one of his reasons for proceeding this way is, I take it, to show that there is a natural route from the first standpoint to the second, even for 'the commonest understanding' – and thus to show that the second standpoint is as 'natural to our reason' as the first standpoint (*CPrR* 5.99). And the first standpoint is one that we all clearly do inhabit, for it is the one we occupy while engaged in prosaic everyday cognitive activities.

From this standpoint, we come to recognize that in order to cognize objects, we must be affected by them; and because of this, we cognize objects only if and as they appear to us, not as they are in themselves (*G* 4.450–451). As this is true of everything we are aware of through sensibility, it is true also of myself, since I am aware of myself through sensibility. I accordingly cognize the appearance of myself in the world of sense, not my 'ego as it may be constituted in itself' (*G* 4.451). From this first standpoint, then, the common understanding comes to recognize, even if but dimly, a distinction between what Kant calls the 'world of sense,' the familiar world constituted by appearances and cognized by us, and the 'world of understanding,' a world of things in themselves, conceived of as the metaphysical ground of the world of sense. And we view ourselves as we view other objects of the world of sense: all under 'laws of nature (heteronomy)' (*G* 4.452). We thus relate 'our actions as appearances to the sensible being of our subject' (*CPrR* 5.99).

But something complicates this picture. The 'human being really does find in himself,' Kant says, 'pure self-activity' (*G* 4.451). What is this pure self-activity? It is, I take it, the activity of reason in generating ideas, ideas that could not have originated in sensibility, since they outstrip not only what is given in sensibility but also what could be so given, ideas such as the idea of freedom or the idea that there is a way that the world ought to be.[6] Because we are conscious of this capacity of reason in us, Kant argues, we must think of ourselves, insofar as we are reasoners (or 'intelligences'), as members of the world of understanding. It is here that the transition to the second standpoint starts to occur – but it is far from clear exactly how this second standpoint is to be understood. A key but puzzling passage is the following:

> If we think of ourselves as free [*wenn wir uns als frei denken*], we transfer ourselves as members into the world of understanding, and cognize autonomy of the will, along with its consequence, morality; but if we think of ourselves as bound by duty we consider ourselves as belonging to the world of sense and yet at the same time to the world of understanding (*G* 4.453; translation modified).[7]

I will suggest that to understand this passage, it is necessary to distinguish between the world of understanding, the '*Verstandeswelt*' explicitly mentioned in the first half of the passage, and the intelligible world, or '*intelligibelen Welt*,' which is described, I will argue, in the second half.[8] Kant uses both terms frequently throughout *Groundwork III*, and most interpreters take them to be used interchangeably. But some passages strongly suggest that there is a difference the terms. For example, Kant writes that

The concept of a world of understanding is thus only a *standpoint* that reason sees itself constrained to take outside appearances *in order to think of itself as practical*, as...is...necessary insofar as he is not to be denied consciousness of himself as an intelligence and consequently as a rational cause active by means of reason, i.e., operating freely. This thought admittedly brings with it the idea of another order and another lawgiving than that of the mechanism of nature, which has to do with the sensible world; and it makes necessary the concept of an intelligible world (i.e., the whole of rational beings as things in themselves) (*G* 4.458).[9]

This passage, naturally read, suggests that there is a distinction between the idea of the world of understanding and a *different* idea that it brings in its train, viz., the idea of an intelligible world. So how should these two ideas be understood?

The thought of a world of understanding arises, as we have seen, from the standpoint of the common understanding engaged in everyday cognition. It is the thought of the metaphysical ground of the world of sense. Thus, insofar as there must be a metaphysical ground to my existence as a member of the world of sense, I locate it in the world of understanding. Moreover, insofar as I am conscious of myself as a reasoner, I must regard myself as reasoner to be free from 'alien influence', independent of the world of sense, and thus a member of the world of understanding. Whenever I reason, then, I take myself to do so as a free member of the world of understanding, and with the thought of my freedom comes, as Kant noted in the beginning of *Groundwork III*, the 'consciousness of a law for acting' (*G* 4.449). But I cannot get further than the mere thought of myself as free. I cannot cognize myself as free, since for that, as Kant puts it in the *Second Critique*, 'an intellectual intuition would be required' (*CPrR* 5.31). The world of understanding therefore remains something that I think myself into, but which is of unclear relevance and reality to me.

What about the intelligible world? Here we can find some clues in Kant's use of the term 'intelligible' in other contexts. In the Antinomies, for instance, Kant writes, 'I call intelligible *that in an object of sense* which is not itself appearance' (A538/B566; my emphasis). Notice the reference to an 'object of sense.' A similar connection with the sensible occurs in Kant's characterization of an 'intelligible cause': an intelligible cause is the non-sensible cause of an event *in the world of sense*, whereby the event is rightfully said to be 'free in regard to its intelligible cause' (though *also* fully determined by the order of efficient causes in the world of sense) (A537/B565). The same point is made in metaphysics lectures delivered by Kant while drafting the *Groundwork*. 'A foreigner called it wild fantasy to speak of the intelligible world,' he reportedly says, 'but this is just the opposite, for one understands by it not another world, but rather *this world* as I think it through the understanding' (*M-Mrong.* 29.850; emphasis mine). I will argue that the intelligible world, unlike the world of understanding, pertains specifically, in some sense, to the sensible world; and that it is specifically the idea of an intelligible world, not the idea of the world of understanding, that provides the second standpoint from which we can resolve the difficulties of *Groundwork III*.[10]

Recall that Kant says that it is 'when…we think ourselves as causes efficient a priori' that we 'take a different standpoint' (*G* 4.450). But what is it that we 'think ourselves…causes' of? It must be our existences as sensible beings. When the existence of a being in the sensible world is taken to be the appearance of an intelligence that is 'efficient a priori', the sensible existence itself is rendered the intelligible existence of a being determined (at least in part) by reason and comprehensible (at least in part) as the appearance of a free intelligence in the world of sense.[11] When we thus think ourselves members of such an intelligible world, we 'consider ourselves as belonging to the world of sense and yet at the same time to the world of understanding,' as Kant puts it (*G* 4.453).

To summarize the two standpoints, then: from the first standpoint, we view our existence in the world of sense as the existence of a purely sensible being, and we relate 'our actions as actions as appearances to the sensible being of our subject.' But from the second standpoint, we view our existence – again, our existence *in the world of sense* – as the existence of an intelligible being, for 'this sensible being is itself referred to the intelligible substratum in us' (*CPrR* 5.99). From the first standpoint, 'we represent ourselves in terms of our actions as *effects*' unfolding in the order of efficient causes; from the second, 'we think ourselves as *causes* efficient a priori' (*G* 4.450, emphases mine). From the first standpoint, we view ourselves 'under laws of nature (heteronomy)'; from the second, we view ourselves under a law 'grounded merely in reason' (*G* 4.452), which law 'is to furnish the sensible world, as a *sensible nature*…with the form of a world of understanding' and thus render it, on the reading I'm proposing, intelligible (*CPrR* 5.43).

The question that now arises is, Why is it legitimate to take myself to be a member of the intelligible world? I am essentially identifying the intelligence in the world of understanding that I think myself to be with the metaphysical ground of my existence. But though I must think that the metaphysical ground of my existence lies in the world of understanding, I have no knowledge of it – the metaphysical ground of my existence might well be an intelligence that is not me, for instance. Thus again, what licenses such an identification?

I take it that Kant's answer in the *Groundwork*, much like his answer in the *Critique of Practical Reason*, points to the reality of our experience of moral obligation. Recall that Kant says that 'when we think of ourselves as bound by duty we consider ourselves as belonging to the world of sense and yet at the same time to the world of understanding (*G* 4.453; translation modified) – that is, we consider ourselves members of an intelligible world. To experience moral obligation is to be conscious of the moral law as *actually* binding on me. It is an experience that is possible only for someone who is a member of both the world of understanding and the world of sense 'at the same time' *and* who is, as member of the world of understanding, the 'efficient cause a priori' of her appearance in the latter. That is, moral obligation is an experience that is possible only insofar as I do inhabit an intelligible world. For only a sensible self can feel constraint; but the constraint can be moral only when it arises from the autonomous self in the world of understanding. Thus, moral constraint arises because I am, as intelligence, 'efficient cause a priori' of the appearance of my sensible self. What therefore secures my right to take myself as inhabiting an intelligible world is everyday moral experience, my repeated encounters with the demands of duty as real constraints. Kant thereby returns to the common moral cognition with which he opened the *Groundwork* and reveals that our everyday moral experience of duty *is* the experience of a member of an intelligible world.[12] As Kant puts it a little later, through our consciousness of the moral law as binding on us,

> that unconditioned causality and the capacity for it, freedom, and with it *a being (I myself) that belongs to the sensible world but at the same time to the intelligible world*, is not merely thought indeterminately and problematically...but is even determined with respect to the law of its causality and cognized assertorically; and thus the reality of the intelligible world is given to us (*CPrR* 5.105; emphasis mine).[13]

Thus in the experience of moral obligation, the reality of the intelligible world and the validity of the moral law is established. So, too, is the value of *humanity*. It is not as mere intelligence that I am an end-in-itself; rather, it is in my humanity, as a human being existing in the intelligible world, that I am an end-in-itself.[14]

§3. A New Problem, Left for Speculative Philosophy

Though *Groundwork III* thus resolves many of the problems it so acutely raised in its opening, a new problem is generated. We have left the subject, Kant says, with a 'seeming contradiction.' For 'if we think of ourselves as put under obligation we regard ourselves as belonging to the world of sense and yet at the same time to the world of understanding' (*G* 4.453). But can we really regard ourselves in this way? As both free and not free?

Kant says that in this case, it is actually the appearance of a contradiction that is illusory: 'something that is unifiable is represented as contradictory' (*Prol.* 4.343). And it is a 'duty incumbent upon speculative philosophy to remove the seeming conflict' (*G* 4.456). Kant scholars often take the Third Antinomy to be where theoretical reason discharges this duty (e.g., Timmermann 2007, 146–147). But what Kant demands is not just the proof that it's possible for freedom and determinism both to be true. As Kant puts it,

> it is an indispensable task of speculative philosophy *at least* to show that its illusion about the contradiction rests on our thinking of the human being in a different sense and relation when we call him free and when we hold him, as a part of nature, to be subject to its laws, and to show that both not only *can* very well coexist, but also must be thought as *necessarily united* in the same subject (*G* 4.456; see also *G* 4.457).[15]

The Third Antinomy accomplishes only part of this task: it shows that it is *possible* that we are both free and determined, but not that freedom and determinism 'must be thought as necessarily united.' How is this further task to be discharged? Kant hints at an answer in the *Groundwork*:

> The human being...puts himself in a different order of things and in a relation to determining grounds of an altogether different kind when he think of himself as an intelligence endowed with a will...than when he perceives himself as a phenomenon in the world of sense....and subjects his causality to external determination.... Now he soon becomes aware that both *can* take place at the same time, and indeed *must* do so. For, that a thing in appearance...is subject to certain laws from which as a thing or a being in itself it is independent contains not the least contradiction; *that he must represent and think of himself in this twofold way, however, rests as regards the first on consciousness of himself as an object affected through the senses and as regards the second on consciousness of himself as an intelligence* (*G* 4.457; my emphases).[16]

This passage begins by reiterating the compatibility of freedom and determinism; it then points to the nature of self-consciousness to account for the necessity of thinking the necessary unity of freedom and determinism. Just such self-consciousness is, as Kant first makes clear in the B-Transcendental Deduction, a necessary condition of the possibility of cognition. It is not just the moral subject but also the cognizing subject who is necessarily conscious of herself as *at once* an intelligence *and* an appearance among other appearances in the sensible world, the former through apperception and the latter through inner sense. Thus the cognizing subject must think of herself as a subject in whom freedom and determinism are 'necessarily united' – and it is naturally the task of speculative reason to demonstrate that this is so. Kant sets himself to this task in the B-Transcendental Deduction; and it is to that difficult chapter of the B-*Critique of Pure Reason* that I now turn.

Part II: The B-Transcendental Deduction

The Transcendental Deduction aims to show that the categories apply to 'all appearances of nature' (B165) and make experience, 'cognition through connected perceptions,' possible (B161). The first half of the B-Deduction is centered on one kind of self-consciousness: apperception, the consciousness we have of ourselves as thinking. The second half focuses on a second kind of self-consciousness: the consciousness we have of ourselves in inner sense. If Kant is pursuing the program I have suggested he sets for himself in the *Groundwork*, we would expect him to argue that the consciousness of ourselves in apperception as thinking grounds or otherwise forms the consciousness of ourselves in inner sense as beings in the world of sense, and that we thus take ourselves as beings in the world of sense as appearances of ourselves as thinking subjects. In the following discussion of the B-Deduction, my aim is to explore whether there is room in the text for such a reading.[17] I begin by discussing Kant's understanding of apperception; I then segue into a discussion of the argument of the B-Transcendental Deduction, pausing occasionally to compare it to the argument in the *Groundwork*.

Pure apperception is the 'pure consciousness of the activity that constitutes thinking' (*Anth.* 7.141), 'the consciousness of myself in mere thinking' (B429; see also B157-158, B413, *Anth.* 7.135fn and 7.142).[18] As thinking is, in turn, 'an act of the spontaneity of the power of representation' (B130), so apperception is consciousness of the spontaneous 'activity that constitutes thinking' (*Anth.* 7.141).

As Kant noted in the *Groundwork*, the spontaneity of understanding, the faculty of thinking, is not unfettered. For the categories of understanding 'serve merely to bring sensible representations under rules...without which use of sensibility it would think nothing at all' (*G* 4.452). Thus the consciousness of myself in thinking is also presumably the consciousness of spontaneous but not unfettered activity. But in the B-Deduction, Kant introduces another element of spontaneity. '[O]riginal apperception,' he says, 'in an act of spontaneity...produces the representation I think,' a representation that 'cannot be regarded as belonging to sensibility' but is an expression of the very spontaneous and self-conscious thinking that it represents (B132). This introduction of the 'I think' into the Transcendental Deduction is, I note, new to the B-*Critique*; in the A-*Critique*, the 'I think' is first encountered in the Paralogisms (A341/B399). But what motivates its introduction into the B-Transcendental Deduction? And is this a significant change? To answer this question, I will pick out a path through the B-Transcendental Deduction that mirrors, to some degree, the argument of the *Groundwork*. The significance I attribute to this, and the reason I take the 'I think' to end up being central to the argument of the B-Transcendental Deduction, will hopefully become apparent as I proceed.

I begin with a quick synopsis of the relevant argument in *Groundwork III*. Kant begins by defending the claim that the 'free will and a will under moral laws are one and the same' (*G* 4.447). His next move is to argue that this premise does indeed apply to me, for I am subject to the moral law. That is clearly a synthetic claim. How can Kant assert it? What is the 'third thing' that puts me in relation to the moral law and thus grounds the synthetic claim? I suggested above that it is the intelligible world, which I occupy when I take myself, as intelligence and moral subject, to be the ground of my sensible existence. Perhaps it is not too much of a stretch to say that to take this second standpoint is to engage in a kind of practical 'synthesis' of the world of sense and the world of understanding.

Compare now the B-Transcendental Deduction. It also begins with a claim that Kant explicitly calls 'analytic': 'the I think must be able to accompany all my representations' (B131; for 'analytic', see B135 and B138). The 'I think' 'accompanies' representations that are combined in a judgment. Judgments combine representations by bringing them into a kind of unity that Kant calls the 'objective unity of apperception' (B141): a unity that obtains when representations are all united in the concept of an object, i.e., in a way that is determined *by* the object, not by the subject (B137, B139). When objective unity obtains, representations relate *to* the object in a way that is 'objectively valid' (B142) and amounts to cognition *of* the object. In every judgment, then, the 'I' that thinks 'accompanies' all the representations taken up in its judgment, which representations that 'I' calls '*my* representations'. And for any 'I' that takes itself to make several judgments, it must be able to combine them all in a single objective unity; and all the representations thereby taken up in this unity will be called 'my representations' by that judging 'I'.[19] What makes Kant's analytic claim analytic, then, is Kant's conception of judgment: for any 'I' that judges, all her manifold of representations 'has a necessary relation to the I think in the same subject in which this manifold can be encountered' (B132).[20]

Kant then argues that this analytic principle presupposes a synthesis (B132, B133, B134, B135, B138 and B143). As Kant puts it, 'the thought that these representations given in intuition all together belong to me [i.e., are *my* representations] means...the same as that I unite them in a self-consciousness' (B134); or again, 'only because I can comprehend their manifold in a consciousness do I call [these representations] all together *my* representations (B134, emphasis mine; see also B132 and B133). The claim is that a synthesis is necessary in order to make it possible to speak of 'my representations' in the first place. But why might this be? Recall that apperception is a consciousness of myself that accompanies thinking. I am thus conscious of myself as long as I am engaged in an activity of synthesizing or thinking. But it is only if I go on to *effect* a synthetic unity that I first become conscious of my *identity*: that the 'I' who thinks the effected synthetic unity is the 'I' who synthesized the manifold into the unity and the 'I' for whom each of the manifold representations is 'my representation'. This synthesis therefore first makes it possible to talk of 'my representations' because it makes it possible to talk of an 'I'; until such a synthesis takes place, there is as 'multicolored, diverse a self as I have representations' (B134).

The analytic premise thus presupposes a synthesis. Kant calls this synthesis the 'original-synthetic unity of apperception' (B131, B136). And he argues that the 'supreme' principle of the understanding is, simply, to bring all manifold of intuition to the original-synthetic unity of apperception, and thus to the synthetic unity that is necessary for judgment to be possible (B135; see also B136 and B137). The original-synthetic unity of apperception is thus a synthesis that must obtain in order for there to be a self-conscious cognizer, an 'I' that can think, an 'I' to whom the 'supreme' principle of the understanding is addressed; it is also the synthesis that the supreme principle of understanding enjoins us to realize. It is thus akin to the idea of the intelligible world: we must think ourselves into the intelligible world in order to undertake the standpoint of moral agency, the standpoint of a subject to whom the moral law is addressed; and what the categorial imperative enjoins is that we act *as* members of the intelligible world, as free intelligences answering only to principles of reason.[21] It is this idea of the original-synthetic unity of apperception that I focus on in the rest of this discussion.

At the very end of the B-Transcendental Deduction, Kant characterizes the original-synthetic unity of apperception as 'the form of the understanding in relation to space and time, as original forms of sensibility' (B169). This is the claim that Kant needs to defend to complete the argument of the Transcendental Deduction. For if space and time and everything given *in* space and time stand under the original-synthetic unity of apperception, then, given what Kant has already shown, it follows that judgment about such spatiotemporal objects is always possible and that the categories apply to them.

It is time that is of central interest to this project. Time is the form of inner sense; it is thus, Kant says, the 'fundamental' form of sensibility – presumably because everything given in space is also given in time (B150). But space and time are also themselves intuitions, with the unity of an intuition (B136n; also B160-161 and B160-161fn). Now Kant has already argued that 'all manifold of intuition has a necessary relation to the I think in the same subject in which this manifold is to be encountered' (B132). This is as true for the intuition of time as it is for our other representations, and it is true in

TRANSPARENCY AND APPERCEPTION

virtue of the nature of our understanding and its requirements. As Kant puts it,

> time...merely as intuition in general, which contains a given manifold, stands under the original unity of consciousness, solely by means of the necessary relation of the manifold of intuition to the one I think, thus through the pure synthesis of the understanding (B140).[22]

But how is it possible to bring time, 'as intuition in general', to the original-synthetic unity of apperception? What does that mean, when time is also the form of intuition?

Here is one way I think the account might be fleshed out. Kant writes that

> The understanding, as spontaneity, can determine inner sense through the manifold of given representations in accord with the synthetic unity of apperception, and thus think *a priori* synthetic unity of the apperception of the manifold of sensible intuition, as the condition under which all objects of our (human) intuition must necessarily stand, through which then the categories... acquire objective reality (B151).

Kant points here to the doctrine of self-affection: that our apperceptive activities of reasoning and of judging affect us and are represented in inner sense. Perhaps one way to understand the passage above is to take it as saying that insofar as we are thinking as we should, bringing representations given in outer sense to the unity of apperception, the manifold of inner sense, which is populated by the workings of the understanding, will also stand under the unity of apperception (see also B153 and B155). Another piece of the account is given by Kant's introduction of the 'transcendental synthesis of the imagination'. He characterizes this synthesis as 'an effect of the understanding on sensibility' that 'determine[s] the form of sense a priori in accordance with the unity of apperception' (B152). The understanding's activity of synthesis affects sensibility to produce a succession of representations. Insofar as the understanding synthesizes the spatial manifold in the way it ought to, bringing it to the unity of apperception, the activity produces a single temporal succession in inner sense, again in accordance with the unity of apperception, that relates to and unifies the spatial manifold.

On the account roughly sketched out, the form of inner sense and its unity is determined by the unity of apperception. Here, as in the case of the intelligible world, I am thus a unity *in* the sensible world only insofar as the 'I' as intelligence and its demand for unity is the ground of this appearance. In the moral case, a causally determined heap of desires and impulses can be rendered the intelligible appearance of a finite and flawed but moral agent whose commitment to the moral law confers unity on this sensible existence. In the case at hand, a set of perceptions and other mental representations, loosely related by associative ties, is rendered the intelligible appearance of a finite but rational thinking subject insofar as the thinker brings these representations to the unity of apperception. The supreme principle of the understanding thus applies to us, and judgment is possible, insofar as our existence in the sensible world is determined by our rational activity as intelligences. If this condition obtains, however, my sensible existence *is* that of a rational thinker: 'I as a thinking being am one and the same subject with myself as a sensing being' (*Anth.* 7.142; see also B156, B157-158, and B429).

I have been arguing that it is possible to see striking similarities between the arguments of the *Groundwork* and the B-Deduction; and I have suggested that this reflects an ongoing project on Kant's part to sketch out and clarify the nature of self-consciousness. There is, however, one important difference between the two contexts. In its account of theoretical reason and the cognizing subject, the *Critique of Pure Reason*, Kant says, 'place[s] reason in its proper territory, namely the order of ends that is yet at the same time an order of nature' (B425). In our various cognitive activities, we may think of ourselves as free intelligences in the world of understanding, and we may drive our inquiry in various self-determined ways, but we cannot thereby gain cognition of our freedom. Thus, in the *Metaphysics of Morals*, Kant writes that

> although a human being has, in his understanding, something more than [animals] and can set himself ends, even this gives him only an *extrinsic* value (*MM* 6.434; also 6.418).

It is only in moral contexts, according to Kant, that the reality of our freedom is secured. But of course, 'moral contexts' are not isolable aspects of life; we thus find ourselves encountering our moral obligations – and our freedom – when we are engaged in our aesthetic and scientific projects just as much as when we are involved in the more practical matters of life.

Conclusion

In this paper, I argued that the *Groundwork* and the B-Deduction both develop an account of our moral and cognitive life as driven by the consciousness of ourselves as at once sensible and spontaneous beings, members of both the world of sense and the world of understanding. This is a point Kant returns repeatedly to in years to come. In a late metaphysics lecture series, for instance, Kant reportedly says,

> *the striking phenomenon with a human being is that freedom united with natural necessity is found in him.* [...] [H]e is...affected by lower powers but determines himself by the independence of reason, and so he appears as ordered under reason and nature not successively, but rather at the same time (*M-Vig.* 29:1019-20; see also Bxxvii-xxviii, *CPrR* 5.6fn, and *M-L2* 28.583).

Kant says that to be conscious of oneself in this way, a person just needs to view his 'existence as determinable only through laws that he gives himself' (*CPrR* 5.97). I have argued that it is specifically our sensible existence that we thereby come to see as intelligible. And though much more work would need to be done even to characterize this conception of self-consciousness adequately, one attractive feature of this view, at least from my perspective, is that it makes it possible to encounter people and projects with absolute value, dignity, and moral worth in *this* world: the world that we're living in.

Notes

1. Owen Ware makes the interesting observation that there is no indication that Kant's earliest readers saw an inconsistency between the two texts (Ware 2017, 117–119). Ware traces the debate back to the 1960 publication of now-seminal studies of the *Second Critique* by Dieter Henrich (1994) and Beck (1960).
2. For readings that find continuity between the two texts, see Onora O'Neill (2002) and cf. Sergio Tenenbaum (2012) and Ware (2017).
3. Some take the *Second Critique* to give up altogether on the project of justification that is central to the *Groundwork*. Among these, Ameriks (2000, 2003, 161–192, 255–258), Beck (1960, 166–175); Paul Guyer (2016, 127–145), and Henrich (1994) take this to be progress; Allen Wood disagrees, memorably saying that the *Second Critique* retreats to mere 'moralistic bluster' (2007, 134–135). Others find a slightly less-radical change between the two texts – less 'reversal' than 'retreat,' as Jens Timmermann puts it (2010, 89). Some argue, for instance, that the justificatory project remains in place but is re-conceived, shedding some of the misplaced aspirations of the *Groundwork*. Henry Allison's interpretation falls in this category; he takes the *Groundwork* argument to be deeply problematic, though he mitigates his criticisms some-what in his latest study (2011, 330n58; cf., 1986; 1990, 288, 230, 234–239). Timmermann can also be put in this category, though he finds the argument of the *Groundwork* less hopeless than Allison does (Timmermann 2007, 133–144, 2010).
4. Many difficult issues are sidestepped in the above. I mention just one: are negative and positive freedom two different kinds of freedom, or are they two ways of conceiving one and the same freedom? After all, as Paul Guyer observes, what Kant says is that these are two concepts of freedom (2018, 129). Positive and negative freedom are treated as two conceptions of the same freedom by O'Neill (1989, 52–53) as well as Guyer; they are taken to be two kinds of freedom by Allison (1995, 18–21).
5. It is sometimes argued that Kant is talking specifically about theoretical reason (except when he explicitly refers to 'practical reason'). Henry Allison, for instance, accordingly takes this passage to be pointing to 'the necessity of reason to regard itself as free in its epistemic capacity' (1990, 217–218; also, 2013, 289). Allen Wood agrees (2007, 130–131). But during this period, Kant appears to assume that reason is a unity – indeed, a unity that might one day be demonstrable (*CPrR* 5.91). As he puts it in the Preface to the *Groundwork*, 'there can, in the end, be only one and the same reason, which must be

distinguished merely in its application' (*G* 4.391; see also Bxxxviii, A811/B839-A812/B840, A840/B868; and *CPrR* 5.89, 5.91, and 5.121). And in the *Critique of Pure Reason*, Kant often talks about 'reason' as a single faculty that has two uses: a 'speculative use' in which it 'accomplishes nothing' with respect to its highest metaphysical aspirations, and a 'practical use' in which it eventually finds its 'ultimate end' (A795/B823-A797/B825). (For a helpful discussion of these passages, see Timmermann 2019.) Though the distinction between the two kinds of reason becomes sharper in the *Critique of Practical Reason*, it is not until the *Critique of the Power of Judgment* (1790) – e.g., *CJ* 5.174–5.176 – that the unity of reason is clearly a problem.

6. Kant's talk of 'reason' is again often taken to refer specifically to theoretical reason (e.g., Allison, 1990, 221–223, 2013, 289; Hill 1992, 120; Korsgaard 1996, 170). (Indeed, some who deny that the earlier passage (*G* 4.448) refers specifically to theoretical reason do make that claim here (see Guyer 2018, 155; Timmermann 2007, 137).) For a dissenting view that takes 'reason' to be pure practical reason, cf. Tenenbaum (2012) and Ware (2017). But again, I think that Kant might be thinking of reason as a single faculty (albeit one with an ultimately practical use). Thus note the similarity in language between the *Groundwork*, where Kant writes that 'reason...shows in what we call "ideas" a spontaneity so pure that it thereby goes far beyond anything that sensibility can ever afford it' (*G* 4.452), and the *First Critique*, where he writes that 'reason does not give in to...grounds which are empirically given, and it does not follow the order of things as they are presented in intuition, but with complete spontaneity it makes its own order according to ideas' (A548/B576). Here Kant is speaking specifically of reason insofar as it generates 'the ought' – reason in its practical use (see, e.g., A547/B575).

7. For a different reading that also takes this passage to be significant, especially the reference to obligation, see Tenenbaum (2012, 580–581).

8. In *Kant's Theory of Freedom*, Henry Allison also argues that Kant distinguishes between the world of understanding and the intelligible world. According to Allison, the world of understanding is a noumenon in the negative sense, viz., a non-sensible world, whereas the intelligible world is a noumenon in the positive sense, a 'supersensible realm governed by moral laws,' i.e., the Kingdom of Ends (1990, 227; Allison has since rejected this view – cf. his, 2011, 338n28). In the above, I propose a different reading of this distinction; however, my interpretation of the intelligible world draws on an understanding of what Kant means by 'intelligible' that is close to what Allison says in his analysis of 'intelligible character' (1990, 29–53).

9. Allison also puts a lot of weight on this passage (1990, 227).

10. A similar reading of the 'intelligible' is given by Onora O'Neill, who writes that '[t]he intelligible world is not a transcendent realm beyond this world, but the system of formal conditions that our understanding of the empirical world presupposes; it is precisely intelligible, not supersensible' (1989, 69).

11. Thanks to Alix Cohen for helping me clarify this point.

12. This is in fact what Kant, in the Preface to the *Groundwork*, says he will do in *Groundwork III*: there, he says, the argument will proceed 'synthetically from the examination of [the moral] principle and its sources back to the common cognition in which we find it used' (*G* 4.392).

13. As is clear from the above, I take there to be continuity between the *Groundwork* and the *Second Critique*. On the reading I am proposing, in the

Groundwork, the argument runs from freedom to the moral law – but not from the proof of my freedom. Rather, it runs from the *use* of my freedom that is necessary to have the experience of moral obligation, to the consciousness of the moral law as binding on me. And this is consistent with the argument of the *Second Critique*. For as Kant puts it there, 'had not the moral law already been distinctly thought in our reason, we should never consider ourselves justified in assuming such a thing as freedom…. But were there no freedom, the moral law would not be encountered at all in ourselves' (*CPrR* 5.4fn).

14. In *Groundwork II*, Kant says that the task of grounding the claim that 'rational nature exists as an end in itself' is undertaken in *Groundwork III*. I take it to be in the idea of the intelligible world that this promissory note about 'rational nature' is discharged (*G* 4.428–429 and 4.429fn; emphasis mine).

15. Ameriks says that in this passage, Kant identifies a 'crucial' or 'real' need that is *not* met by the arguments of the *Groundwork*. I agree with this, but Ameriks goes on to suggest that this reveals a weakness in the argument of the *Groundwork*, whereas I think it does not. See Ameriks (2003, 175).

16. In texts that post-date the *Groundwork*, Kant frequently emphasizes the fact that the human being must be conscious of herself as *at once* free and not free. Thus in Bxxvii-xxviii, he writes, 'I…say of one and the same thing, e.g., the human soul, that its will is free and yet that it is simultaneously…not free.' And in *CPrR* 5.6n, the connection is made again with the nature of self-consciousness: 'the union of causality as freedom with causality as natural mechanism…in one and the same subject, the human being, is impossible without representing him with regard to…the former in *pure*, the latter in *empirical* consciousness.' See also *G* 4.453, 4.454, 4.455; *CPrR* 5.97, 5.105; *M-L2* 28.583; and *M-Vig.* 29.1019–1020, *inter alia*.

17. My discussion thus focuses on the subjective strand of the argument; the question of how experience is thereby made possible is largely set aside, and the further tasks of defending the interpretation and the theory that emerges from it is not even embarked upon.

18. Kant uses a number of terms for this kind of consciousness, including 'logical' or 'discursive' consciousness (*Anth.* 7.141), the 'consciousness of understanding' (*Anth.* 7.135fn), 'intellectual consciousness' (*Leningrad Fragment I, M-D* 28.670–671). And though Kant's emphasis remains on apperception as consciousness of an activity, some cryptic remarks suggest that this consciousness is not entirely metaphysically noncommittal. Consider, for instance, Kant's claim that 'in the consciousness of myself in mere thinking I am the being itself' (B429), or that 'apperception is something real' (B419).

19. The kind of unity that obtains when a single 'I think' accompanies several judgments is the 'analytical unity of apperception' mentioned in B133; and the point I discuss in the next paragraph above – that a synthesis is necessary for the analytic premise to obtain – is Kant's claim that 'the analytic unity of apperception is only possible under the presupposition of some synthetic one' (B133-134).

20. For three different interpretations of the analytic principle, see Allison (2004, 166–167), Kitcher (2011, 124–126) and Longuenesse (2017, 177–181). In my analysis, I take Kantian 'judgment' the way it is defined in the B-*Transcendental Deduction*, which I think involves a shift from the view of the *Prolegomena* (see, e.g., *Prol.* 4.298, 4.300–4.306). See Pollok (2008) for an argument for this

claim; for a defence that the *Prolegomena* view is consistent with the B-*CPR* view, cf. Longuenesse (1998, 167–195).

21. I thank Thomas Land for suggesting I make this connection explicit.
22. This point touches on issues that are central to the conceptualism/non-conceptualism debate, which has recently focused on the unity of time and space and whether such unity has its source in intuition itself or whether it is conferred by the faculty of understanding (or perhaps apperception). I believe that what I say above remains neutral. When Kant talks about the 'pure synthesis of the understanding', for instance, in the passage quoted above, I take him to be referring not to the synthesis that makes time a unity, but the synthesis that brings the intuition of time to the original-synthetic unity of apperception. For arguments that space and time have their own unity, see, e.g., Allison (2004, 191–193), Colin McLear (2015), and James Messina (2014); for arguments that take the unity of space and time to be generated by a synthesis that is in some sense informed by the understanding (though not itself a conceptual synthesis), see, e.g., Thomas Land (2015), Longuenesse (1998, 214–241, 2005, 105–106), Michael Friedman (forthcoming).

Acknowledgments

Thanks to Angela Breitenbach, John Callanan, Alix Cohen, Samantha Matherne, and especially Thomas Land for helpful suggestions and discussions of these issues; to Chen Liang for a thoughtful response to a very early version of this paper at the German Philosophy Workshop in Chicago; and to other participants of the German Philosophy Workshop, the Berlin Summer Colloquium, and conferences at Ryerson University and the University of Southampton.

References

Allison, H. 1986. "Morality and Freedom: Kant's Reciprocity Thesis." *Philosophical Review* 95 (3): 393–425. doi:10.2307/2185466.

Allison, H. 1990. *Kant's Theory of Freedom*. Cambridge: Cambridge University Press.

Allison, H. 1995. "Spontaneity and Autonomy in Kant's Conception of the Self." In *The Modern Subject: Conceptions of the Self in Classical German Philosophy*, edited by K. Ameriks and D. Sturma, 11–29. Albany: SUNY Press.

Allison, H. 2004. *Kant's Transcendental Idealism*. 2nd ed. New Haven: Yale University Press.

Allison, H. 2011. Kant's *Groundwork for the Metaphysics of Morals: A Commentary*. Oxford: Oxford University Press.

Allison, H. 2013. "Kant's Practical Justification of Freedom." In *Kant on Practical Justification: Interpretive Essays*, edited by M. Timmons and S. Baiasu, 284–299. Oxford: Oxford University Press.

Ameriks, K. 2000. *Kant's Theory of Mind*. 2nd ed. Oxford: Oxford University Press.

Ameriks, K. 2003. *Interpreting Kant's Critiques*. Oxford: Oxford University Press.

Beck, L. W. 1960. *A Commentary on Kant's* Critique of Practical Reason. Chicago: University of Chicago Press.

Friedman, M. Forthcoming. "Space and Geometry in the B-Deduction." In *Kant's Philosophy of Mathematics, Volume I*, edited by C. Posy and O. Rechter. Cambridge: Cambridge University Press.

Guyer, P. 2016. *Virtues of Freedom*. Oxford: Oxford University Press.

Guyer, P. 2018. "The Struggle for Freedom: Freedom of Will in Kant and Reinhold." In *Kant on Persons and Agency*, edited by E. Watkins, 120–137. Cambridge: Cambridge University Press.

Henrich, D. 1994. "The Concept of Moral Insight and Kant's Doctrine of the Fact of Reason." In *The Unity of Reason: Essays on Kant's Philosophy*, edited by, R. L. Velkley translated by Manfred Kuehn, 55–87. Cambridge, MA: Harvard University Press.

Hill, T. 1992. *Dignity and Practical Reason*. Ithaca: Cornell University Press.

Kitcher, P. 2011. *Kant's Thinker*. Oxford: Oxford University Press.

Korsgaard, C. 1996. *Creating the Kingdom of Ends*. Cambridge: Cambridge University Press.

Land, T. 2015. "Nonconceptualist Readings of Kant and the Transcendental Deduction." *Kantian Review* 20 (1): 25–51. doi:10.1017/S1369415414000272.

Longuenesse, B. 1998. *Kant and the Capacity to Judge*. Trans. Charles T. Wolfe. Princeton: Princeton University Press.

Longuenesse, B. 2005. *Kant on the Human Standpoint*. Cambridge: Cambridge University Press.

Longuenesse, B. 2017. *I, Me, Mine*. Oxford: Oxford University Press.

McLear, C. 2015. "Two Kinds of Unity in the *Critique of Pure Reason*." *Journal of the History of Philosophy* 53 (1): 79–110. doi:10.1353/hph.2015.0011.

Messina, J. 2014. "Kant on the Unity of Space and the Synthetic Unity of Apperception." *Kant-Studien* 105 (1): 5–40. doi:10.1515/kant-2014-0002.

O'Neill, O. 1989. *Constructions of Reason*. Cambridge: Cambridge University Press.

O'Neill, O. 2002. "Autonomy and the Fact of Reason in the *Kritik der Praktischen Vernunft* (§§7-8, 30-41)." In *Kritik der praktischen Vernunft: Klassiker Auslegen*, edited by O. Höffe, 81–97. Berlin: Akademie Verlag.

Pollok, K. 2008. "'An Almost Single Inference' – Kant's Deduction of the Categories Reconsidered." *Archiv für Geschichte der Philosophie* 90 (3): 323–345. doi:10.1515/AGPH.2008.013.

Tenenbaum, S. 2012. "The Idea of Freedom and Moral Cognition in *Groundwork III*." *Philosophy and Phenomenological Research* 84 (3): 555–589. doi:10.1111/phpr.2012.84.issue-3.

Timmermann, J. 2007. *Kant's* Groundwork of the Metaphysics of Morals: *A Commentary*. Cambridge: Cambridge University Press.

Timmermann, J. 2010. "Reversal or Retreat? Kant's Deductions of Freedom and Morality." In *Kant's* Critique of Practical Reason: *A Critical Guide*, edited by A. Reath and J. Timmermann, 73–89. Cambridge: Cambridge University Press.

Timmermann, J. 2019. "Emerging Autonomy: Dealing with the Inadequacies of the 'Canon' of the *Critique of Pure Reason*." In *The Emergence of Autonomy in Kant's Moral Philosophy*, edited by S. Bacin and O. Sensen, 102–121. Cambridge: Cambridge University Press.

Ware, O. 2017. "Kant's Deductions of Freedom and Morality." *Canadian Journal of Philosophy* 47 (1): 116–147. doi:10.1080/00455091.2016.1235856.

Wood, A. 2007. *Kantian Ethics*. Cambridge: Cambridge University Press.

'I do not cognize myself through being conscious of myself as thinking': Self-knowledge and the irreducibility of self-objectification in Kant

Thomas Khurana

ABSTRACT
The paper argues that Kant's distinction between pure and empirical apperception cannot be interpreted as distinguishing two self-standing types of self-knowledge. For Kant, empirical and pure apperception need to co-operate to yield substantive self-knowledge. What makes Kant's account interesting is his acknowledgment that there is a deep tension between the way I become conscious of myself as subject through pure apperception and the way I am given to myself as an object of inner sense. This tension remains problematic in the realm of theoretical cognition but can be put to work and made productive in terms of practical self-knowledge.

It seems natural to think that the distinct immediacy and authority with which we know ourselves has to be due to a special theoretical capacity granting us a unique view of ourselves, unavailable to the gaze of others. The fact that we know ourselves in a more immediate way and with an authority that outranks the authority of others must have something to do with the privileged spectator position we have with regard to our own inner life, the stage of the 'internal theatre' to which we can direct our inner eye. As suggestive as this inner perception model may seem, the fundamental problems that it raises are well known. In recent years, Richard Moran has proposed a radical alternative to this approach, suggesting that the true root of these problems does not just reside in the misleading implications of the metaphors of an inner eye or an internal theatre, but in the even more general issue that this model misconstrues our self-knowledge by understanding it as a form of *theoretical* cognition. If we try to explain self-knowledge in terms of a 'purely theoretical or spectator's stance toward the self', whatever its concrete form or shape, we distort the fundamental character of self-knowledge (Moran 2001, 3): 'Modelling self-consciousness on the *theoretical awareness of objects* obscures the specifically first-person character of the phenomenon' (Moran 2001, 32). To understand the immediacy and authority of first-person knowledge, we rather need to recognize the extent to which self-knowledge is due to a *practical* stance. That I have distinct access to my own beliefs and intentions is not due to the fact that I am in a privileged position to observe them, but due to the fact that I am the very person determining and maintaining them. My self-knowledge is thus not based on special *evidence* available only to me or an exclusive *point of view*. Rather, it is based on the special way in which the determination of my own attitudes is *up to me* and the *point of agency* that I have with regard to these attitudes. I know my 'beliefs, desires, intentions' (Moran 2001, xxxiii) immediately and with authority, because I am the agent determining them. The peculiar features that distinguish knowledge of myself from knowledge of others are thus to be explained in terms of the specific agential character that self-knowledge involves. The agential stance that I have in view of my own attitudes becomes evident in the way in which I can identify them not merely by observing them and attributing them to myself as anyone else might, but by determining and avowing the.

There are a number of different inspirations Moran cites for this fundamental idea – the idea that self-knowledge is rooted in a specific form of *practical* self-relation – but one especially salient source is Kant.[1] Matthew Boyle (2009) has suggested that returning to Kant may not only allow us to better understand the underlying intuition guiding Moran's account, but in addition will lead to a clarification that helps to defend Moran against an important objection, namely the worry that Moran's account cannot explain the privilege the first person has with regard to knowing one's own basic sensations. Boyle reminds us that Kant distinguishes between two fundamentally different 'kinds of self-knowledge: knowledge of ourselves through "inner sense" and knowledge of ourselves through "pure apperception."' Whereas knowledge through inner sense 'gives us knowledge of our sensations, knowledge of ourselves as passive beings', the self-knowledge granted by pure apperception 'gives us knowledge of what we think and judge, knowledge of our own spontaneity' (Boyle 2009, 133). The latter self-knowledge – that granted by pure apperception – could thus help to elucidate the agential mode in which we know our own beliefs and intentions on Moran's account. By distinguishing this type of self-knowledge from another type, Kant makes explicit that not all self-knowledge is of the active sort Moran is interested in. Kant thereby contests what Boyle has termed the *Uniformity Assumption*: the assumption that we need to 'seek some common explanation of all of the cases in which we speak immediately and authoritatively about our own mental states' (Boyle 2009, 141). In addition, Kant suggests that there is an interesting dependency relation between these two forms of self-knowledge such that we can see why the agential self-consciousness granted to us by pure apperception indeed deserves our primary attention – without it, we could not have any self-knowledge at all.

In what follows, I will not discuss Moran's or Boyle's accounts but follow the suggestion of taking a closer look at Kant's alleged distinction of different forms of self-knowledge. I think that it is a deeply intriguing idea that self-knowledge is based on a practical or agential self-relation, and I agree that Kant is a crucial source to consult when we want to get clear about this idea. As his conception of pure apperception indeed indicates, Kant suggests that our self-knowledge depends on an agential stance: on consciousness of ourselves as self-active, as spontaneous. However, I want to contest the idea that Kant's distinction of pure apperception and inner sense can be understood as pointing us to two self-standing types of self-knowledge. Boyle himself already draws on the fact that self-knowledge of our sensations presupposes self-consciousness of our thinking and judging I. Here I am more interested, however, in the reverse dependency. For Kant it is not the case that pure apperception as such gives one *cognition* of one's self, 'Erkenntnis seiner selbst' (Kant 1998, B158).[2] Although Kant's conception of pure apperception indeed gives us an account of the awareness we have of our agential self, it renders problematic the idea that this awareness by itself amounts to *knowledge* or *cognition* of ourselves. In merely being conscious of my pure apperceptive activity, I do not yet cognize my 'I'. In order for us to know not only *that* we think and judge, but *what* it is that we think and judge we are dependent on the mediation of inner sense. To yield *cognition* or *knowledge* of ourselves, our apperception is thus dependent on a given sensible manifold and on the articulation of our thoughts in inner sense.[3]

Kant's significance for the current debate is thus not that through his conception of pure apperception he has specified a form of immediate self-knowledge. Rather, his significance resides in the fact that he has characterized our self-knowledge as inherently double: it is based on two forms of self-relation that are in seeming tension with one another, but only jointly give us knowledge of ourselves. In what follows, I will (I) first retrace the way in which Kant distinguishes and relates pure apperception and inner sense. Next (II), I will highlight the way in which Kant's distinction implies that we are conscious of ourselves in two ways that, in the context of Kant's theoretical philosophy, remain in a problematic tension. I will close (III) with a discussion of the way Kant tries to elaborate this tension through an account of practical self-consciousness in his conception of practical reason.

I.

Kant's most extended discussion of consciousness of ourselves through inner sense and of consciousness of our 'I' through pure apperception can be found in the *Critique of Pure Reason*. This discussion is, however, not presented in terms of an independent theory of self-knowledge. Rather, Kant introduces these notions in his attempt to specify the transcendental conditions of possibility of cognition of objects in general. He first introduces his notion of an inner sense in the context of the Transcendental Aesthetic and specifies pure apperception in the context of the Transcendental Analytic. The Transcendental Aesthetic highlights that due to the nature of our intuition, consciousness of ourselves as an object of inner sense requires inner perception of a manifold, antecedently given sensibly in the subject and not self-actively produced. To intuit ourselves we have to affect ourselves; we cannot intuit ourselves as we would immediately and spontaneously think ourselves, but only according to the way in which we affect ourselves through inner sense.[4] The Transcendental Analytic, in turn, highlights the way in which the objectivity of our cognition ultimately depends on the original synthetic unity of pure apperception.[5] Only through the synthetic activity of conjoining representations and being conscious of my conjoining them (Kant 1929, B133) – that is, only through the 'unity of consciousness in the synthesis' – can I 'constitute the relation of representations to an object, and therefore their objective validity' (Kant 1929, B137). 'Thoroughgoing identity of the apperception of a manifold ... is possible only *through* the consciousness of this synthesis.' (Kant 1929, B133, emphasis added) Pure apperception is thus the *vehicle* or *medium* through which the objects of our cognition can take shape and appear to us. Kant thus does not focus on the way in which this pure apperception may give us access to ourselves, but rather the way in which it allows us to constitute our experience such that it gives us access to objects in general. As Kant writes in the *Paralogisms*: 'We can thus say of the thinking "I" ... that it does *not* know *itself through the categories* but knows the categories and through them all objects, in the absolute unity of apperception, and so *through itself*.' (Kant 1929, A402) Pure apperception is, in other words, what makes the mind transparent to the objects given in its cognition.[6]

I recall this framing only to remind us that self-knowledge is not in and of itself Kant's topic. He is not concerned to explain the immediacy or authority with which we speak about our mental attitudes or sensations, and he is not concerned with a comprehensive account of the different ways in which we relate to ourselves (as a thinking I, as a person, as a sensible being, as a body, etc.), although his account touches on all of these ways in which we might be an issue for ourselves. His immediate topic is the conditions of possibility of objective knowledge in general.

And it turns out that the forms of intuition and the understanding that are required for knowledge of objects, in general, involve certain forms of self-consciousness. Given our forms of intuition, we can become a determinate object for ourselves through inner sense; and given the synthetic activity of understanding, our cognitive activity involves a pure form of self-consciousness expressed in the 'empty representation' or 'mere consciousness' I (Kant 1929, B404), the 'concept' or 'judgment' 'I think' (Kant 1929, B399). This is not to say that we cannot try to develop a comprehensive theory of self-consciousness from Kant's reflections,[7] but it reminds us that this requires careful attention to the way in which self-consciousness becomes a topic for Kant. Given the distinction Kant makes between self-consciousness through inner sense and through pure apperception, leading to a consciousness of the '"I" as *object* of perception' and the '"I" as *subject* of thinking' (Kant 2006, 7:134FN) respectively, it is suggestive to think that Kant's account implies the idea that there are two self-standing types of self-knowledge with distinct contents. Boyle suggests such an understanding when he reformulates Kant's distinction as one of two forms of self-knowledge, one concerning our *sensations*, the other regarding our *thoughts and judgments*.[8] As a closer look at Kant's discussion makes clear, however, the types of self-consciousness are neither self-standing nor can they properly be distinguished simply in terms of these contents. The two types of self-consciousness rather involve two fundamentally different modes of self-relation that have to co-operate to produce substantial self-knowledge, be it of our sensations or our thoughts.

Let me briefly point out the way in which these two types of self-consciousness depend on one another in bringing forth self-knowledge. Kant distinguishes '*inner sense*' or '*empirical apperception*' on the one hand, from '*pure*' or '*transcendental apperception*' on the other (Kant 1929, A107). Whereas empirical apperception is consciousness of myself according to the always changing 'determinations of our state in inner perception', transcendental apperception is a 'pure, original, immutable consciousness' of my 'I' (Kant 1929, A107). Now, it is probably not very controversial that empirical apperception depends upon pure apperception, since it is Kant's explicit aim in the first *Critique* to show that pure apperception is a transcendental requirement for any form of objective knowledge. For our experiences in inner sense to amount to cognition of ourselves – cognition of an aspect of our empirical I, given as an object of our inner sense – our experiences require a certain type of unity that is based on the unity of pure apperception. In the absence of the original synthetic unity of apperception, no objective knowledge, be it about other objects in the world or myself, is possible. Kant makes this particularly clear in a letter to Marcus Herz from 1789 in which he contemplates a possible cognizer lacking pure apperception: If I abstract from the synthetic activity of my understanding and imagine myself to be a mere animal, I may still assume that the sense data given in my mental life could 'carry on their play in an orderly fashion', but in the absence of the synthetic activity of the understanding this could only happen 'without my cognizing the slightest thing thereby, not even what my own condition is.'[9] Without the synthetic activity of the understanding, the data of sense could never represent objects: 'They would not even reach that unity of consciousness that is necessary for cognition of myself [*Erkentnis meiner selbst*] (as object of inner sense)' (Kant 1999, 11:52).

Let us, therefore, assume that there cannot be any knowledge of myself as an object of my inner sense without pure apperceptive consciousness of myself as the subject of my thoughts. This is a fact that the contemporary debate seems fully aware of, wherever it takes up Kant's distinction.[10] Less noted, however, is the extent to which that pure apperception is in turn also dependent on the given manifold of intuition. To elaborate this, it is helpful to take note of the distinction that Kant draws between the *analytic unity* of pure apperception, expressed in the 'I think' which must be able to accompany all my representations, and the *synthetic unity* of apperception which is presupposed by this analytic unity (Kant 1929, B133). In general, an analytic unity can be understood as the unity of a one contained in many: a shared feature or mark common to a multiplicity of instances. A synthetic unity, by contrast, is the unity of many contained in one, a unity of conjunction.[11] The analytic unity of the 'I think' – the one trait accompanying all of my representations insofar as they are mine – presupposes the synthetic unity of apperception: my operation of self-consciously conjoining these representations in one consciousness. Kant writes:

> The thought that the representations given in intuition one and all belong to me, is therefore precisely the same as the thought that I unite them in one self-consciousness, or can at least so unite them; and although this thought is not itself the consciousness of the *synthesis* of the representations, it presupposes the possibility of that synthesis. In other words, only in so far as I can grasp the manifold of the representations in one consciousness, do I call them one and all *mine*.' (Kant 1929, B134)

The simple unity of the *I think* thus does not precede the synthetic activity of the understanding, it rather results from the synthetic activity of *my thinking something*, actualizing the original synthetic unity of apperception. However, if the 'I think' indeed depends upon the possibility of such self-conscious synthesis, it seems dependent upon a given manifold that lends itself to this synthetic activity. Pure apperception cannot itself produce the matter for its synthetic activity, but has to rely on receptivity to attain the manifold it can unite:

> For through the 'I', as simple representation, nothing manifold is given; only in intuition, which is distinct from the 'I', can a manifold be given; and only

through *combination* in one consciousness can it be thought. An understanding in which through self-consciousness all the manifold would *eo ipso* be given, would be *intuitive*; our understanding can only *think*, and for intuition must look to the senses. (Kant 1929, B135)[12]

The point here is not just that pure apperception is dependent on the cognitive matter to be provided from elsewhere. Kant also wants to point us to the fact that pure apperception, taken in abstraction, grants us only a very peculiar access to 'ourselves' that Kant himself would not venture to call cognition of myself (*Erkenntnis meiner selbst*) and that does not yield substantive knowledge of myself.[13] For Kant, cognition by definition requires the unity of sensibility and understanding, intuition and concept (Kant 1929, A51/B75). Kant does think that the understanding can be *conscious* of the mere unity of its action in abstraction from sensibility, that is to say: it can be conscious of the unity of its operation directly just by virtue of the thought 'I think.' With this consciousness abstracting from sensibility altogether, the understanding, however, does not cognize (*erkennt*) anything determinate of the putatively represented object (the 'I'). In abstraction from all sensibility, all that the understanding becomes conscious of with regard to its synthesis is the mere form and the sheer unity of its action (*Einheit der Handlung*): The synthesis of the understanding is 'nothing but the unity of the act, of which, as an act, it is conscious to itself, even without [the aid of] sensibility' (Kant 1929, B153). But such consciousness of the mere unity of the act – consciousness of the 'I' as the vehicle of all concepts – cannot be called *cognition* of myself. As Kant writes explicitly in § 25 of the deduction: 'Consciousness of one's self is ... very far from being cognition of one's self [*Erkenntnis seiner selbst*]' (Kant 1929, B158, transl. modified). And in the Paralogism section he underlines: 'I do not cognize [*erkenne*] myself through being conscious of myself as thinking' (Kant 1929, B406, transl. modified), for I do not cognize or know any object by merely thinking, but 'only in so far as I determine a given intuition with respect to the unity of consciousness in which all thought consists' (Kant 1929, B406).[14] The awareness of myself I gain by virtue of the transcendental synthesis of the manifold of the representations is not consciousness of myself as an object – neither an object of inner sense, nor a thing in itself – it is rather merely consciousness of the actuality of a distinct activity: 'In the ... synthetic original unity of apperception, I am conscious of myself, not as I appear to myself, nor as I am in myself, but only *that I am*.' (Kant 1929, B157, emphasis added) The consciousness of the 'I think' as such thus makes me aware *that* I think and *that* I am but does not amount to *cognition* of *what* I think or *what* I am.

This awareness is certainly not without import. It does not determine my existence such that I can cognize given features of myself, but it makes me aware of a distinct mode of my existence that distinguishes me: it reveals me as activity, as spontaneity, as a self-given unity. Moreover, it gives me access to the pure form of this fundamental activity that I am. But this spontaneous mode of existence and this pure form is not disclosed as a content of this consciousness which I cognize, but rather as the mode of this consciousness: as the agential form of my knowing things. It is through this active or performative character of this consciousness that this 'I think' in some very specific sense entails that I exist.[15] By means of the 'I think' I do not become aware of an object that I can know to exist, I rather become aware of the 'I' of the 'I think' as something that 'exists in the deed' ('*etwas, was in der Tat existiert*', Kant 1998, B423FN). Pure apperception thus reveals to me the extent to which I, qua subject, exists as pure activity.[16] Kant explicitly rules out that the 'I' of the 'I think' is here given as an *object* of my cognition at all: it is neither given 'as appearance, nor as thing in itself (*noumenon*)' (Kant 1929, B423FN); neither 'as we appear nor as we are' (Kant 2005, 364).

The self-consciousness of pure apperception thus gives me access to my existence in a certain distinct mode or voice, but it does not grant me knowledge of any determinate features that characterize me apart from my being a thinker.[17] As such, transcendental apperception only gives us consciousness of the form of the activity of the 'I think', but not knowledge of the characteristics of the 'I' as an object: Neither knowledge of the soul as the general type of object that may underlie this 'I', as the Paralogisms show, nor cognition of the particular self that I am. Although transcendental apperception puts me in a relation to myself that is indispensable for me to be a cognizer at all, including me being a cognizer of myself, on its own, it does not suffice to yield cognition of myself. In §25 of the deduction Kant gives the following explanation of why this is:

> Now in order to *cognize* ourselves [*zum* Erkenntnis *unserer selbst*], there is required in addition to the act of thought, which brings the manifold of every possible intuition to the unity of apperception, a determinate mode of intuition, whereby this manifold is given; it therefore follows that although my existence is not indeed appearance (still less mere illusion), the determination of my existence can take place only in conformity with the form of inner sense, according to the special mode in which the manifold, which I combine, is given in inner intuition. Accordingly I have no *cognition* of myself *as I am* but merely as I *appear* to myself [*ich habe also demnach keine* Erkenntnis *von mir wie ich bin, sondern bloß wie ich mir selbst* erscheine]... Just as for cognition of an object distinct from me I require, besides the thought of an object in general (in the category), an intuition by which I determine that general concept, so for cognition of myself I require, besides the consciousness of myself, or the fact that I think, an intuition of the manifold in me, by which I determine this thought. I exist as an intelligence which is conscious solely of its power of combination; but in respect of the manifold which it has to combine I am subjected to a limiting condition (entitled inner sense), namely,

that this combination can be made intuitable only according to relations of time, which lie entirely outside the concepts of understanding, strictly regarded. Such an intelligence, therefore, can cognize itself only as it appears to itself in respect of an intuition which is not intellectual and cannot be given by the understanding itself, not as it would cognize itself if its *intuition* were intellectual. (Kant 1929, B157f.)

As Kant makes clear in this passage, pure apperception alone is insufficient for self-cognition. Besides the thought of myself, cognition of myself requires an intuition of the manifold in me. Only thereby can my thought of myself attain determinacy. Note that Kant is here not distinguishing pure apperception of our thoughts, which may not be cognition strictly speaking, from a different form of self-consciousness of other items – say sensations – which does constitute self-cognition. Rather, he considers the possibility that the synthetic activity of apperception itself may become known to us *through inner sense*: 'this combination can be made intuitable according to relations of time, which lie entirely outside the concepts of understanding strictly regarded.' The subject can thus cognize itself as an intelligence, but only 'as it appears to itself in respect of an intuition.' (Kant 1929, B157f) This seems to suggest that Kant does not think that we have one way of accessing our thoughts and judgments and quite another one of knowing our sensations, one relying on pure apperception and one relying on inner sense. Whatever we become aware of in inner sense presupposes pure apperception to become an object of knowledge; and whatever we want to know through our power of thinking or judging can only be known 'as it appears in respect of an intuition' and by making itself intuitable according to relations of time.[18]

II.

As we have seen, the two forms of self-consciousness – pure apperception and inner sense – need to co-operate in order to grant us cognition of ourselves. Whereas it is widely recognized that inner sense presupposes the synthetic unity of apperception, it is less commonly taken into account that pure apperception only leads to a determinate cognition of myself – instead of mere consciousness of my pure I – by reference to an 'intuition of the manifold in me, by which I determine this thought.' It is only when we realize this that we see the true problematic force of Kant's fundamental distinction of the two modes of self-relation. Kant is not distinguishing two types and regions of self-knowledge that could happily co-exist alongside one another, one concerning our sensations knowable through inner sense and one concerning our thoughts and judgments knowable through the pure force of thinking. Rather, he describes two ways in which we relate to ourselves that need to co-operate for us to know anything about ourselves at all, be it about our sensations or about our thoughts and judgments.

Only now am I arriving at the aspect that interests me most in Kant's account: Kant does not only require that these two forms of self-relation should co-operate, he also characterizes them in a way that makes it hard to see how they can, in fact, give rise to a unified perspective on the same subject. On Kant's account, humans can only know themselves on account of a double consciousness of themselves: Consciousness of ourselves as the purely active, spontaneous thinkers of our thoughts and consciousness of ourselves as the objects of our inner sense. Only to the extent that we become an object to ourselves is there something to know at all. But to the extent that we become an object to ourselves we can only know ourselves as an appearance, and even more to the point: we become accessible to ourselves merely as the *result* of an activity, not as the activity itself. Even though it is our very own activity, we cannot *cognize* it directly. It thus seems that, on Kant's account, it is impossible for us to cognize ourselves *as subjects*. To cognize ourselves, we have to turn ourselves into objects. Yet, through the self-consciousness of pure apperception, we are aware of ourselves qua subjects. To unify both self-relations into a coherent form of self-knowledge we would need to find a way of cognizing ourselves in such a manner that, *qua subjects*, we know ourselves as objects. It is not immediately clear, however, how this should be possible. There is a deep sense in which it seems that 'awareness of something as an object and awareness of it *qua* subject are mutually exclusive modes of awareness', to borrow a formulation by Quassim Cassam (1997, 5).

Recall once again the fundamental way in which Kant distinguishes, even opposes the form of pure apperception and empirical apperception such that it can give rise to the impression that these two forms of self-knowledge have different objects: As Kant proposes, pure apperception is a consciousness of the 'I' as the *subject* of thought, whereas empirical apperception makes me aware of the 'I' as the *object* of awareness (Kant 2006, 7:134FN).[19] In pure apperception, I become conscious of *what I do*, whereas inner sense gives me access to *what I undergo*.[20] Pure apperception gives me awareness of the *determining self*, where I may cognize the *determinable self* through inner sense (Kant 1929, B407; B157FN). And in pure apperception I become aware of something that exists *in the deed* without becoming conscious of it as either appearance or thing in itself (Kant 1929, B423FN); in inner sense, I become aware of myself *as a fact*, knowing it inevitably only as an appearance. It thus seems that these two modes of self-awareness give me access to two fundamentally different types of being, such that the unity of the 'I' that we are conscious of in these two ways becomes mysterious. As Kant grants in the *Anthropology*, it at least seems that the 'I' here is 'double', 'which would be contradictory'

(Kant 2006, 7:134FN). What is this 'I' that is supposed to be both the subject of my thinking and the object of my perceptions, both only existent in the act and a resultant fact, both a spontaneous act and the being affected by such a spontaneous act?

Given this duplicity, it is not entirely clear in what sense we can identify the active subject of my thinking with the constituted object of my perceptions such that we can say that what I come to know in inner sense is my very own active self. Even though it is the indispensable condition of my cognitive activity, it seems that the 'I' of the 'I think' can only be known in a distorted form: I cannot *cognize* it on its own terms as the pure act that it is, but only come to know it by turning it into an *object* of knowledge, a determinable self, an *appearance*, and a *fact*. It thus seems that I cannot know myself directly to be the very sort of thing that makes me a knower. Or, put differently, to know myself, I have to become something else: I have to turn myself into a phenomenon, fall into nature, manifest myself as an object of my perception. To fully understand myself as the being that I am would therefore mean to realize that my self-awareness has an irredeemably double, even ironic structure; it is split between, and yet fated to hold together, my transcendental consciousness of myself as the thinker of my thoughts and my empirical knowledge of myself as the object of inner sense.[21]

In Kant's treatment of these issues, it becomes clear that Kant has an acute sense of the possible tension between these two ways of relating to myself. It is, however, not entirely clear what he wants to make of this. He seems to oscillate between three strategies: (i) first, downplaying the tension such that it is not that mysterious after all how we come to identify the 'I' of pure apperception and the intuited 'I' of inner sense. (ii) A second, competing strategy we find in Kant is to embrace the very split as our true condition which defines us as human beings and demonstrates the truth of transcendental idealism. (iii) A third strategy is to embrace this split, but still recognize that something more needs to be said in order to make sense of this condition.

The first strategy turns on Kant neglecting the contrast of subject and object, activity and passivity, determining self and determinable self, deed and fact, and employing the distinction of thing in itself and appearance to make sense of the split. Since it is a general and familiar feature of Kant's account that we can only know appearances, it should not puzzle us that this is true for ourselves as well. To become an object of knowledge requires us to become an appearance and hence we cannot know ourselves as we are but can only know ourselves as appearance. In this way, Kant hopes to resolve the apparent 'paradox' of inner sense (Kant 1929, B152f.). However, this response fails to address the fact that the problem, in this case, is much more specific: In order to appear, the 'I' has to take on the shape of an object being thought. But we are at the same time aware of the 'I' as existing as a pure activity. How is it, then, that 'I, *as intelligence and thinking subject*' can in fact truly '*cognize myself* as an object that is thought' (Kant 1929, B155, emphasis added, transl. modified)? Appearance in this specific instance seems to verge on dissimulation or distortion since it portrays what is the thinking subject as merely an object being thought. The 'I' as intelligence does not actually seem to appear, but rather manifests itself in an indirect form that presents us with a being of a fundamentally different kind. The object of inner sense is not so much the appearance of the intelligence but rather its symptom or trace.[22] If we are, however, required to identify this intelligence and its symptom, this puts us under a restriction far more difficult to meet than the idea that we should identify a thing and its appearance as being of the same subject. I am not sure if Kant really captures the contrast that he has described, when he suggests that the contrast between the two I's is one merely in form, not in content.[23] In addition, it is puzzling how Kant could think that the distinction between appearances and things in themselves could be helpful here given that he had explicitly argued that the 'I' of the 'I think' is not a thing at all – *neither* appearance *nor* thing in itself – but something that exists only in the deed. In what sense can we take this I that is a pure deed and the active synthetic origin of all our cognition to be identical in content with the thing that we grasp in empirical apperception as an object of cognition?

These difficulties suggest that it may not work to downplay the tension. One should rather embrace it as part of the distinctive finite character of human cognition. Kant's way of arguing for this is his insistence that the human cognizer is fated to become conscious of itself in this double way since intellectual intuition for us is not even a conceivable possibility.[24] As we do not have intellectual intuition the 'I think' cannot lend manifold content to itself but has to rely on sensible intuition. This does not only mean that the 'I' cannot create the world by simply thinking it. It also implies that the 'I' can only come to know itself in a distinctly indirect or mediated fashion. To become something known the 'I' needs to affect its inner sense and appear as an object of inner sense. It thus seems that by virtue of lacking intellectual intuition human cognizers are incapable of an immediate form of self-cognition.

This limitation quite naturally produces the urge to supersede the Kantian framework by questioning whether intellectual intuition is indeed impossible for us. This is a route that the German Idealists explored in various ways. Fichte, for example, thinks that to give a full account of the 'I' requires us to see that a certain form of intellectual intuition underlies its originary form. He repeatedly raises doubts as to whether Kant was indeed justified in denying us any form of intellectual intuition. Fichte's point, however, is not to suggest that we can, in fact, create the world just by thinking it and that our intellect is thus indistinguishable from a divine intellect. His suggestion is actually much more internal to Kant's own project: he thinks that what Kant calls pure apperception is a form of original self-consciousness that is itself evidence of the actuality of an intellectual intuition in human cognition.[25]

Be that as it may, Kant himself certainly continues to deny that there is anything close to intellectual intuition in our theoretical cognition. For Kant himself, this lack points us to the limitations that any form of theoretical cognition imposes upon our capacity for self-knowledge. According to the theoretical model, knowledge requires a subject thinking an object given to it. In order to know myself, I need to become an object to myself, thereby effectively separating myself from myself, the object known from the subject knowing this object. I can only know the active subject obliquely through the object known. If we try to apply this theoretical model to the original self-consciousness of pure apperception itself, it seems obvious that it is inadequate to capture its structure. All of this might suggest that in order to make sense of our self-relation, we need to turn to practical cognition instead. In practical cognition – in determining myself through knowledge of what I should do and who I ought to be – I may become an object to myself in a different sense and I may gain a different understanding of the original self-consciousness of the 'I think' (or rather: the 'I will'). Kant suggests that our practical form of cognition indeed gives us access to an original self-consciousness 'through which our reality would be determinable, independently of the conditions of empirical intuition' (Kant 1929, B430). Kant insists that in the practical context he is still not attributing intellectual intuition to us,[26] but he is specifying a type of cognition that comes close to a functional equivalent. Consider this passage from the *First Critique*:

> Should it be granted that we may in due course discover, not in experience but in certain laws of the pure employment of reason – laws which are not merely logical rules, but which while holding *a priori* also concern our existence – ground for regarding ourselves as *legislating* completely *a priori* in regard to our own *existence*, and as determining this existence, there would thereby be revealed a spontaneity through which our reality would be determinable, independently of the conditions of empirical intuition. And we should also become aware that in the consciousness of our existence there is contained a something *a priori*, which can serve to determine our existence – the complete determination of which is possible only in sensible terms – as being related, in respect of a certain inner faculty, to a non-sensible intelligible world. (Kant 1929, B430f.)[27]

This brings us to a third possible strategy: embracing the split without denying that a different way of relating to it or of putting it to work is needed in order for it to make sense. With this we return to the very basic idea with which I started: that self-knowledge is fundamentally *practical*. Even though there already is an agential aspect in pure apperception, in the context of Kant's theoretical philosophy this agential aspect seems curtailed, since theoretical cognition always includes a peculiar disjunction between the subject and the object of cognition. This agential aspect can thus only become manifest in the indirect form of the consciousness of an object symptomatic of, but at the same time reifying and obfuscating, the pure self-activity of the 'I'. The only paradigm of an object of knowledge that is available in theoretical cognition seems inadequate to the thing to be known. The question is whether practical cognition offers a different understanding of the object of cognition and the disjunction of subject and object of knowledge, which affords us a different sense of the I's activity and a fuller conception of how this activity can be known.

III.

At crucial points in the *Groundwork* and in his *Critique of Practical Reason*, Kant returns to the thought that the 'I' is accessible to itself in two fundamentally different ways. The 'I' knows itself through its appearances in inner sense and thus knows itself as an object in nature; in virtue of pure apperception, however, the human being becomes aware of 'what there may be of pure activity in him (what reaches consciousness immediately and not through affection of the senses)' (Kant 1996a, 4:451; cf.1996, 5:114). This gives the human being reason to consider itself as an intelligence. In his practical philosophy Kant shifts the perspective on the relation of these two stances toward the self in three fundamental ways: first (i) he does not limit his consideration to the way in which the appearance of ourselves necessarily falls short of giving us adequate cognition of the 'I' of pure apperception, but explores the way in which the 'I' of the 'I think' grants us a standpoint from which we may transcend and practically liberate ourselves from our own appearance. Secondly, (ii) Kant re-describes the 'I' that we do not cognize but already become conscious of through pure apperception as our *'proper* self' (Kant 1996a, 4:452, emphasis added). Only as an intelligence – only as the 'invisible self', as the second Critique has it (Kant 1996, 5:162) – am I my proper self; as a human being, I am a merely derivative 'appearance of myself'. And thirdly (iii), the unity of these two selves is neither downplayed as unproblematic nor simply stipulated as necessary, it is presented as a task. We thereby not only grasp the proper self as the source of the determination of the 'appearance of ourselves', but also disclose the task of bringing forth a type of appearance that can be understood as expressive of the activity that underlies it. In Kant's practical philosophy, we are thus not simply left with the disjunction of my intelligible and my empirical self, the 'I' of pure activity and its reification as a sensible object, but confronted with the task of their mediation. It is from the point of view of his practical philosophy that we see Kant developing a response to the question how spontaneity itself may appear and how we may know of ourselves, *qua subjects*, as objects.[28]

To enact these three shifts, we need to gain a more determinate consciousness, if not knowledge, of our proper self. The awareness of the 'I' of pure apperception might open up the possibility of a different standpoint, but it gives us no positive determination of this stance. It is the crucial advancement of practical over theoretical philosophy that it provides us with 'a fact that points to a pure world of the understanding and, indeed, even *determines* it *positively* and lets us cognize something of it, namely a law.' (Kant 1996, 5:43) This gives us a more robust way of understanding the way in which our empirical self is an appearance of our proper self not just in the sense that it is a derivative effect of it, but also in the sense that it can be grasped as its expression. And finally, Kant's practical philosophy tries to bring into view the operations that bring about an empirical order in which the proper self might manifest itself in such a way that it actualizes itself in it.[29]

The more determinate consciousness of the proper self becomes available to us in the form of the fact of reason: the consciousness of the moral law by means of which we finally become aware of a positive determination of the intelligible realm. For us to know this law, our faculty of reason again has to affect us; this affection does not result in mere facts of inner sense, but in what Kant calls the sole *factum* of reason, which we subjectively grasp by means of a distinctive kind of feeling Kant calls *Achtung*. This feeling, according to Kant, allows us to become aware of ourselves not only as the being affected but also as therein affecting ourselves.[30] The factum of reason that gains subjective reality by means of this feeling is neither a *datum* nor a *construct* of reason, but the very deed of reason itself. That we do not perceive the deed of reason as a dead fact or object is plain from the form our awareness of it takes. It presents itself as a task to us, as what is to be done. In my moral consciousness, the deed of reason thus does not present itself as a fact but as a command calling for further deeds.

According to the second Critique, this law requires us 'to furnish the sensible world, as a *sensible nature* (in what concerns rational beings) with the form of a world of the understanding' (Kant 1996, 5:43). Applying this general understanding of the task of the moral law to the problem of the self, it seems to require that one inform one's empirical self in such a manner that it becomes the expression and the reflection of the very form of a proper self. I take this not only to mean that the empirical self should abide by rules given from somewhere else but requiring that the empirical self takes on the very shape of the proper self: the very shape of an active self. This would seem to require that it would need to reflect its inherent dependence on, and determination by, the pure practical self in the very mode in which it is an appearance and an object. This presents us with the task of rearticulating the empirical self as the manifestation of the very difference between proper and empirical self, as the re-entry of this difference into the world of appearance. Note the fact that Kant ties our capacity of reason to our ability to distinguish ourselves from ourselves: As he writes in the *Groundwork*, 'the human being ... finds in himself a capacity by which he distinguishes himself from all other things, *even from himself* insofar as he is affected by objects, and that is *reason*' (Kant 1996a, 4:452, first emphasis added), and the *Prize Essay* seconds that by pointing to the unexplainable but undoubted fact that 'I, who think, can be an object (of intuition) to myself, and thus distinguish myself *from* myself' (Kant 2002a, 20:270). Expressing a proper self thus seems to require an empirical self that internalizes this self-distinction.[31]

How exactly to think of this and how to relate this form of ethical elaboration of one's self-difference back to one's theoretical self-relation is far from fully developed in Kant's practical philosophy, and only partially advanced in his third Critique. My complaint here is not that Kant has failed to demonstrate how we can ultimately overcome the duplicity, but merely that he has not told us enough about putting it to work. If Kant's account is right, simply superseding the double sense of myself might well amount to losing myself. It is thus key to acknowledge that Kant is committed to the idea that the unity of our self-knowledge can only be the unity of a difference, and that even the practical determination of our existence does not proceed by means of intellectual intuition, but has to go through the trouble of taking up and transforming the sensible world such that it becomes expressive of its rational ground. In other words, to require that Kant should tell us more about the relation of the proper and the empirical self cannot mean that the distinction between pure and empirical self-consciousness, and between the theoretical and the practical articulation of this difference, should be extinguished. It must rather be *sublated*: We need to understand pure apperception in a way that is reflective of its dependence on empirical apperception; and awareness of my own appearance is to be conceived in such a way that it does not become the reification or obliteration of the active self but a way for its activity itself to gain objective consistency.[32]

We started with the diagnosis that modeling self-knowledge on '*theoretical awareness of objects*' obscures the distinctive character of self-knowledge and suggested that we have to understand self-knowledge in practical terms instead. To the extent that transcendental apperception on Kant's account is awareness of myself as pure activity, it is natural to assume that we may be able to derive such a practical understanding of self-knowledge from Kant's notion of pure apperception. I have tried to cast some doubt on this hope by investigating Kant's account of pure apperception. I have first tried to show that pure apperception alone yields no cognition of myself and that self-cognition on Kant's account seems to require the co-operation of pure apperception and inner sense. Secondly, I have suggested that in the context of Kant's theoretical philosophy this co-operation seems to leave us with a split sense of our own selves. A sense of the practical that is derived from pure apperception alone is thus revealed to be insufficient. It is a form of the practical still tied to a theoretical framework, governed by an irreducible gulf between subject and object. In the third section, I have suggested that we can think of Kant's practical philosophy as a response to this problem, developing a form of cognition by means of which the subject actualizes itself objectively and in knowing its practical objects can come to know itself *qua subject*. The self-knowledge delineated here is practical, but not in the sense of an immediate awareness of my pure activity; it is practical in the deeper sense of coming to know myself through my deeds.

Notes

1. I will cite Kant's first critique according to the pagination of the A and the B edition. Other writings by Kant will be cited according to volume and page number of the *Akademieausgabe*, with the exception of the *Leningrad Fragment I* and the *Rostocker Handschrift* cited according to the page number of the respective cited sources.
2. Our discussion in the following is complicated by a certain terminological issue: What Kant denies is that pure apperception amounts to *Erkenntnis*, which I will usually translate as *cognition*. Many English translations, including that of the first critique by Norman Kemp Smith, employed in the following, translate this term with *knowledge*. This translation has the disadvantage of not differentiating *Erkenntnis* from *Wissen*, but I do not think that this is misleading in all cases. As will become clear in the following, I take it that Kant's denial that pure apperception is cognition of myself indeed implies that it does not in and of itself constitute self-*knowledge* in the sense the contemporary discussion is most interested in. There is, however, a certain distinct kind of formal self-knowledge that rests upon pure apperception, namely: the transcendental knowledge of what characterizes me as a thinker as such, developed in Kant's transcendental philosophy. Against this background, there is a sense in which Kant's denial that pure apperception is cognition of oneself (*Erkenntnis seiner selbst*) leaves open the possibility that it still involves or discloses a certain type of pure formal self-*knowledge*. For an instructive attempt to clarify the terminological difference between *Erkenntnis* and *Wissen* in Kant see Watkins and Willaschek (2017).
3. Cf. Kant (1929) B138, B154.
4. Cf. Kant (1929, B68, transl. modified): 'The consciousness of oneself (apperception) is the simple representation of the "I", and if all that is manifold in the

subject were thereby given *self-actively*, the inner intuition would be intellectual. In man this consciousness demands inner perception of the manifold which is antecedently given in the subject, and the mode in which this manifold is given in the mind without spontaneity must be entitled sensibility. If the faculty of coming to consciousness of oneself is to seek out (to apprehend) that which lies in the mind, it must affect the mind, and only in this way can it give rise to an intuition of itself. But the form of this intuition, which exists antecedently in the mind, determines, in the representation of time, the mode in which the manifold is together in the mind, since it then intuits itself not as it would represent itself if immediately self-active, but as it is affected by itself, and therefore as it appears to itself, not as it is.'

5. '[A]n *object* is that in the concept of which the manifold of a given intuition is *united*. Now all unification of representations demands unity of consciousness in the synthesis of them. Consequently, it is the unity of consciousness that alone constitutes the relation of representations to an object, and therefore their objective validity and the fact that they are modes of cognition.' (Kant 1929, B137, transl. modified).

6. This characterization of pure apperception is related to what Moran has called 'the transparency condition', but obviously makes a different use of the term 'transparency'. On Moran's account, the question whether I believe that p 'is "transparent" to' (Moran 2001, 66) the question whether p is to be believed. In order to answer whether I believe that p I thus do not have to observe myself and investigate whether I have this belief. Rather, I have to attend to the fact of the matter itself and deliberate whether p is true. In order to determine my self-knowledge in this regard, I have to look to the world, as it were. The point that Kant makes in the cited passage may help to explain how this becomes possible: pure apperception is what makes the mind transparent to the objects given in its cognition. What underlies transparency on Kant's account is the specific agential self-relation of pure apperception. This comes close to Moran's important suggestion that the transparency condition is not a simple given but an achievement: It depends on the deliberative stance which can be regarded as the 'vehicle of transparency' (Moran 2001, 63).

7. Cf. Powell (1990); Ameriks (2000); Keller (2001); Kitcher (2011); Longuenesse (2017).

8. The issue with Boyle's account on this point is not that he contrasts the two types of self-knowledge only in terms of their contents – in terms of giving us knowledge of our thoughts and judgments on the one hand *or* our sensations on the other, knowledge 'of what we do' *or* 'what we undergo', knowledge of ourselves as spontaneous beings *or* as passive beings (Boyle 2009, 133, 157). He does take into account the mode of self-knowledge as well by characterizing the two forms in terms of 'an active kind' and 'a passive kind' of knowledge (Boyle 2009, 133; 134; 158). The issue is that he short-circuits active form and active content, passive form and passive content, effectively excluding the possibility of active self-consciousness of our sensations and emotions and passive self-awareness of our thoughts. However, as the passage from the *Anthropology* Boyle himself refers us to makes clear, inner sense does not only give us knowledge of our sensations, but also of our thoughts in so far as they affect us: 'Inner sense' is, as Kant writes, a consciousness of what the human being 'undergoes, in so far as he is *affected by the play of his own thoughts*.'

(Kant 2006, 7:161, emphasis added). For a more elaborate critical assessment of Boyle on this point see Renz (2015, 589–90).

9. Letter to Marcus Herz, 26 May 1789; Kant (1999), 11:52, transl. modified. On the significance of this letter see Fisher (2017) and Villinger (2018, 121ff.). In a related discussion in one of his *Lectures on Metaphysics*, Kant (1997, 28:276) denies that we can think of animals as having inner sense at all. He there connects this lack of inner sense to a lack of consciousness of oneself, more precisely, lack of the concept of 'I'. This just underlines the extent to which Kant's notion of inner sense depends upon pure apperception. Compare Kant's definition of inner sense as 'the mode in which the mind is affected *through its own activity* (namely, through this positing of its representation), and so is affected *by itself*' (Kant 1929, B67f., emphasis added). Whatever it is that remains, when we subtract pure apperception, it cannot be an inner sense of the sort we possess.

10. See Longuenesse (2017, 32) for a clear exposition of the way in which the various forms of empirical awareness of myself 'depend on ... the activity in which alone, in Kant's terms, I am "conscious of myself as subject"', i.e. 'the activity of thinking'.

11. For this way of elucidating the contrast cf. Engstrom's distinction between 'a one that essentially contains many (synthetic unity) and a one that is essentially contained in many (analytic unity).' (Engstrom 2013, 39f.)

12. Cf. also the parallel rejection from the Aesthetic (Kant 1929, B68) already quoted in fn. 4.

13. As Henry Allison writes, pure apperception yields 'the thought, though not the cognition, of the self' (Allison 2004, 280), since 'self-knowledge requires sensible intuition' (Allison 2004, 282). Or, as Robert Pippin puts it: Even though it may seem 'as if I must be able to know myself without the aid of sensation by pure reflection alone', it defines Kant's account of the human mind that he 'must deny that this appearance is correct' (Pippin 1982, 173). On the necessity to hold apart self-*consciousness* and self-*knowledge* at this point since the latter requires a certain form of self-objectification, see Keller (2001), 104, 106.

14. Kant is not completely consistent in terms of terminology here, since we find one passage in the first critique where he explicitly speaks about the human being *cognizing* itself through pure apperception – Kant (1998, B574, emphasis added): 'Allein der Mensch, der die ganze Natur sonst lediglich nur durch Sinne kennt, *erkennt sich selbst auch durch bloße Apperzeption*, und zwar in Handlungen und inneren Bestimmungen, die er gar nicht zum Eindrucke der Sinne zählen kann, und ist sich selbst freilich eines Teils Phänomen, anderen Teils aber, nämlich in Ansehung gewisser Vermögen, ein bloß intelligibeler Gegenstand'.

15. Kant makes explicitly clear that existence is here not to be taken in the sense of the category of existence, but in a different, pre-categorical manner: 'the existence here [referred to] is not a category' (Kant 1929, B423FN). It is, of course, a difficult issue to determine whether Kant has succeeded in substantiating this sense of existence that we do not cognize but become aware of through awareness of our own activity. In this regard compare also Kant's characterization of this awareness as 'a feeling of an existence without the least concept' (Kant 2002, 4:334). On the broader significance of such a 'feeling' for Kant's conception of self-consciousness, see Emundts (2013, 70).

TRANSPARENCY AND APPERCEPTION   103

16. Regarding this understanding of I as an activity which characterizes especially the paralogisms of the B edition, see Horstmann (1993, 2010, 453).

17. Given that the 'I think' expresses the transcendental unity of apperception, we might suggest that I actually know quite a bit about myself by means of this pure apperceptive self-consciousness: I know myself to be engaged in an activity that is informed by the categories. This certainly is a merely *formal* kind of self-knowledge, but one with far-reaching consequences. It is important to note, however, that in order for the 'I think' to yield even this transcendental kind of self-knowledge we have to consider the act of pure apperception in relation to intuition, if Kant is right in suggesting that the categories are the elementary concepts of *transcendental* logic, a type of logic that does not abstract from cognition's relation to its object.

18. Since Kant holds that the *combination* of the understanding itself can become intuitable in inner sense, it seems obvious that he assumes that thoughts themselves can affect us through inner sense. Cf. again the passage from the *Anthropology*, already mentioned in fn. 8 where Kant explicitly describes a 'play of *thoughts*' as the content of inner sense (Kant 2006, 7:161, emphasis added). Compare also Kant's famous reflection on the question whether we can *experience* thinking. In this reflection, he imagines a case in which we think of a square *a priori* and considers whether this amounts to an experience. Neither the thought itself nor my consciousness of having this thought is in itself something empirical, he argues. However, this thought at the same time can produce ('*hervorbringen*') a product of experience or a determination of our mind ('*Gemüt*') that can be observed 'insofar it is affected by the capacity of thought' ('*sofern es nämlich durch das Denkungsvermögen afficiert wird*') (Kant 1928, No. 5661, 18:319). On the passive knowledge of our thoughts in Kant, see also Renz (2015).

19. 'Now here the "I" appears to us to be double (which would be contradictory): 1) the "I" as *subject* of thinking (in logic), which means pure apperception (the merely reflecting "I"), and of which there is nothing more to say except that it is a very simple idea; 2) the "I" as *object* of perception, therefore of inner sense, which contains a manifold of determinations that make an inner *experience* possible.' (Kant 2006, 7:134FN). Compare the related opposition of the self *as subject* and the self *as an object* in the *Prize Essay* on the progress of metaphysics: 'That I am conscious of myself is a thought that already contains a twofold self, the self as subject and the self as object. How it should be possible that I, who think, can be an object (of intuition) to myself, and thus distinguish myself *from* myself, is absolutely impossible to explain, although it is an undoubted fact; it demonstrates, however, a power so far superior to all sensory intuition, that as ground of the possibility of an understanding it has as its consequence a total separation from the beasts, to whom we have no reason to attribute the power to say "I" to oneself, and looks out upon an infinity of self-made representations and concepts. We are not, however, referring thereby to a dual personality; only the self that thinks and intuits is the person, whereas the self of the object that is intuited by me is, like other objects outside me, the thing.' (Kant 2002a, 20:270).

20. Cf. Kant (2006, 7:161); Kant (1996a, 4:451).

21. On the problem of negotiating these two perspectives on the self, see Ginsborg (2013, 119). Ginsborg suggests that, in the final analysis, we should become able to identify the I that thinks with a particular human being in

space and time but emphasizes that on Kant's account there is a deep difficulty standing in the way of this identification: Knowledge of myself as an object seems 'on the face of it to be incompatible with understanding myself as a thinking subject, endowed with the spontaneity characteristic of the I that thinks.'

22. In a reflection on inner sense, Kant makes the related point that through inner sense we only cognize ourselves as *being affected*, but we do not directly become accessible to ourselves as the ones affecting ourselves: 'In the case of inner experience ... I affect myself insofar as I bring the representations of outer sense into an empirical consciousness of my condition. Thereby I cognize myself *but only insofar as I am affected by myself*, whereby I am not so much appearance to myself as I affect myself through representations of outer sense ..., for that is spontaneity, *rather insofar as I am affected by myself, for that is receptivity*.' (Kant 2005, 365, emphasis added, translation modified).

23. Cf. Kant (2006), 7:134FN: 'The human "I" is indeed twofold according to form (manner of representation), but not according to matter (content).' See also the *Rostocker Handschrift* of Kant's Anthropology in which he notes that there is in fact 'not a double I', but merely a 'double consciousness of the I' (Kant 1977, 427).

24. Cf. Kant (1929, B138f., emphasis added): 'The synthetic unity of consciousness is, therefore, an objective condition of all knowledge... This principle is not, however, to be taken as applying to every possible understanding, but only to that understanding through whose pure apperception, in the representation "I am", nothing manifold is given. An understanding which through its self-consciousness could supply to itself the manifold of intuition an understanding, that is to say, through whose representation the objects of the representation should at the same time exist would not require, for the unity of consciousness, a special act of synthesis of the manifold. For the human understanding, however, which thinks only, and does not intuit, that act is necessary. It is indeed the first principle of the human understanding, *and is so indispensable to it that* we *cannot form the least conception of any other possible understanding*, either of such as is itself intuitive or of any that may possess an underlying mode of sensible intuition which is different in kind from that in space and time.'

25. § 5 of Fichte's second introduction to the *Wissenschaftslehre* makes it clear that he uses the term intellectual intuition in order to give a modified account of what Kant calls 'pure apperception': 'This intuiting of himself that is required of the philosopher, in performing the act whereby the self arises for him, I refer to as *intellectual intuition*. It is the immediate consciousness that I act, and what I enact: it is that whereby I know something because I do it... Everyone, to be sure, can be shown, in his own admitted experience, that this intellectual intuition occurs at every moment of his consciousness. I cannot take a step, move hand or foot, without an intellectual intuition of my self-consciousness in these acts; only so do I know that I do it, only so do I distinguish my action, and myself therein, from the object of action before me. Whosoever ascribes an activity to himself, appeals to this intuition.' (Fichte 1982, 38) Compare also his *Wissenschaftslehre nova methodo*: 'The I is by no means a subject; instead it is a subject-object... We must possess some knowledge of this ultimate ground, for we are able to talk about it. We obtain this knowledge through immediate intuition... Pure intuition of the I as

a subject-object is therefore possible. Since pure intuition of this sort contains no sensible content, the proper name for it is intellectual intuition. Kant rejected intellectual intuition ... Kant too has such intuition but he did not reflect upon it.' (Fichte 1992, 114–15)

26. Cf. Kant (1996a, 4:452, 4:458); Kant (1996, 5:31).
27. Fichte himself has pointed out that the type of intellectual intuition he is aiming at has its true place in practical cognition: 'The intellectual intuition alluded to in the *Science of Knowledge* refers, not to existence at all, but rather to action, and simply finds no mention in Kant (unless, perhaps, under the title of *pure apperception*). Yet it is nonetheless possible to point out also in the Kantian system the precise point at which it should have been mentioned. Since Kant, we have all heard, surely, of the categorical imperative? Now what sort of consciousness is that? Kant forgot to ask himself this question, since he nowhere dealt with the foundation of *all* philosophy, but treated in the *Critique of Pure Reason* only of its theoretical aspect, in which the categorical imperative could make no appearance; and in the *Critique of Practical Reason*, only of its practical side, in which the concern was solely with content, and questions about the type of consciousness involved could not arise.' (Fichte 1982, §6, 46)
28. For these ways of putting the problem cf. Ginsborg (2013: 'Appearance of Spontaneity'); Cassam (1997, 8: 'awareness of oneself *qua* subject as a physical object among physical objects'), and following Cassam, Longuenesse (2006).
29. Cf. Kant's distinction of theoretical and practical cognition from the first critique: Whereas theoretical cognition relates to its object by merely determining it and its concept, practical cognition also 'makes it actual' (Kant 1929, Bx).
30. Respect is a peculiar feeling that is 'self-wrought by means of a rational concept' (Kant 1996a, 4:402), 'produced solely by reason' (Kant 1996, 5:76), 'produced by an intellectual ground' (Kant 1996, 5:74) and to be distinguished from any 'feeling of pleasure based on the inner sense' (Kant 1996, 5:80). In Khurana (2017), § 42, 207ff. I argue that in order to make sense of respect as a feeling, and not just as an intellectual estimation, we have to reconsider the way in which we are given to ourselves by means of what Kant's third critique calls 'feeling of life'.
31. Note that Kant understands being under obligation as a mode of actualizing this self-distinction: 'if we think of ourselves as put under obligation we regard ourselves as belonging to the world of sense and yet at the same time to the world of understanding' (Kant 1996a, 4:453).
32. I think that Hegel's formula of '*the free will which wills the free will*' describes the form of a practical self-consciousness that approaches this desideratum. For a reconstruction of this formula as an elaboration of the self-consciousness of desire see Khurana (2018).

Acknowledgments

I had the great opportunity to discuss versions of this paper at Ryerson University, the University of Leipzig, and the University of Essex. Many thanks to the participants for their perceptive comments. They have largely helped me clarify my tentative thoughts on the issues discussed above. Special thanks are due to Cristóbal Garibay-Petersen, Thomas Land, Dirk Setton, and Alexey Weißmüller for instructive comments on an earlier draft.

ORCID

Thomas Khurana (iD) http://orcid.org/0000-0003-3149-3787

References

Allison, H. 2004. *Kant's Transcendental Idealism*. Revised and Enlarged Edition. New Haven: Yale University Press.

Ameriks, K. 2000. *Kant's Theory of Mind: An Analysis of the Paralogisms of Pure Reason*. Oxford: Clarendon Press.

Boyle, M. 2009. "Two Kinds of Self-Knowledge." *Philosophy and Phenomenological Research* 78 (1): 133–164. doi:10.1111/j.1933-1592.2008.00235.x.

Cassam, Q. 1997. *Self and World*. Oxford: Oxford University Press.

Emundts, D. 2013. "Kant über Selbstbewusstsein." In *Self, World, and Art. Metaphysical Topics in Kant and Hegel*, edited by D. Emundts, 51–77. Berlin/Boston: De Gruyter.

Engstrom, S. 2013. "Unity of Apperception." *Studi Kantiani* 26: 37–54.

Fichte, J. G. 1982. *The Science of Knowledge*. Translated and edited by Peter Heath and John Lachs. Cambridge: Cambridge University Press.

Fichte, J. G. 1992. *Foundations of Transcendental Philosophy (Wissenschaftslehre) Nova Methodo (1796–99)*. Translated and edited by Daniel Breazeale. Ithaca: Cornell University Press.

Fisher, N. 2017. "Kant on Animal Minds." *Ergo* 4 (15): 441–462. doi:10.3998/ergo.12405314.0004.015.

Ginsborg, H. 2013. "The Appearance of Spontaneity." In *Self, World, and Art. Metaphysical Topics in Kant and Hegel*, edited by D. Emundts, 119–144. Berlin/Boston: De Gruyter.

Horstmann, R.-P. 1993. "Kants Paralogismen." *Kant-Studien* 84 (4): 408–425. doi:10.1515/kant.1993.84.4.408.

Horstmann, R.-P. 2010. "The Limited Significance of Self-Consciousness." *Revue de Métaphysique et de Morale* 68 (4): 435–454. doi:10.3917/rmm.104.0435.

Kant, I. 1928. "Reflexionen zur Metaphysik." In *Kant's gesammelte Schriften Bd. XVIII*. Edited by the Königlich Preußische Akademie der Wissenschaften, 3–725. Berlin/Leipzig: De Gruyter.

Kant, I. 1929. *Critique of Pure Reason*. Translated by Norman Kemp Smith. London: Macmillan.

Kant, I. 1977. "Anthropologie in pragmatischer Hinsicht." In *Schriften zur Anthropologie, Geschichtsphilosophie, Politik und Pädagogik. Werkausgabe XII*, edited by W. Weischedel, 399–690. Frankfurt am Main: Suhrkamp.

Kant, I. 1996. "Critique of Practical Reason." In *Practical Philosophy*. Translated and edited by Mary J. Gregor, 133–271. Cambridge: Cambridge University Press.

Kant, I. 1996a. "Groundwork of the Metaphysics of Morals." In *Practical Philosophy*. Translated and edited by Mary J. Gregor, 37–108. Cambridge: Cambridge University Press.

Kant, I. 1997. *Lectures on Metaphysics*. Translated and edited by Karl Ameriks and Steve Naragon. Cambridge: Cambridge University Press.

Kant, I. 1998. *Kritik der reinen Vernunft*. Edited by Jens Timmermann. Hamburg: Meiner.

Kant, I. 1999. *Correspondence*. Edited by Arnulf Zweig. Cambridge: Cambridge University Press.

Kant, I. 2002. "Prolegomena to Any Future Metaphysics that Will Be Able to Come Forward as Science (1783)." In *Theoretical Philosophy after 1781*. Edited by H. Allison, P. Heath, translated by G. Hatfield, M. Friedman, H. Allison, P. Heath, 29–169. Cambridge: Cambridge University Press.

Kant, I. 2002a. "What Real Progress Has Metaphysics Made in Germany since the Time of Leibniz and Wolff? (1793/1804)." In *Theoretical Philosophy after 1781*. Edited by H. Allison, P. Heath, translated by G. Hatflield, M. Friedman, H. Allison, P. Heath, 337–424. Cambridge: Cambridge University Press.

Kant, I. 2005. "Leningrad Fragment I: On Inner Sense." In *Notes and Fragments*. Edited by Paul Guyer, translated by C. Bowman, P. Guyer, F. Rauscher, 364–366. Cambridge: Cambridge University Press.

Kant, I. 2006. *Anthropology from a Pragmatic Point of View*. Edited and translated by Robert B. Louden. Cambridge: Cambridge University Press.

Keller, P. 2001. *Kant and the Demands of Self-Consciousness*. Cambridge: Cambridge University Press.

Khurana, T. 2017. *Das Leben der Freiheit. Form und Wirklichkeit der Autonomie*. Berlin: Suhrkamp.

Khurana, T. 2018. "The Self-determination of Force: Desire and Practical Self-consciousness in Kant and Hegel." *International Yearbook of German Idealism* 13/2015: 179–204. https://doi.org/10.1515/9783110579802-009.

Kitcher, P. 2011. *Kant's Thinker*. Oxford: Oxford University Press.

Longuenesse, B. 2006. "Self-Consciousness and Consciousness of One's Own Body. Variations on a Kantian Theme." *Philosophical Topics* 34: 283–309. doi:10.5840/philtopics2006341/210.

Longuenesse, B. 2017. *I, Me, Mine: Back to Kant, and Back Again*. Oxford: Oxford University Press.

Moran, R. 2001. *Authority and Estrangement: An Essay on Self-Knowledge*. Princeton: Princeton University Press.

Pippin, R. 1982. *Kant's Theory of Form. An Essay on the Critique of Pure Reason*. New Haven: Yale University Press.

Powell, C. T. 1990. *Kant's Theory of Self-Consciousness*. Oxford: Oxford University Press.

Renz, U. 2015. "Becoming Aware of One's Thoughts: Kant on Self-Knowledge and Reflective Experience." In *Mind, Language and Action*, edited by D. Moyal-Sharrock, V. Munz, and A. Coliva, 581–599. New York: De Gruyter.

Villinger, R. 2018. *Kant und die Imagination der Tiere*. Konstanz: Konstanz University Press.

Willaschek, M., and E. Watkins. 2017. "Kant on Cognition and Knowledge." *Synthese*. doi:10.1007/s11229-017-1623-5.

Kant's "I think" and the agential approach to self-knowledge

Houston Smit

ABSTRACT

This paper relates Kant's account of pure apperception to the agential approach to self-knowledge. It argues that his famous claim 'The **I think** must be able to accompany all of my representations' (B131) does not concern the possibility of self-ascribing beliefs. Kant does advance this claim in the service of identifying an a priori warrant we have as psychological persons, that is, subjects of acts of thinking that are imputable to us. But this warrant is not one to self-knowledge that we have as critical reasoners. It is, rather, an a priori warrant we have, as thinkers, to prescribe to given representations their conformity to principles of thinking inherent in our capacity of understanding itself.

Directly and indirectly, Kant's critical philosophy has inspired an important approach in contemporary theorizing about the nature of our self-knowledge, one to which I will refer as 'the agential approach'. The self-knowledge in question is a distinctive sort of knowledge that each of us has, *de se*, of her own beliefs. On the agential approach, one has this self-knowledge in virtue of being a critical reasoner. To be a critical reasoner, in turn, is to have the ability to adopt beliefs out of one's own recognition of how reasons dictate that one ought to. And a critical reasoner has this ability only if her conceptual awareness of herself as exercising this control and agency over her thinking is correct and justified. Proponents of the agential approach contend that a critical reasoner has the right, or a priori warrant, to take herself to in fact have the thoughts and attitudes that do, or can, enter into her critical reasoning, because, if she did not have this right, she would not be subject to rational norms in the way that is constitutive of her being a critical reasoner. It follows that each critical reasoner has, as a critical reasoner, a certain kind of nonobservational knowledge of her own beliefs.[1] In the case of at least some proponents of the agential approach, Kant's account of self-consciousness, and in particular of pure apperception and the 'I think', seems to have played a role in inspiring them to take this approach.[2]

In what follows, I examine whether, and if so just how and to what extent, the account of self-consciousness Kant advances in the first *Critique* is continuous with the agential approach to self-knowledge. And in doing so, I will be focusing on Kant's famous claim 'The **I think** must be able to accompany all of my representations' (B131), one to which many proponents of the agential approach allude as expressing the core idea of behind this approach.[3] My goal in doing so is not to question the Kantian heritage of the agential approach. It is, rather, to further our understanding of Kant. For it will prove illumining to see that Kant does indeed develop his account of self-consciousness – in particular, of pure apperception and its original synthetic unity – in the service of articulating and establishing an a priori warrant that is, in a crucial respect, of the same sort as that with which proponents of the agential approach to self-knowledge are concerned: namely, an a priori warrant that each of us has simply as a subject that is able to engage in thinking that is responsive to grounds of thought and cognition in the way that is characteristic of persons. This is a deep point of continuity between Kant, on the one hand, and proponents of the agential approach, on the other.

At the same time, two fundamental and closely related points of discontinuity will emerge. First, the a priori warrant that Kant aims to establish is not, I will argue, one specifically for claims to self-knowledge, or even necessarily for knowledge claims at all. It is, rather, a de se a priori warrant that each of us has, as a person, to put her capacity of understanding to use in acts of thinking that are imputable to her.[4] Now, on Kant's account, our capacity of understanding is conceptual, where a concept is a rule that constitutes the predicate of a possible judgment. And we have a genuine capacity of understanding at all only if we can correctly and legitimately take manifolds of representations that are given to us as ones that are subject to concepts. Indeed, Kant maintains that our capacity of understanding itself is the capacity to prescribe, correctly and legitimately, to particular manifolds as they are given to our consciousness – where the manifold may be one of concepts or the manifold of a given sensible intuition – their objectively necessary conformity to certain fundamental purely intellectual principles of our thinking. The categories number among these principles. Second, the a priori warrant that Kant sets out to establish does not, as on the agential approach to self-knowledge, have its ultimate ground in the nature of our cognitive agency in making inferences that are subject to rational norms. Rather, as we will see, Kant argues that the a priori warrant I have for any and all uses of my capacity of understanding has its ultimate ground in the nature of the cognitive activity that realizes in me my capacity of pure understanding. This activity is the operation of the spontaneity of cognition that first brings manifolds of representations given to me in intuition under certain purely intellectual principles of our thinking, the highest of which is the principle of the synthetic unity of apperception.

Transparency and the agential approach to self-knowledge

Many philosophers have espoused the idea that a subject's beliefs are transparent to her: that the question whether one believes a certain proposition P is to be answered, not by introspection, but simply by thinking about whether P is true.[5] Different philosophers have been led to this idea in rather different ways. But a number of those who champion the doctrine of the transparency of belief take their inspiration, at least in part, from Kant. Gareth Evans, in particular, espouses this doctrine in developing his influential account of the self-ascription of belief (Evans 1982, 225–6). In doing so, he makes reference to what he takes to be Kant's views about the 'I think'. According to Evans, a subject can use 'I believe' or 'I think' in attributing a belief to herself only if she can, in conjunction with physical predicates, use cognates of 'believe' and 'think' to attribute beliefs to others (Evans 1982, 226–8).[6]

Richard Moran retains the core idea of Evans' account of the transparency of beliefs in his influential development of the agential approach to self-knowledge (Moran 2001). On his view, beliefs are essentially states that a critical reasoner can author in herself on the basis of reasons that this subject can determine, in an exercise of her rational agency, to be reasons that tell in favor of her adopting that belief. Moran maintains that, to the extent that the beliefs we are to ascribe to a critical reasoner are, in this way, ones that are to be imputed to her, they must be transparent to her. For a critical reasoner, as such, has the right to take her beliefs to be subject to her critical reasoning, and thus to take reasons she has to hold a belief as evidence that she in fact holds that belief. This right is the basis of the distinctive sort of self-knowledge that, on Moran's view, any critical reasoner as such can, and must be able to, have of the beliefs that belong to her, merely by thinking about the reasons she has for adopting those beliefs.

But the agential approach to self-knowledge can be pursued without retaining the doctrine of the transparency of belief. Consider here Tyler Burge, to whom we owe the richest account on offer of the nature of the epistemic right to self-knowledge that, on the agential approach, each of us has as a critical reasoner. In Burge's terminology, 'entitlements are epistemic rights or warrants that need not be understood by, or even accessible to, the subject' (1993, p. 458); an individual's epistemic entitlement, unlike her epistemic justification, 'consists in a status of operating in an appropriate way in accord with norms of reason, even when the norms in question cannot be articulated by the individual with that status' (Burge 1996, 93). On Burge's view, each of us, as a critical reasoner, has a certain sort of a priori entitlement to claims, made in a distinctively first-personal way, about her own beliefs, which entitlement is grounded, at least in part, in what is necessary to our being critical reasoners: one is a critical reasoner only if one's thinking is subject to rational norms that govern how one is to change one's beliefs based on one's critical reflection, but one is subject to rational norms in this way only if one has a certain a priori entitlement to take one's judgments about one's own thoughts to be true, which entitlement is 'stronger than that involved in perceptual judgments' (Burge 1996, 98).

Burge, however, denies that a critical reasoner's beliefs, even those that are hers because she arrived at them through her reasoning, are transparent to that reasoner. He does so on the grounds that a critical reasoner's ability to review her own reasoning critically, an ability essential to her being a critical reasoner, also requires that she be able to distinguish between how she ought to reason and how she, in fact, has reasoned. On Burge's account, then, a critical reasoner must have another mode of epistemic access to how she in fact reasons, in addition to the distinctively agential and nonobservational one she has in and through thinking about how she ought to reason.[7]

Is Kant a precursor to the agential approach to self-knowledge?

Now one might well be tempted to take the agential approach to self-knowledge, and indeed even the transparency thesis, as coming to expression in Kant's famous claim, mentioned earlier, about 'the **I think**'. This claim (hereafter, 'the Claim') opens Section 16 of the Transcendental Deduction of the Categories in the B-Edition of the *Critique of Pure Reason*:

> The **I think** must **be able** to accompany all my representations [*muss alle meine Vorstellungen begleiten können*]; for otherwise something would be represented in me that could not be thought at all, which is as much as to say that the representation would either be impossible, or at least nothing for me. (B131-2)

Here Kant asserts that the possibility of the <*I think*> accompanying a representation is a necessary condition of that representation being mine. A representation's being mine, in the relevant sense, is incompatible with my not being able to think what that representation represents, an inability that entails, in turn, that representation's being, at best, 'nothing for me'. It isn't obvious just what Kant is saying. But it seems plausible that a representation's being mine requires that I be able to put it to some use in my thinking, and in particular in thinking in which I am responsive to reasons in the right way. And it is certainty tempting to interpret what it is for the <I think> to actually accompany a representation in me to consist in my self-ascribing that representation. What it is more, one could make the case that what Kant here requires, as a condition of a representation's being mine, is the possibility of a self-ascription that constitutes knowledge of one's own representations. For a representation to have a use in my thinking, I must, in fact, have that representation. And it seems plausible that Kant advances the Claim in the service of identifying an a priori epistemic right or warrant that each of us has, merely as a thinker, to ascribe to herself representation that she puts to use in her thinking to herself as ones that do, in fact, have a use for her in her thinking. On such a line of interpretation, then, the Claim advances a position strikingly similar to that taken by proponents of the agential approach to self-knowledge. It parallels the contention, made both by Burge and Moran, that a critical reasoner must be able knowledgeably to self-ascribe any beliefs she has as a critical reasoner.[8]

To be sure, even if we adopt this reading of the Claim, it isn't clear just how strong its continuity with the agential approach to self-knowledge is. In particular, is the conception that Kant is invoking of what it is for me to be a thinker, and thus a subject that can have a representation in the way I take myself to in calling that representation mine, the same as that which informs the agential approach to self-knowledge? It is tempting to answer this question in the affirmative. There is, however, an obvious point of discontinuity between the Claim and the position advanced by proponents of the agential approach to self-knowledge that should immediately give us pause. The Claim asserts the necessity of the possibility of the <I think> accompanying *all my representations*. And Kant famously provides a taxonomy of all our representations that divides all our representations with consciousness, or *perceptiones*, into two fundamental kinds, cognition and sensation, and then cognition, in turn, into concept and intuition (A320/B376).[9] The Claim, then, would seem, on the face of it, to hold for sensations and intuitions, as well as for thoughts and attitudes. Indeed, once we have examined Kant's conception of what it is for the <I think> to accompany one of my representations, we will be in a position to see that even *my* sensations, as *my* representations, must, on Kant's account, meet conditions of the possibility of being accompanied by the <I think>. Burge and Moran, by contrast, explicitly restrict their account of self-knowledge to one's knowledge of one's own thoughts and attitudes, to the exclusion of our sensations.[10] This raises the suspicion that the concept of what it is to be a thinker that motivates Kant's claim that the <I think> must be able to accompany all my representations cannot be entirely the same as that which informs the agential account of self-knowledge.[11]

Kitcher's answer

In her recent work, Patricia Kitcher answers our last question in the affirmative. She develops an original reading of Kant's account of the transcendental unity of apperception on which it amounts to an account of rational thinking of the same sort that underlies the agential approach to self-knowledge. On her reading, the transcendental unity of apperception is a unity of a subject's mental states that constitutes him as a subject of what she dubs 'rational cognition'. In her parlance, rational cognition is cognition of the sort humans have in and through making judgments and drawing inferences – where this is understood, in turn, as performing acts of 'making and recognizing relations of dependence and so necessary connection across their states' (Kitcher 2017, 170). As Kitcher reads him, Kant maintains that a thinker, in consciously drawing inferences from her various mental states, thereby creates and recognizes 'the relation of necessary connection across them that makes them the states of a single thinker' (Kitcher 2017, 171). The necessary unity of apperception, on Kitcher's interpretation, is the necessary unity that a thinker realizes in her mental states when she uses them, in her rational thinking, to produce her beliefs. Kitcher grants that Kant himself held that a thinker self-ascribes representations only in being aware of them through inner sense, and so through a sort of observation of her own mental states. Nonetheless, she contends, his account of higher cognition is consonant with the agential approach to self-knowledge. Since judging and inference require conscious acts, 'whenever a subject is consciously thinking that p, she can self-ascribe the activity and the thought' (Kitcher 2017, 171): the consciousness had in consciously believing p, gives her grounds for self-ascribing this belief. But, she claims, Kant's doctrine of the unity of apperception is, at the same time, incompatible with Evans's transparency thesis, because it makes all of a subject's beliefs, including those about the world, dependent on a prior de se consciousness she has of herself, in engaging in rational thought, as the subject that engages in this thought.[12] Finally, she brings this reading to bear specifically on the Claim by suggesting that the scope of the Claim, and indeed more generally of what she terms Kant's 'I-think doctrine', is restricted to 'the set of representations that can participate in cognition' (Evans 1982, 144). On her reading, what makes an intuition that is in me a rational cognition, and so mine, is my being able to bring it under a concept so as to 'combine it with other representations in a resultant representation' (ibid). Kitcher contends that, in this way, Kant's position is opposed to Evans's, in that Kant's position on higher cognition is incompatible with the doctrine of the transparency of belief: contrary to what Evans thought, Kant was 'no friend of transparency, but its natural enemy.'[13]

Kitcher's reading has many virtues, not least that it represents a serious, and philosophically resourceful, attempt to identify a single cogent, and well-motivated, account of self-consciousness and cognition in the many bewilderingly difficult texts in which Kant presents this complex account. Moreover, as advertised, Kitcher's reading recognizes, and tries to do justice to, how Kant's account of the possibility of our thought and cognition makes the synthetic unity of apperception explanatorily fundamental (cf. Kitcher 2011, especially Chapter 9). And in doing so, it relates Kant's work to contemporary debates, including those about self-knowledge, in intriguing ways. Nonetheless, we have reason to worry that Kitcher's reading fundamentally mischaracterizes

Kant's account of pure apperception and its synthetic unity. Indeed, once we have examined this account, we will see that we have reason to question an assumption made, not just by Kitcher (as well as other proponents of the agential approach to self-knowledge who look to Kant as an ally), but by most of Kant's readers: namely, that in accompanying one of her representations with the <I think>, a thinker is, whatever else, doing something above and beyond what she is doing in using that representation to think of what that representation is a representation of; and that one can, thus, put a representation to use in thinking without actually accompanying it with the <I think>. Examining the Claim, and the one-clause argument for it that immediately follows it, will suggest otherwise: any act of thinking in which a thinker relates one of her representations to an object consists, in respect of its intellectual form, in the <I think> accompanying that representation. But before we are in a position to examine the Claim, I need to take care of some preliminaries. The first is to explain, if only briefly, some of the terminology that it employs, as well as the treatment of the concept of combination in Section 15 that sets the stage for Section 16.

Representation, thought, and combination

Kant characterizes representation (*Vorstellung*) as 'what has a relation to an object [*eine Beziehung auf ein Object hat*]' (cf., e.g. 24: 805). I take this to amount to the characterization of representation as what the subject of a capacity to represent (which capacity may be that of a brute animal) *is to relate* to an object in exercising that capacity. Here – and unless I specify otherwise, in what follows – I will use 'object' to translate Kant's Latinate '*Object*'. '*Gegenstand*' is another term in Kant that is often translated with 'object'; but a *Gegenstand*, in his sense, is the real – the subject of activity and power – considered insofar as it is given as such in representation. In the case of any conceptual understanding, Kant holds that a *Gegenstand* can be given to it only in an operation of its ability of sensibility. An object, in his sense, in turn, is whatever a subject is conscious of, insofar as that subject is conscious of it (A189/B234). Since our capacity of understanding is conceptual, a *Gegenstand* that is given to you constitutes an *Object*, only insofar as you are conscious of it.

Any representation can be considered as an operation of a subject's capacity or ability of representation; to do so, in Descartes' famous terminology, is to consider it in its formal reality. But what makes it a representation, on Kant's account, is its being such that this subject is to relate it to an object, and to consider it insofar as it has this relation is to consider the representation in its objective reality. For example, Kant characterizes a sensation 'as an effect of an object [*Gegenstand*] on the ability for representation insofar as we are affected by it' (A19/B34). This is a sensation's formal reality. But what makes such an effect a representation is, in the case of an objective sensation, its providing the matter of appearance: as such matter, an objective sensation (the green of the field) is to be related to an object (*Gegenstand*) of experience (the field) in an act of thinking that does not constitute an act of cognizing that object (*Gegenstand*).

Thinking (*Denken*), in Kant's sense of the term, is representing through concepts. And for a representation to be mine – that is, to belong to me *qua* thinker and indeed as the subject to whom acts of thinking are imputable and so as what Kant calls a psychological person – is for it to be one that I *am to* relate to an object, somehow, in an act of thinking. So, for example, in making the perceptual judgment 'This rose is red', I relate to an object, in this act of thinking, not just all the representations that make up the concepts <rose> and <red> as they make up these concepts (i.e. as general marks, marks that are common to more than one possible thing), but also those that make up my present empirical intuition (e.g. the perceptually presented token instances of shapes characteristic of a rose, which, as singular marks, are not common to more than one thing). And, in relating these representations to the rose in this judgment, I think, not just these concepts, but also this empirical intuition, along with the objective sensation <red> that belongs to this intuition. To be sure, the sensation <red> does not, of itself, have any relation to the rose; it is only insofar as it constitutes the matter of an appearance of the rose that the sensation has any relation to the rose. And I think it as having this relation when, in making this perceptual judgment, I subsume it under the concept <red>, the concept of the quality (redness) of the sensation that, as a 'predicate of appearance,' 'can be attributed [*beigelegt werden*] to the object [*Object*] in itself, in relation to our sense' (B69-70n).

Kant maintains that to think 'is to unite representations in a consciousness,' and that 'the unification of representations in a consciousness is judgment' (4: 304). Moreover, he distinguishes different actions of combination according to the unity of representations in a consciousness that it determines as its effect. He terms the most general such action 'combination in general [*Verbindung überhaupt*],' and examines the possibility of this combination in Section 15 of the B-edition Deduction (entitled 'On the Possibility of a Combination in General'). Kant opens this section with the claim that 'Only the combination [*die Verbindung*] (*conjunctio*) of a manifold in general can never come to us through sense ...; for it is an *actus* [*Aktus*][14] of spontaneity of the power of representation' (B130). Kant tells us that he gives this 'act of the understanding [*Verstandeshandlung*]' 'the general title **synthesis**' to indicate

> that we can represent nothing as combined in the object [*im Object*] without having previously combined it ourselves, and that among all representations **combination** is the only one that is not given through objects [*Objecte*], but can be executed only by the subject itself, because it is an *actus* [*Actus*] of its self-activity. One can here easily see that this action must originally be unitary [*einig*] and equally valid for all combination .... (B130)

Any token act of thinking is, on Kant's account, an act of combining (uniting representations in a consciousness) in which the subject is conscious of a manifold of representations given to her through an object, and in doing so represents that manifold 'as combined in' that object. *My* determined thinking is thinking in which I determine my representation of how the manifold is combined in the object out of my consciousness of how a principle of thinking requires me to do so. Here, and throughout what follows, I use 'determine' in Kant's technical sense, on which to determine is 'to posit a predicate to the exclusion of its opposite' (AA 1: 139). On Kant's account, any act of determined thinking consists in the 'orginally unitary' action of 'combination in general' insofar as the subject combines in this action the manifold that an object could through sense supply for this action, which manifold constitutes the content that the subject of this action is subsequently to relate to that object in *her* determined thinking. 'Combination in general,' out of which any act of determined thinking consists, is thus the subject's self activity in thinking considered in itself and so insofar as it is not, itself, determined.

I am proposing, then, that not every act of determined thinking that occurs in me is, on Kant's account, an act of what Kant calls 'my determined thinking' (B134). As we will see, *my* determined thinking is that in which I relate some particular manifold of representations that is given to my consciousness to an object in and through prescribing to that manifold its conformity either to a logical form of judgment (in the case of a manifold of concepts) or to a category (in the case of the manifold of an intuition). For it is only in such prescription that I posit a unity of the given manifold in the object to the exclusion of its opposite, and this by correctly and legitimately representing some ground (not necessarily in the object) as one sufficient to determine this unity. My determined thinking constitutively employs the most fundamental concepts of an object in general [*Object überhaupt*] that are inherent in the discursive capacity of understanding of the kind we have, as purely intellectual principles of our thinking. These concepts, Kant argues, are the twelve categories that he exhibits in the Table of Categories.

Our main aim in the remainder of this paper will be to present, if only schematically, how Kant argues, over the course of Sections 15 and 16, that my determined thinking is made possible only by pure apperception. Pure apperception is the operation of understanding that combines all manifold of intuition that is to be encountered in me in the concept of an object in general. Indeed – and this is the crucial point – pure apperception combines this manifold as the act that first subjects these manifolds to the categories, an act that Kant terms 'the legislation for nature' (A127). Pure apperception is thereby the operation of my capacity of apperception that realizes it as my capacity of understanding, my first capacity for determined thinking.

Moreover, in legislating for nature, pure apperception also subjects all other manifolds of representations that are to have any use in my thinking to principles of thinking. Pure apperception is thus the act that realizes my capacity of apperception more generally as the power to unite any manifold given to me in combination in general in an a priori consciousness of how this manifold is subject to purely intellectual principles of my thinking. And, in doing so, pure apperception is what constitutes me as the numerically identical subject throughout any manifold of representations given to my consciousness that are to have a use in my determined thinking, and so that are to be anything to me (B134). As such pure apperception is not, and cannot be, itself an instance of *my* determined thinking. It is the single, and original, purely intellectual de se consciousness that first makes any of my determined thinking possible by subjecting a manifold given to my consciousness to intellectual conditions to which it must conform, if the representations that make up that manifold are to have any use in my determined thinking. And, on Kant's account, because it is the self-consciousness that constitutes me as the numerically identical subject of thinking throughout the manifold of representations given to me in combination in general as a manifold I can relate to an object in and through determining (in reflection) how I am to do so, Kant says that the 'the identity of apperception' 'precedes all *my* determined thinking a priori' (B134).

'Previously,' 'first,' 'precede' – all have here an explanatory, and not a temporal, sense. Indeed, Kant stresses that the 'combination of a manifold in general' in which a manifold of representations must be given to a thinker's consciousness to be combined in the object is as such fundamentally constitutive of all combination of a given manifold in the object. This is why he says combination in general 'must be originally unitary and equally valid for all combination' (B130). And this holds for any combination of a manifold of representations – whether 'we are conscious of the combination or not, whether it is a combination of the manifold of intuition or of several concepts' (ibid)

In the closing sentences of Section 15, Kant sets the task of Section 16 as explaining how, in being added to the representation of the manifold, and to the synthetic unity that combination in general gives this manifold, 'the representation of this synthetic unity' 'first makes the concept of combination possible':

> But the concept of combination includes, besides the concept of the manifold and of synthesis, also the concept of the unity of the manifold. Combination is the representation of the *synthetic* unity of the manifold. The representation of this unity cannot, therefore arise from the combination; rather, by being added to the representation of the manifold, it first makes the concept of combination possible. This unity, which precedes all concepts of combination a priori, is not the former category of unity (Section 10); for all categories are grounded on logical functions in judgments, but in these combination, thus

the unity of given concepts, is already thought. The category therefore already presupposes combination. We must therefore seek this unity (as qualitative, Section 12) somewhere higher, namely in that which itself contains the ground of the unity of different concepts in judgments, and hence of the possibility of the understanding, even in its logical use. (B130-1)

What Kant seeks in Section 16 and there identifies as the original synthetic unity of apperception, is this representation of the synthetic unity of the manifold (i.e. of the synthetic unity that combination in general gives to the manifold) that first makes *the concept* of combination possible. And he identifies pure apperception as that in which we are to find this unity, and this as what 'itself contains the ground' even of the unity of different concepts in judgment. Pure apperception, then, is what Kant contends adds the original synthetic unity of apperception to what is given in the 'originally unitary' action of combination in general. And pure apperception's representation of this unity is 'the actus of spontaneity' that, in bringing forth the representation <I think> (B132), 'first makes the concept of combination possible.'

Principles of thinking, reflection, and intellectual form

Before we turn to the Claim, we need, finally, to fill out somewhat Kant's account of what thinking consists in. I will do so by explaining some more crucial terminology that, despite not occurring in the Claim itself, will prove useful to have in hand in interpreting the Claim. I start with his notion of a principle of thinking.

Kant characterizes principles (*Principien*) as 'cognitions that are grounds of grounds that follow a certain rule' (AA 27: 749). And a rule, in turn, is 'an assertion under a universal condition' (AA 9: 121). The concept *<gold>* is a rule, in this sense, one that specifies that the marks it contains (<body>, <yellow>, <dense>, <malleable>, <dissolves in *aqua regia*>, etc.) constitute the universal condition of something's being gold. The principle of contradiction is the principle of our analytic cognition in that it is the cognition that is the ground of a discursive mark being the ground of an analytic cognition: this principle is, for example, the ground of the discursive mark <malleable> being, in the analytic cognition <All gold is malleable>, the ground of this cognition that follows the rule <gold>. The force of 'a priori' in 'a priori principle' is to specify that the principle is as such a cognition that makes what is a ground in the objective order of explanation the ground of the cognition and this out of a consciousness of how that ground objectively necessitates its consequence (Smit 2009). An a posteriori principle, by contrast, takes what is, in the objective order of explanation, a consequence, and makes it the ground in the order of one's cognition. Thus Kant tells us that the particular law of nature <All bodies are heavy> serves as an a posteriori principle when one derives from it the cognition <This body is heavy> (AA 27: 749): the synthetic a posteriori cognition <All bodies are heavy> is the ground of this cognition one has of the individual body one designates with 'this body' as heavy. But our cognition of the particular law of nature <All bodies are heavy> is, as such, a cognition we take from particular successively given appearances as we are acquainted with them in taking them to belong to what Kant terms 'our complete possible experience' (A232/B283): what makes these successively given appearances particular experiences just is, on Kant's account, their belonging, as its parts, to this universal possible human experience. In the cognition <All bodies are heavy>, then, we make what is, in the objective order of explanation, a consequence (namely, actual experiences) the ground of our cognition <This body is heavy>, which is just to say that this cognition is an a posteriori principle. By contrast, purely intellectual principles of thought (*Principien des Denkens*), such as the principle of contradiction, are a species of a priori principles: namely, ones inherent solely in our higher capacity of cognition (as against those that are further determined by the addition of sensible content, such as the transcendental schemata and the principles of pure understanding) that make our acts of thinking first possible. In the case of the principle of contradiction, the possibility is the formal possibility merely of an act of thinking in general. In the case of the categories, the possibility is that of the thinking that constitutes the formal possibility of our experience in general, and thus the formal possibility of a certain act of cognizing a thing. Any principle of thinking is a priori: it is a cognition in which the subject is conscious of how the ground in the objective order of explanation objectively necessitates its consequence.

'Reflection' (*'Überlegung,' 'reflexio'*) is Kant's term for a subject of discursive understanding's consciousness of how the sources of her cognition (understanding and/or sensibility) objectively necessitate how she is, as a person and so in acts of thinking that are imputable to her, to relate given representations to an object (*Object*). Kant thus characterizes reflection as 'the consciousness of the relation [*Verhältnis*] of given representations to our various sources of cognition, through which alone their relation [*Verhältnis*] among themselves can be correctly determined' (A260/B316). A subject's determined thinking is the act in which she aims, in and through reflection, to determine correctly the relation among representations that are given to it in combination in general. Successful thinking realizes form, that is, determination (positing to the exclusion of the opposite), in some matter, that is, the determinable manifold of representations given in combination in general, to determine a thought (A261/B317). So, for example, the logical form of categorical judgment is a form, in this sense, that one realizes in some matter (the concepts <horse> and <mammal>) to determine the relation they have to one another in a categorical judgment ('Horses are mammals'). The principles of our thinking are given to us in reflection on the form that is determined solely by the nature of our understanding. Let's call such form 'intellectual form'.

A subject's determined thinking consists, not just in reflection, but in that subject's determining its own act of thinking out of its *de se* consciousness of how principles of thinking objectively necessitate that it do so. This follows from Kant's theory of concepts, on which a concept is a rule that a thinker gives to herself in logical consciousness – that is, her consciousness of how the principles of thinking given to her in logical reflection, as intellectual form, determine how she, in her thinking, is to relate representations that are given to her to an object. Here a passage in the *Anthropology* – in which, to look ahead, Kant specifies that logical, or discursive, consciousness is 'pure apperception of one's mental action' – is helpful:

> Because experience is empirical cognition, but for cognition (since it rests on judgments) (*reflexio*), and consequently consciousness of the activity [*Tätigkeit*] in the composition [*Zusammenstellung*] of the manifold of representations according to [*nach*] a rule of the unity of the same [i.e. the manifold], that is, concepts and (from intuition distinct) thought in general, is required: so consciousness is divided up into discursive consciousness (which as logical consciousness must lead the way, since it gives the rule), and intuitive consciousness. Discursive consciousness (pure apperception of one's mental action [*Gemüthshandlung*]) is simple. The I of reflection contains no manifold in itself and is always one and the same in every judgment, because it is merely the formal element of consciousness. On the other hand, inner experience contains the material of consciousness and a manifold of empirical inner intuition, the I of apprehension. (7: 141-2)

The intellectual form of a cognition is a purely intellectual principle of thinking that a thinker realizes in some matter (a manifold of representations given to it in combination in general) to determine that matter (the relation among these representations) a priori. One species of such form is the logical form of our thinking in general (which belongs to the subject matter of pure formal logic, as well as transcendental logic). Another is the intellectual form of our pure thinking of a thing (treated only in transcendental logic). The latter, in us, are the categories, concepts that are particularly fundamental species of principles of our thought, that is, 'self-thought a priori first principles of our cognition' (B167).

The Claim

I want now to sketch a reading of the Claim on which the possibility that it specifies as a necessary condition of a representation being mine is determined purely intellectually, and indeed one that is determined solely by the nature of discursive understanding (of which our higher capacity of cognition is

TRANSPARENCY AND APPERCEPTION

a species). Appreciating this point will allow us to see that the accompaniment of a representation with the <I think> is what brings forth, and constitutes, the intellectual form of the act of thinking in which a thinker relates that representation to an object. This form is, itself, the determination of an objectively necessary relation that a representation of the sort in question (i.e. a concept, an intuition, or a sensation) must stand in with the other representations with which it is, in synthesis, given successively, if it is to be one that is given to that thinker in such a way as to constitute a representation that has a use for that thinker. It will prove illumining to start by considering what Kant means by 'Das: **Ich denke**'.

I propose that Kant uses '**Ich denke**' to refer to a subject of discursive understanding's purely intellectual de se consciousness of itself merely as the subject of spontaneity (self-activity) in pure thinking itself, and so apart from how, in its thinking, it realizes this activity in any of its sensible representations. This echoes the sense in which Descartes uses '*cogito*.' Indeed, that it does helps to explain why Kant does not, at B131, pause to explain what he means by '**Ich denke**,' despite this being the first appearance of this terminology in the (B-edition) *Critique*. I propose, moreover, that in adopting this terminology Kant means to invoke a neo-Platonic tradition (which stretches through Descartes back to Augustine and Plotinus) on which any thinker can – and must, in order, in the course of first philosophy, to come to cognize how it is properly to employ its mind – withdraw its mind from the senses to isolate its pure understanding.[15] Indeed, he has, in introducing the project of the Transcendental Analytic, clearly signaled that this project is, in this crucial respect, continuous with this tradition: in completing this project, he tells us, 'the pure understanding separates itself completely not only from everything empirical, but even from all sensibility' (A65/B89; cf. A65-6/B90-1).

We are now finally in a position to appreciate the sense and motivation of the Claim.

> The **I think** must **be able** to accompany all my representations [*muss alle meine Vorstellungen begleiten **können**]; for otherwise something would be represented in me that could not be thought at all, which is as much as to say that the representation would either be impossible, or at least nothing for me. (B131-2)

The Cartesian-Augustinian connotations of 'I think' suggest that the Claim is, itself, concerned only with the most general *purely intellectual* condition of the possibility of thinking the representations that are to be given to me for this thinking in combination in general. The Claim's place in the argument of the B-edition Deduction confirms that his aim in Section 16 is to isolate purely intellectual conditions of this sort: we have seen that this section aims, in particular, to identify the original synthetic unity of apperception, a unity that has pure apperception as its source, as the original representation of synthetic unity – a contribution of the pure understanding – that, 'by being added to the representation of the manifold, first makes the concept of combination possible' (B130). Moreover, the condition that the Claim itself specifies is the *most general* such condition in that it holds for *all* representations that can be given, in combination in general, to a thinker for its use in thinking, regardless even of whether those representations are concepts, intuitions, or sensations. To be sure, one actually accompanies a representation with <I think> only in determining, under some more determined principle of thinking, the relation (*Verhältnis*) it stands in, as the sort of representation it is, to other representations with which it is given to one in combination in general.[16] But the Claim itself prescinds from any differences among these principles. As such, it must be distinguished from all other purely intellectual conditions that we can specify in doing logic. And, in specifying the most general purely intellectual condition that *all* representations that are to be given to me in combination in general must satisfy, if they are to have any use in my thinking, the Claim constitutes the principle of thinking under which all other principles of my thinking fall, merely as principles of my thinking.

Even the principle of contradiction is a principle of thinking that, itself, determines the formal logical possibility of *concepts*, and thus one that has a more limited scope than does the Claim. Here it is important to recognize that Kant states this principle as 'the proposition that no predicate pertains to a thing that contradicts it' (A151/B190). He thus conceives of this principle, in traditional Aristotelian fashion, as one that concerns things (*Dinge, res*) – that is, subjects of activity and power. And what, on his account, this principle determines is, at bottom, the formal logical possibility of concepts having their proper and defining use as concepts – namely, that in a thinker's act of relating *sensible intuitions* that can be given to that thinker to a thing in an act of thinking that thing. In this way, Kant holds that the principle of contradiction owes its standing as a principle of our thinking to the standing that the categories have as principles of thinking that determine the purely intellectual possibility of given sensible intuitions having a relation to objects (*Gegenstände*) in our thinking.[17]

On Kant's account, our higher capacity of cognition itself contains the a priori concepts <concept> <intuition>, <sensible intuition>, <sensation> – indeed all the concepts included in our a priori and purely intellectual concept of a possible experience in general. Our higher capacity even includes a purely intellectual concept <succession>. It must include all these concepts, in order to be able, purely a priori, to prescribe to the manifold of representations that are to be encountered in me their conformity to purely intellectual conditions of their having a relation to an object in a thought of the same. Moreover, because the intellectual conditions that determine the possibility that the Claim asserts to be necessary are specified in purely intellectual principles of thought, it is only insofar as 'all my representations' fall merely under these purely intellectual concepts <concept>, <intuition>, <sensation>, etc. that these principles set the intellectual conditions of the possibility of these representations being 'anything to me.' The conditions that the distinctive nature of our pure understanding itself sets, conditions that render more determinate the possibility that the Claim asserts, thus, are not only impersonal (in that they hold for possible human subjects other than myself).[18] They hold for any representations of the relevant sort (concept, intuition, or sensation) that can be given to me, merely as transcendental subject, in combination in general, on pain of their not being mine. And they do so while prescinding from all determinate sensible conditions of the possibility of my thought and cognition that are set by my sensibility, whether by its nature or in and through its operation.

Kant uses 'accompany' to convey that my thinking a manifold given to me for thinking in combination in general does not, in any way, alter what is so given, or the giving of it in combination in general. The force of the Claim, then, is that for manifolds of representation that are given to me in combination in general to have any use for me, the thinker, they must conform to the intellectual conditions that our higher capacity of cognition itself sets on their having this use.

Consider now the argument Kant gives for the Claim. Kant advances the Claim as an analytic cognition, one that we can cognize a priori as necessarily true under the principle of contradiction by analyzing the concept <my representation> and bringing to light that it contains the concept <representation that it is possible for the <I think> to accompany>.

> The **I think** must **be able** to accompany all my representations [*muss alle meine Vorstellungen begleiten **können***]; for otherwise something would be represented in me that could not be thought at all, which is as much as to say that the representation would either be impossible, or at least nothing for me.

In the second clause, Kant gives a brief *reductio* argument for the Claim. Suppose that the <I think> could not accompany one of my representations, <r > . In that case, something would be represented in me – that is, the predicates that make up the representational content of <r> – that could not be thought at all. In the case of a concept, this amounts to its not being a possible representation at all, since a concept has a relation to an object only in thinking. In the case of a sensible intuition, or a sensation, however, all that follows is that it cannot have any use in my thinking, and so is 'nothing for me,' the thinker. It may still have a use in an operation of my lower capacity of cognition, which operation relates sensible intuitions and sensations to objects in and through a merely associative synthesis of the imagination.

On the present reading, the possibility of the <I think> accompanying one of my representations <r> constitutes the purely intellectual possibility of my being able to think <r > . Moreover, the <I think>'s actually accompanying a representation <r> in the synthesis, and so together with the other representations that make up the manifold that is given to me in combination in general, is what constitutes my realizing some intellectual form in this manifold to think <r>, and thereby my putting it to use in relating it to an object in an act of thinking. Contrary to what most readers of Kant have assumed, the <I think>'s actually accompanying a representation that is given to me in combination in general is constitutive, in respect of its intellectual form, of my putting it to any use in my determined thinking. This accompaniment is not to be understood on the model of the sort of explicit self-ascription that one might take to be expressed by 'I think p'.

Pure apperception, original synthetic unity of apperception, and understanding

In the service both of developing the present reading of the Claim and of clarifying his account of pure apperception, and its unity, I want now to sketch, if only briefly, how immediately after stating the Claim Kant goes on to derive this account from the Claim. We will see that the Claims serves, thereby, as the *ratio cognoscendi* of the principle of the original synthetic unity of apperception. But it does so in virtue of an a priori insight, achieved in Section 16, into how my pure apperception is what, in representing the original synthetic unity of the apperception of any manifold *of intuition* that is to be encountered in me, makes all my determined thinking first possible for me. Pure apperception is itself an actus of spontaneity that realizes the synthetic unity of apperception in all manifold of intuition that can be given to me – that is, the original synthetic unity of apperception – as my capacity of understanding itself (B134n). It is also what, in realizing this unity in a manifold of representations that is given to me in combination in general combines it in my concept of an object in general. Indeed, in doing so, it is what brings forth the representation <I think> (B132). But all my determined thinking consists in my accompanying with the <I think>, representations that are given to me in combination in general. In this way, pure apperception is the *ratio essendi* of our capacity of thinking itself.

Recall that these purely logical conditions of the possibility of the <I think> accompanying my representations differ, depending on whether the representations given to me for thinking are intuitions, sensations, or concepts. Immediately after stating the Claim, Kant at B132 draws our attention to the *distinctive* necessary relation (*Beziehung*) that *all manifold of intuition* has 'to the I think in the same subject in which this manifold is to be encountered.'

> That representation that can be given prior to all thinking is called intuition. Thus all manifold of intuition has a necessary relation [*Beziehung*] to **I think** in the same

subject in which this manifold is to be encountered. But this representation is an act [*actus*] of **spontaneity**, i.e. it cannot be regarded as belonging to sensibility. I call it the **pure apperception**, in order to distinguish it from the **empirical** one, or also the **original apperception**, since it is that self-consciousness which, because it brings forth [*hervorbringt*] the representation **I think**, which must be able to accompany all others, and which in all consciousness is one and the same, cannot be accompanied by any further representation.

The necessary relation in question is, as we have seen, one that this manifold has to the subject where it is considered merely as transcendental subject, and so prescinding from all the sensible content of its thought and cognition. To be sure, any transcendental subject is, as such, a subject that has some distinctive sort of sensibility, one that determines the distinctive forms of its sensibility. Moreover, any thinker constitutes a transcendental subject only on the condition that its sensibility is originally affected, timelessly, by some transcendental object (*Gegenstand*) or other that, in this affection, determines all possible appearances that belong to a single universal possible experience. Nonetheless, the nature of the capacity to think that a subject has merely as transcendental subject does not specify either the distinctive nature of its sensibility, or the manner of the original affection of its sensibility. Thus, the scope of 'all manifold of intuition that is to be encountered in it' encompasses, not only all the pure intuitions contained in the forms of that subject's sensibility, but also all the appearances that are determined by whatever transcendental object (*Gegenstand*) originally affects its sensibility.

A thinker's original representation of the necessary relation (*Beziehung*) that all manifold of intuition that is to be encountered in it has to the <I think> is itself, Kant then tells us, 'an *actus* of spontaneity', which he dubs 'pure apperception' (B132). I propose that, on Kant's account, pure apperception (the self-consciousness of an understanding that is discursive, as against intuitive cf. B136 and B138-9) is the single a-temporal mental act in and through which a thinker prescribes to any and all manifold of intuition that can be given to its consciousness (where the thinker is considered merely as transcendental subject) its objectively necessary conformity to *any and all* of the purely intellectual conditions of the possibility of the <I think> accompanying it. These purely intellectual conditions include most fundamentally, but not exclusively, those specified in its concept of an object in general as the purely intellectual conditions of the possibility of the <I think> accompanying the manifold of a given intuition in thinking that constitutes cognition of the object of that intuition.

To be sure, we do not in pure apperception think the conformity that we prescribe *under this description*. Indeed, in pure apperception itself we are not conscious of any determined principle of thinking (i.e. any principle of thinking other than that which the Claim itself states). But, on Kant's account, pure apperception is a thinker's self-activity that, as transcendental consciousness, eminently contains all the purely intellectual principles of its thinking: these principles are contained in this activity (intellectual consciousness itself) as the possible ways in which it can, and must, differentiate itself in uniting manifolds that are given to the subject in combination in general, much as the essences of created beings were thought, in traditional transcendental philosophy, to be contained in God's single unchanging and unchangeable pure act of being. For these principles owe their standing as such principles to their being purely intellectual cognitions that our capacity of the absolute spontaneity of representation brings forth itself to actuate itself as our capacity of understanding.[19] And pure apperception itself only occurs as the formal element that a-temporally realizes in the temporally successive manifolds of representations given to a thinker through its inner sense different purely intellectual principles of thinking as the intellectual form that determines their respective distinctive relations to an object in acts of thinking. The acts of thinking that determine this relation employ the categories, the purely intellectual concepts that constitute our concept of an object in general, and this in representing the purely intellectual conditions of representations that are given in our intuition having any relation to an object in our thinking. The distinctive nature of our discursive understanding, in determining the character of our pure apperception, determines the twelve categories Kant displays in his table of the categories as the fundamental purely intellectual conditions to which all intuitions that are to be encountered in me must conform if they are to be anything to me, and thereby as the 'self-thought a priori first principles of our cognition' (B167).

Pure apperception itself is, on Kant's account, to be distinguished from the categories, and more generally from all the principles of thinking that it brings forth. The act of pure apperception itself does not change, even as it realizes different intellectual forms in different sorts of representations to determine different sorts of acts of thinking. For example, in realizing our capacity of understanding in its real use, pure apperception realizes different categories in different particular given manifolds of intuition, to relate them to (perhaps only merely possible) things (i.e. to *Gegenstände* of an experience that is possible for us). But it does so timelessly, and in doing so does not change, any more than God, according to orthodoxy, changes in timelessly creating and sustaining creation. These intellectual forms, on Kant's account, *flow* from pure apperception. Or, to put the point in terminology that Kant avoids because of its unreconstructed metaphysical implications, pure apperception *emanates* these logical forms to realize them in that thinker's particular acts of determined thinking. In this way, as Kant puts it, pure apperception is a 'pure, original, unchanging consciousness' (A107). And, on his account, it must be, because its numerical unity – one that constitutes a thinker as what is numerically identical in the strict Leibnizian sense throughout all representations that can be given to it, through inner sense, for combination – is what 'grounds all concepts a priori' (A107). Pure apperception is, in short, a distant descendent (through Plotinus, Augustine, Aquinas, and Descartes) of Aristotle's active intellect (*de Anima* III 5). Pure apperception is, however, much more restricted in scope than its predecessors, in that all this *actus* eminently contains are the purely intellectual principles of thinking – the purely intellectual a priori principles of our thought and cognition. Moreover, Kant identifies it only as what our capacity of understanding itself *would have to* consist in, and thus as what we have an a priori entitlement to presuppose, transcendentally, as an *actus* of spontaneity in which we actually realize ourselves a subjects of thought and cognition, even though, on his account, we cannot, in any way, prove that such an actus is really possible, let alone actual.[20]

B132-3 also expresses Kant's view that the *de se* consciousness that a thinker has, in pure apperception, of itself as the subject of pure thinking – and this, in virtue of pure apperception's bringing forth its representation <I think> – is what constitutes that thinker as the numerically identical thinker throughout all its acts of determined thinking. I am proposing, then, that the force of 'in all consciousness is one and the same' at B132 is 'numerically the same.' I am proposing, moreover, that this consciousness must, on his account, be actually present, in all of that thinker's thinking, as what constitutes the intellectual consciousness it has as the individual thinker it is. We can appreciate this by attending to how Kant goes on, in B133, to identify the unity of the purely intellectual self-consciousness had in pure apperception – one that is to constitute the 'thoroughgoing identity of the apperception of a manifold in intuition' – with the consciousness of *a certain synthesis* of the representations that make up this manifold, a synthesis the consciousness of which makes this identity possible:

> Namely, this thoroughgoing identity of the apperception of a manifold given in intuition contains a synthesis of the representations, and is possible only through the consciousness of this synthesis. For the empirical consciousness that accompanies different representations is by itself dispersed and without relation to the identity of the subject. The latter relation therefore does not yet come about by my accompanying each representation with consciousness, but rather by my adding one representation to the other and being conscious of their synthesis. (B133)

This synthesis is what Kant later terms the intellectual synthesis, in distinguishing it from the figurative (B151). Pure apperception just is, on Kant's account, the *de se* consciousness I must have of what I am doing in this synthesis – that is, prescribing to the manifold I unite in this synthesis its conformity to whatever particular purely intellectual conditions I think in this synthesis. And this *de se* consciousness, as applied in the thinking in which I unite the representations that make up this manifold in one consciousness, is what gives the representations I unite in this synthesis their relation to myself, as the numerically identical thinker throughout the successive consciousnesses of those representations – even though I am not thereby conscious of these representations as my representations. And the synthetic unity of one's apperception that one realizes throughout one's in-themselves-discrete consciousnesses of each element of the manifold one unites consists in the single actus he has dubbed 'pure apperception.' And as the act that timelessly realizes the original synthetic unity of this apperception itself in all manifolds of intuition that are to be given to me in the synthesis of my imagination, my pure apperception constitutes my capacity of understanding itself: Kant thus tells us that the original synthetic unity of this apperception, considered as capacity (the inner possibility of my power to understand), 'is the understanding itself' (B134n). This parallels how, in the A-edition Deduction, Kant draws on his account of how original apperception sets purely intellectual conditions on a representation 'representing something in me' (A116) to argue that 'the unity of apperception in relation to the synthesis of imagination is the understanding' (A119). The exercise of our capacity of apperception, insofar as it realizes synthetic unity of the apperception of all intuition that is to be given to one in this synthesis, is what constitutes our capacity of understanding itself.

Consider now briefly the sense and motivation of Kant's claim that what makes the representation <I think> the representation of ourselves as the subject of thinking that it purports to be can only be its originating in pure apperception, the actus of spontaneity that realizes our capacity of appercep-tion as our capacity of understanding. Recall that a representation is what *is to be* related to an object. What makes the representation <I think> a represen-tation, then, is its being such that the subject that has this representation is to relate it to itself in thinking itself as the subject that has and exercises the capacity of thinking itself. And there must be an intellectual principle under which it is to do so, that is, a principle that makes the <I think>, as it is thought assertorically by a subject, a *de se* representation of that subject as the subject to whom acts of thinking are to be imputed. This principle is the principle of the original synthetic unity of apperception. The sense of Kant's claim, then, is that pure apperception is, in and through its original synthetic unity, the *ratio essendi* of the representation <I think>.

We can now see how, on Kant's account, even sensations have a use in my thinking, and are anything to me, only in virtue of having a relation to things that we are to determine under a principle of thinking that derives its standing as such a principle from the Claim. The Claim, as applied to all manifold of intuition, yields the principle that this manifold has a use for me only as representations that I am to determine under the categories in cognition of their objects. But for this to be possible, the sensations that provide the matter of the appearances that make up the manifold of a given empirical intuition must, as such (and so as objective sensations), have a relation to objects in thinking, albeit thinking that does not constitute cognition of these objects. Recall that sensations are subjective perceptions (*perceptiones*) (A320/B376), in that they are to be related to objects of our experience in thinking, but only in thinking that attributes these sensations to these objects in relation to the character of our sensibility; they are merely subjective, and not objective, determinations of these objects. The principle of thought under which sensations have this relation, and through which concepts of objective sensations are possible, is thus a principle of thought that is subordinate to, and derives from, the Claim, via the principle of the synthetic unity of apperception (B135-6).

The obscurity of pure apperception

The present reading of Section 16 confirms my contention that all my determined thinking, on Kant's account, consists in my actually accompanying representations with the <I think>. On this reading, Kant argues in B132-3 that pure apperception is a thinker's actus of spontaneity in which, in bringing forth the representation <I think>, that thinker is conscious *de se*, and purely intellectually, of itself, as it is the subject of the actus of spontaneity in virtue of which it constitutes an individual thinker that is numerically identical throughout all its thinking. But one might worry that the position I am ascribing to him is so manifestly mistaken that we shouldn't ascribe it to Kant – at least as his considered position. Isn't it obvious that we commonly employ our understanding to form concepts of all sorts of subject-matter without being conscious of our doing so? Indeed, it isn't obvious that we ever are, or even can be, conscious of ourselves, in thinking, as subjects of the activity that constitutes us as numerically identical subjects throughout our thinking.

First, let me note that the present reading finds ample confirmation in the Paralogism chapter. There Kant tells us that the I of <I think> 'occurs in all thinking,' when he characterizes rational psychology as attempting to derive a purely intellectual science of the soul as a rational doctrine that 'independently of all experience can be inferred from this concept I insofar as it occurs in all thinking' (A342/B400). Indeed, he implies that the categories are essentially actually accompanied by <I think> when he describes these concepts, referring to them as 'transcendental concepts,' as ones 'which say "I think substance, cause, etc."' (A343/B401): indeed, this is what he means in describing the categories as '*self-thought* a priori first principles of our cognition' (B167, my italics). A few paragraphs later, he tells us that 'the simple and in content for itself wholly empty **I**' is 'a mere consciousness that accompanies every concept' (A346/B404). He continues 'Through this I, or He, or It (the thing) which thinks, nothing further is represented than a transcendental subject of thoughts = x′ (ibid). He then, speaking of this consciousness – i.e. pure apperception, or transcendental consciousness, consciousness of oneself as transcendental subject – remarks 'the consciousness in itself is not even a representation distinguishing a particular object [*Object*], but rather a form of representation in general, insofar as it is to be called a cognition [*Erkenntnis*]; for of it alone can I say that through it I think anything' (ibid).

My reply to the worry, briefly, is that it is predicated on a misunderstanding of Kant's position. Kant agrees that we are not, and indeed cannot, be conscious of ourselves as transcendental subjects, *provided 'conscious' is used in the sense that requires the degree requisite for clarity*. On his view, the exercise of the spontaneity that is pure apperception, and that, in realizing the intrinsic unity of this apperception, constitutes (in relation to the synthesis of imagination) our capacity of understanding, is, as such, obscure. It is only the self-consciousness I can, in realizing pure apperception in some particular manifold given to me through my inner sense, have of myself as the subject of *that* manifold – an empirical consciousness of myself – that can be clear. Consider here a stretch of the A-edition Deduction that parallels much of Section 16 of the B-edition Deduction:

> All empirical consciousness has, however, a necessary relation to [*Beziehung auf*] a transcendental (preceding all particular experience) consciousness, namely the consciousness of myself, as original apperception. It is therefore absolutely necessary that in my cognition all consciousness belong to one consciousness (of myself). Now here is a synthetic unity of the manifold (of consciousness) that is cognized a priori, and that yields the ground for synthetic a priori propositions concerning pure thinking in exactly the same way that space and time yield such propositions concerning the form of mere intuition. The synthetic proposition that every different empirical conscious-ness must be combined into a single self-consciousness is the absolutely first and synthetic principle of all our thinking in general. But it should not go unnoticed that the mere representation I in relation to all others (the collective unity of which it makes possible) is the transcendental consciousness. Now it does not matter here whether this representation be clear (empirical con-sciousness) or obscure, even whether it be actual; but the possibility of the logical form of all cognition necessarily rests on the relation [*Verhältnis*] to this apperception [what he here refers to as 'transcendental consciousness' but also as 'pure apperception'] *as a capacity*. (A117n)

The consciousness – pure apperception – relation to which grounds 'the possibility of the logical form of all cognition' is transcendental, and not empirical. But this transcendental consciousness itself, as it represents and prescribes to all manifold of intuition that is to be encountered in one (merely as transcendental subject) its necessary conformity to principles of thinking (as the purely intellectual conditions of their being anything to me), is obscure. And to say that it is obscure just is to say that the *de se* consciousness of myself, as thinker, in which it consists, does not suffice to provide me with a representation by means of which I can represent myself as the same or different though different representations. It is only as this consciousness takes up some particular manifold given to me in my inner sense that it provides me with grounds for distinguishing myself – and this, only in inner experience – as a subject that is different from other (perhaps merely possible) subjects. So Kant's account of how, in doing transcendental logic, I am to isolate pure apperception, or even the <I think>, had better *not* be one on which I am supposed to draw on a clear self-consciousness of myself as the subject of thinking. Notice that the reading I sketched of Section 16 is one on which I am not.[21]

The recognition that, on Kant's account, pure apperception is itself essentially obscure has direct bearing on Kitcher's proposal that his account of higher cognition is consonant with the agential approach to self-knowledge. On this account, as Kitcher interprets it, judging and inference require conscious acts in such a way that 'whenever a subject is consciously thinking that p, she can self-ascribe the activity and the thought' (Kitcher 2017, 171). Now the consciousness that, according to Kant, one must have in consciously believing p gives one grounds for self-ascribing the belief p only if that consciousness is clear. But, as we have seen, the purely intellectual consciousness that, on Kant's account, one must have, *de se, of oneself* in thinking, as the subject of that thinking, is itself obscure. On his account, it is only the logical consciousness in which one gives oneself the rule for that thinking that is, and need be, clear. In this way, Kant has a principled reason to maintain, as Kitcher herself recognizes that he does, that a thinker self-ascribes representations only in being aware of them through inner sense, and so through a sort of observation of her own mental states.

Moreover, we can see that Kitcher is also mistaken in reading Kant as holding that a thinker, in consciously drawing inferences from her various mental states, thereby creates and recognizes 'the relation of necessary connection across them that makes them the states of a single thinker' (Kitcher 2017, 171). What makes the various mental states that a thinker has, in succession, its states is not the determined thinking in which that thinker relates their representational contents to an object or, for that matter, to one another. It is, rather, the thinker's exercise of its originally unitary actus of combination in general in pure apperception, that, in prescribing to these representations their objectively necessary conformity to the purely intellectual conditions of their being accompanied with <I think>, makes possible their collective unity in that thinker that makes them its representations. The consciousness of this collective unity – the original synthetic unity of the apperception of these representations – is obscure. Nonetheless, it must be present in all my thinking, as the *de se* consciousness that makes my representations mine (gives them use in my determined thinking) in timelessly taking them up into itself.

The a priori warrant for principles of thinking, and a defense of Kant's account of pure apperception

Some will balk at reading Kant's account of the intellectual conditions of possibility of our thinking as grounded in pure apperception, where pure apperception is understood as I propose: that is, as a single supersensible, and so a-temporal, exercise of the spontaneity of our cognition that, in an Aristotelian vein, constitutes a thinker as the numerically identical subject of all its thinking. For to do so will seem to many to read this account as making a posit that is, by Kant's own lights, far too metaphysically extra-vagant – one more fitting of a dogmatic rationalist such as Leibniz. For these claims about our capacity of understanding would, it seems, have to consist of theoretical cognition of ourselves as subjects of supersensible acts. How, they will ask, can Kant advance such cognition without violating the central negative tenet of his critical philosophy – namely, that we cannot have any theoretical cognition of things in themselves? I cannot hope to provide a fully adequate reply to this worry here. But let me briefly sketch a line of interpretation that promises to explain how Kant does not, and given his purposes need not, advance his account of pure apperception as a body of cognition of the thing that thinks – or indeed, of any thing at all, let alone a supersensible thing in itself. He need not, because he does not aim to establish that we are subjects of apperception, or indeed that what we conceive of in thinking of pure apperception is even really possible. Kant aims only to establish our a priori warrant *to presuppose* that we are, as thinkers, subjects of pure apperception. And this a priori warrant is, he contends, sufficient for us to have genuine principles of thinking, as we must if we are to be subjects of acts of thinking that are imputable to us. The most fundamental of these principles, as we have seen, are the purely intellectual ones that constitute all the intellectual forms of acts of thinking of which we are capable, given only the nature of our understanding. These include, most crucially, the categories: the purely intellectual concepts through which we can cognize things in respect of the being they have in appearing to us, in prescribing to manifolds of intuition that can be given to us their objectively necessary conformity to these concepts.

On Kant's account, I have the a priori warrant requisite to have genuine principles of thinking only if I, in fact, have a capacity of understanding. And I have this capacity only in and through the two acts of spontaneity in and through which I bring given representations to the original synthetic unity of apperception: combination in general and pure apperception. But Kant sets a further, broadly internalist, condition I must meet if I am to have this a priori warrant: it must, if only in principle, be possible for me to achieve the rational insight that Kant purports to achieve, in Section 16, into our capacity of understanding – namely, an insight into how their originating in pure apperception is not only necessary but *would*, if actual, be sufficient, for these principles to be the purely intellectual principles of thinking that collectively, under the principle of the original synthetic unity of apperception, constitute the intellectual form of any determined thinking that is to be possible for me. The crucial point to see is that, in achieving this insight, what I *cognize* is only the inner possibility of these principles constituting *my* representations – that is, principles that I am, in my thinking, to relate to manifolds as they are given to me through my inner sense as principles to which these manifolds must conform, if they are to have any use in my thinking. To be sure, on the reading I propose, this insight essentially employs a *representation* of the inner possibility of my being as a thing that thinks. But this insight is not an insight into this inner possibility, and the representations of the spontaneity of our cognition that it employs are not, themselves, cognitions. Nonetheless, this insight suffices to provide an account of an origin in an operation of the spontaneity of our cognition for the purely intellectual principles of my thinking – including the categories – that establishes, entirely a priori, the a priori warrant I have to employ them, a warrant I must have if they are to constitute genuine principles of my thinking.

In short, Kant's account of pure apperception, and the use to which he puts it in the Transcendental Analytic of the first *Critique* is not undermined in any way by his contention that we cannot have any theoretical cognition of the transcendental grounds of the possibility of our thinking that this account specifies. All that Kant's account of pure apperception, and of the transcendental subject of thinking that one constitutes in this *actus*, need do is to provide us a mere representation of these grounds that each of us can, merely in virtue of the purely intellectual principles of thinking contained in the nature of our capacity of understanding itself, employ in an act of self-understanding to establish, *de se*, her own a priori warrant, merely as a thinker, to prescribe to all manifolds of intuition that can be given to her in intuition their objectively necessary conformity to the categories. In establishing this in principle possibility, Kant contends, his transcendental deduction of the categories establishes, for each of us, a de se a priori warrant, merely as a subject that takes herself to be capable of acts of thinking that are imputable to her, to presuppose, as she does in any of her determined thinking, that the conditions of the possibility of her, in fact, being such a subject actually obtain. These conditions include that she be the subject of an act of pure apperception that realizes a capacity of understanding in her, and thereby the transcendental subject of all her determined thinking. And Kant succeeds in establishing our a priori warrant to make this presupposition by employing a representation of pure apperception merely as an act that *would have to* take place in us, if we are to be capable of any acts of thinking that are imputable to us.[22]

Conclusion

We have seen that Kant works with a conception of what it is to be a thinker that is importantly similar to the account of what it is to be a critical reasoner that informs the agential approach to self-knowledge. For, on the reading offered here, the Claim asserts that, unless a representation that is given to a subject of thinking meets the condition that the Claim specifies as necessary to its being a representation that this subject can put to use in thinking that is imputable to her, that representation 'cannot be thought at all' and is 'nothing to her.' In this way, Kant's Claim expresses an idea that parallels, in an important respect, that which animates the agential approach to self-knowledge: a representation that belongs to me, the person, is as such a representation that can play a proper role in the activity that characterizes me as a person (i.e. a subject that is responsive to reasons in the relevant way).

Nonetheless, we have also seen that what lies behind the Claim is a conception of what it is for us to be thinkers that is, in other respects, importantly different from that which animates the agential approach to self-knowledge, one on which we are, as thinkers, subjects of rational belief. What animates Kant's position is, rather, a conception on which what makes us thinkers is our having the authority, as subjects of a capacity of conceptual understanding, to prescribe a priori to manifolds of representations as they are given to our consciousness their conformity to purely intellectual principles of our thinking, inherent in this capacity, that determine conditions of these representations having any use in thinking that is to be imputable to us. Moreover, this a priori warrant that, on Kant's account, we have merely as thinkers is not one to self-knowledge at all. It is, rather, one that each of us, as a thinker, has to take representations as they are actually given to her consciousness as subject to the purely intellectual conditions that our capacity of understanding sets on their having a use in her thinking – as we actually take them to in putting them to use in our thinking.

The reading I propose of the sense and motivation of the Claim has the virtue of helping to clarify the role it plays in the argument of the B-edition Transcendental Deduction of the Categories. We have, if only in outline, seen how on this reading the Claim provides the starting point of Kant's attempt, in Section 16 of this Deduction, to achieve a certain rational insight: cognition of how and why the essence of the capacity of thinking itself – the principle of the synthetic unity of apperception – is as such the *ratio essendi* of all principles of our thinking; it is only in standing under this, the highest principle of all our cognition, that these principles constitute genuine priori cognitions of the objectively necessary unities that manifolds of representations given to us must have if they are to have any use in our thinking. This insight yields an account of what would have to be the case if we are to have the a priori warrant requisite to our being subjects of acts of thinking that are to be imputable to us. This points the way to a new approach to the Deduction, one on which it does not depend on an ultimately undefended assumption that we are, in fact, subjects of experience, or even that we are, in fact, subjects of acts of thinking that are imputable to us. The Deduction, rather, aims to achieve a purely intellectual insight into how having their origin in pure apperception would give what we take to be the purely intellectual principles of our thinking the normative ground they require to constitute genuine principles of our thinking. Moreover, this insight serves to establish, entirely a priori, an a priori warrant we have, merely as subjects of discursive understanding, to presuppose that the conditions of the possibility of our being such subjects actually obtain. And this includes an a priori warrant we have, merely as subjects of thinking that is imputable to us, to take manifolds of intuitions that are, and can be, given to us as subject to the most fundamental purely intellectual principles of our thinking, namely, the categories. It is in this way that Kant's Transcendental Deduction of the Categories specifies an origin for the categories that suffices to establish their a priori objective validity, if only for objects of our experience.[23]

Notes

1. A proponent of the agential approach to self-knowledge need not hold that the only warrant we have, or could have, for self-knowledge derives from our beliefs being embedded in our critical reasoning.
2. The most important such proponent is Tyler Burge, who in a series of influential papers has developed detailed accounts of a priori entitlements that we have as persons, entitlements that include one to self-knowledge. These accounts, as he puts it, 'have a Kantian flavor' (Burge 2003, p. 335 n50). In particular, in 'Our Entitlement to Self-Knowledge,' Burge develops an account of an epistemic entitlement to self-knowledge that turns crucially on the claims that being a critical reasoner requires that one be the subject of 'mental acts and states that are knowledgeably reviewable' (Burge 1996, 98) and that this reviewability requires that one have a certain non-observational entitlement to first-person judgments regarding those acts and states (ibid). Burge's emphasis on the possibility of a subject's applying 'the I think' to her thoughts echoes Kant's famous discussion at B132f. I hasten to add that Burge is careful to distinguish his position from Kant's (see, e.g. Burge 1996, p. 99, n5), and his aim in these papers (Burge 1988, 1993, 1996, 2003, 2011) is not Kant exegesis (although he does offer several penetrating observations about Kant along the way). And I need especially to stress that the reading of B132f., and more generally of Kant's account of the unity of apperception, that I will be rejecting is not one that Burge endorses.
3. See Evans (1982), Boyle (2009), and Setiya (2011).
4. Here 'understanding' is to be taken in the sense in which understanding contrasts with judgment and reason. Kant also occasionally uses this term in a broader sense to refer to our higher capacity of cognition, which encompasses judgment and reason, as well as understanding in the narrower sense of the term. To look ahead, to understand something, in turn, is to represent

its essence positively with a warrant sufficient for that representation to serve as a principle of our cognition. This does not require that the representation constitute cognition of the essence.

5. The term 'transparent' is one coined by Roy Edgley (1969, p. 90).

6. As Patricia Kitcher points out, in reading Kant this way, Evans is following Strawson (see her Kitcher 2017, discussed below).

7. Moran and Boyle are happy to allow that a critical reasoner may have other modes of access to her beliefs in addition to the agential one. All they claim is that agential access is privileged, in that it tracks the proper functioning of the capacity for belief. So the thesis of the transparency of belief to which they subscribe is weaker than that which Evans champions: they claim only that there are some cases in which a critical reasoned can determine what she believes by addressing world-directed questions, and not that the only way in which she can determine what she believes is by addressing such questions.

8. Neither Burge nor Moran reads Kant as advancing, at B131-2 or elsewhere, the claim that our beliefs are transparent.

9. One might worry here that what Kant says in this passage is inconsistent with his famous claim that concepts and intuitions constitute cognitions only in conjunction with one another: this claim seems to entail that concepts and intuitions cannot be species of cognition. But this inconsistency is only apparent. On Kant's account, a concept can be considered either of itself, or as it constitutes a cognition in conjunction with intuition, and the same goes for intuition. At A320/B372, Kant is using 'concept' and 'intuition' to refer to these representations as they constitute cognitions.

10. Burge and Moran, as well as other proponents of the agential approach, maintain that our knowledge of our sensations is of a different character than our knowledge of our thoughts and attitudes. And they exclude sensations from the nonobservational self-knowledge that a critical reasoner can, as such a reasoner, have of her mental acts and states, on the grounds that sensations are not essentially the content of her thoughts and attitudes. See Burge (1996, 107), Moran (2001, 9–10), as well as Aaron Zimmerman (2008) and Matthew Boyle (2009). For a helpful discussion of this point, as well as of what, following Burge, has come to be referred to as the rationalist approach to self-knowledge, see Brie Gertler (2011, especially Chapter 6).

11. A related problem is worth mentioning: Kant distinguishes between two sorts of cognitions – concept and intuition – and it isn't at all clear that to have a *perceptio* that is an intuition is, itself, to think it, or indeed to take any attitude toward it. Kitcher addresses this concern in the course of developing a reading of Kant on which his position is amenable to the agential approach to self-knowledge (Kitcher 2011, 151f).

12. This line of thought seems to raise difficulties only for Evans's transparency thesis, on which the question of what one believes always can, and is to be, settled solely by answering the world-directed question. And, even so, it isn't entirely clear what the difficulty is supposed to be. Kitcher seems to be assuming that the prior de se consciousness one has of oneself as the subject of rational thought that Kant's account posits is either itself a belief that cannot be determined in the world-directed fashion, or a source of such beliefs. Thanks to Thomas Land for raising this worry.

13. This is the central thesis of her (2017). See also Chapter 15 of (2011).

14. '*Aktus*' and '*actus*', in Kant's terminology, signifies, not just any action (*Handlung*), but an actuation, or *inner* action, i.e., a subject's activity (*Activität*) insofar as it suffices to realize its capacity (*Vermögen*) as a power (*Kraft*). See here the final section of my (2009).

15. Where Kant parts company with Descartes, and others, is in denying that <I think> is *cognition* of *the thing* that thinks: it is a *mere representation of the thing that thinks*, because we cannot prove that any such thing is really possible. He maintains that the representation <I think> has the function of making it possible for one to determine one's own thinking out of one's de se consciousness of how one is, in bringing them under intellectual principles, to relate representation to an object. And he holds that the <I think> can serve this function without being cognition of the thing that thinks. It can, and does, serve this function in virtue of constituting cognition that a human being can have, through pure apperception, of herself in respect of 'actions and inner determinations' of which she must, timelessly, be the subject, if she is, as a human being, to be a person at all (A546/B574).

16. Consider here how, in his 4 December 1792 letter to J.S. Beck, Kant reacts to Beck's attempt to gloss the Claim. Kant offers the following emendation to Beck's attempt: 'Instead of … "The I think must accompany all the representations in the synthesis," "must *be able to* accompany [*begleiten können*]"' (11: 395). Notice that Kant does not correct Beck's gloss of the Claim in any way other than to add the modal qualifier '*können*.'

17. One might object that the objective validity of the principle of contradiction cannot depend on our thought's relation to things because pure general logic abstracts 'from all content of our cognition, i.e. from any relation [*Beziehung*] of it to the object [*Object*]' (A55/B79). To be sure, the principle of contradiction does, on Kant's account, abstract from all relation of our cognition to the object. But this is entirely consistent, on his view, with its owing its standing as cognition to its being applicable to objects of our experience, much as pure mathematics owes its objective validity to there being 'things that can be presented to us only in accordance with the form of our sensible intuition' (B147), despite its abstracting from the dynamical character of these things.

18. For a helpful discussion of this point, see Keller (1998).

19. For a reading of Kant's conception of the spontaneity of cognition along these lines, see my (2009).

20. Here it is useful to contrast the present reading with a similar one that Dieter Henrich considers, and rejects, in (Henrich 1976), p. 79f. On this reading, Kant conceives of the subject as having strict Leibnizian identity (one that requires that identicals be indiscernible). Henrich rejects this reading as incompatible with Kant's characterization of the capacity that is essential to the subject as one for altering its condition in and through reflection on how it is to think. The present reading provides the resources for distinguishing between pure apperception itself, which constitutes the thinker as transcendental subject, and the alterations it determines in itself as empirical subject.

21. This provides some indication of how the present reading is not subject to a second worry that leads Henrich to reject his reading of the subject as enjoying strict Leibnizian identity (Henrich 1976, p. 79f.). The worry is, in effect, that Kant cannot provide a case for such an account of the subject because we are not given to ourselves, in consciousness, as transcendental subjects. The

response is that Kant does not purport to arrive at his account from what is given to him, or us, in a *clear* consciousness.

22. For details, see 'Essence, Nature, and the Possibility of Metaphysics,' forthcoming. Here I can, given the constraints of this paper, only gesture at the approach to Kant's critical philosophy that I develop and defend here, and elsewhere.

23. This paper was written for the conference *Transparency and Apperception* held at Ryerson University in May 2018. I thank the organizers of this conference – David Hunter, Thomas Land, and Boris Hennig – and other conference participants for helpful discussion. Part of this paper was presented at the UCLA Kant conference held in February 2019. I thank John Carriero for organizing this conference, and to all its participants for their helpful comments. I also thank Robert M. Adams, Tyler Burge, Tom Christiano, Suzanne Dovi, Frode Kjosavik, Thomas Land, Shaun Nichols, Santi Sanchez, and Mark Timmons for helpful comments and discussion.

References

Boyle, M. 2009. "Two Kinds of Self-Knowledge." *Philosophy and Phenomenological Research* 78: 133–164. doi:10.1111/phpr.2008.78.issue-1.

Burge, T. 1988. "Individualism and Self-Knowledge." *Journal of Philosophy* 85: 649–663. doi:10.5840/jphil1988851112.

Burge, T. 1993. "Content Preservation." *The Philosophical Review* 103: 457–488.

Burge, T. 1996. "Our Entitlement to Self-Knowledge." *Part 1 Proceedings of the Aristotelian Society* 96: 91–116. doi:10.1093/aristotelian/96.1.91.

Burge, T. 2003. "Perceptual Entitlement." *Philosophy and Phenomenological Research* 67: 503–548. doi:10.1111/phpr.2003.67.issue-3.

Burge, T. 2011. "Self and Self-Understanding." *Journal of Philosophy* 108 (6/7): 287–383. doi:10.5840/jphil20111086/715.

Edgley, R. 1969. *Reason in Theory and Practice*. London: Hutchinson.

Evans, G. 1982. *The Varieties of Reference*, edited by J. McDowell. Oxford: Oxford University Press.

Gertler, B. 2011. *Self-Knowledge*. New York, NY: Routledge.

Henrich, D. (1976) *Identaet Und Objectivitaet*. Heidelberg: C. Winter Universitätsverlag.

Keller, P. 1998. *Kant and the Demands of Self-Consciousness*. New York: Cambridge University Press.

Kitcher, P. 2011. *Kant's Thinker*. New York, NY: Oxford University Press.

Kitcher, P. 2017. "A Kantian Critique of Transparency." In *Kant and the Philosophy of Mind: Perception, Reason, and the Self*, edited by Anil Gomes and Andrew Stephenson, 158–172. Oxford: Oxford University Press.

Moran, R. 2001. *Authority and Estrangement: An Essay on Self-Knowledge*. Princeton, NJ: Princeton University Press.

Setiya, K. 2011. "Knowledge of Intention." In *Essays on Anscombe's Intention*, edited by Anton Ford, Jennifer Hornsby, and Frederick Stoutland, 170–197. Cambridge, MA: Harvard University Press.

Smit, H. 2009. "Kant on Apriority and the Spontaneity of Cognition." In *Metaphysics and the Good: Themes from the Philosophy of Robert Merrihew Adams*, edited by Samuel Newlands and Larry M. Jorgensen, 188–251. New York, NY: Oxford University Press.

Zimmerman, A. 2008. "Self-Knowledge: Rationalism Vs. Empiricism." *Philosophy Compass* 3 (2): 325–352. doi:10.1111/j.1747-9991.2008.00125.x.

Transparency and reflection

Matthew Boyle

ABSTRACT

Much recent work on self-knowledge has been inspired by the idea that the 'transparency' of questions about our own mental states to questions about the non-mental world holds the key to understanding how privileged self-knowledge is possible. I critically discuss some prominent recent accounts of such transparency, and argue for a Sartrean interpretation of the phenomenon, on which this knowledge is explained by our capacity to transform an implicit or 'non-positional ' self-awareness into reflective, 'positional' self-knowledge.

'[T]he mode of existence of consciousness is to be consciousness of itself [*conscience de soi*]... [But] this consciousness of consciousness – except in the case of reflective consciousness, on which we shall dwell shortly – is not *positional*, which is to say that consciousness is not for itself its own object. Its object is by nature outside it.'

Sartre, *The Transcendence of the Ego*[1]

1. Transparency as phenomenon and as problem

In an influential discussion of first-person belief ascriptions, Gareth Evans observed that we are normally in a position to ascribe beliefs to ourselves, not by seeking evidence concerning our own psychological states, but by looking to the realm of non-psychological facts:

> In making a self-ascription of belief, one's eyes are, so to speak, or occasionally literally, directed outward – upon the world. If someone asks me "Do you think there is going to be a third world war?", I must attend, in answering him, to precisely the same outward phenomena as I would attend to if I were answering the question "Will there be a third world war?" (Evans 1982, 225)

Evans also held that a similar point applies in the case of first-person ascriptions of perceptual appearances:

> [A] subject can gain knowledge of his [perceptual] states in a very simple way... He goes through exactly the same procedure as he would go through if he were trying to make a judgment about how it is at this place now, but excluding any knowledge he has *of an extraneous kind*... The result will necessarily be closely correlated with the content of the [perceptual] state which he is in at that time. (Ibid., 227–228)

The phenomenon Evans describes here has come to be known as the 'transparency' of (certain kinds of) self-knowledge. Our knowledge of our own mental states is said to be *transparent* inasmuch as we can knowledgeably answer questions about these states by attending in the right way, not to anything 'inner' or psychological, but to aspects of the non-mental world.[2]

Although Evans discusses only our knowledge of our own beliefs and perceptual appearances, there is reason to think his point may have wider application. For instance, the mind-focused question whether I intend to ϕ is arguably normally transparent for me to the world-focused question whether I will ϕ (when the latter question is answered subject to certain restrictions),[3] and the mind-focused question whether I want X is arguably normally transparent for me to the world-focused question whether it would be desirable for me to have X (again, answered subject to certain restrictions).[4] Each of these formulations is rough and incomplete, and the task of making them sharp and complete would be little easier than, and closely related to, the task of giving a philosophical account of intention and desire. But while there is room for dispute about how to characterize specific relations of transparency, it is widely accepted that there is an important phenomenon here for which a theory of self-knowledge must account. The phenomenon is this: I seem to be able to know various facts about my own mind simply by considering questions about the non-mental world. To obtain this knowledge, I look, as it were, not inward but outward. I will refer to knowledge of my own mental states that is available in this sort of way as *transparent self-knowledge*.

Evans regarded his observations as demystifying our capacity for certain kinds of privileged self-knowledge. It can seem mysterious how we are able to say what we believe without observing ourselves, even though we must observe another person to determine what she believes; but, Evans suggests, this should not seem strange once we recognize that a person can answer the question whether she believes *p* by 'putting into operation whatever procedure [she has] for answering the question whether *p*'. For where *p* is a proposition about the non-mental world, it is no surprise that a subject can answer the question whether *p* without needing evidence about her own psychology.

Many subsequent writers, however, have thought of Evans's observations, not primarily as providing the solution to a puzzle, but as presenting a puzzle in their own right. After all, where *p* is a proposition about the non-mental world, it is generally possible for it to be the case that *p* although I do not believe that *p*. Indeed, this is surely my actual situation for many values of *p*: I am very far from omniscient (or omnicredent, for that matter). And similarly, there are often states of affairs that hold in my environment although I do not perceive them: I am very far from omnipercipient. So what justifies me in answering such questions about my own psychology by looking to seemingly independent facts about the world?[5]

It will not suffice, as an answer to this question, simply to point out that the contents of our beliefs and perceptions are systematically related to the contents we would express in answering corresponding world-directed questions. This is certainly true, and it is part of what gives Evans's proposals their initial appeal, but it does not address the heart of the puzzle. If I reach the conclusion that there will be a third world war, or judge on the basis of perception that there is a table in front of me, I become cognizant of an apparent fact that is in fact the *topic* of a certain belief I hold or a certain perceptual experience I am having. But the procedures Evans outlines instruct me to lay claim to a further item of knowledge: knowledge *that I believe* that there will be a third world war or *that it perceptually appears to me* that there is a table strewn with papers in front of me.[6] It is this psychological knowledge whose warrant is in question, and the *problem of transparency* is that nothing in my apparent basis seems to supply a ground for it.

This problem of transparency has, in the last two decades, become a principal focus in discussions of self-knowledge, succeeding and to some extent supplanting more generic debates about the basis of 'first person authority', whether 'privileged access' is compatible with externalism about mental content, and so on. I believe this is a valuable development, not because those earlier debates were misconceived, but because focusing on transparency sharpens our sense of a crucial issue at stake in them. What is at stake is not merely how we know a certain special range of facts (viz., facts about our own present mental states), but how this variety of knowledge is related to our capacity to engage, theoretically and practically, with the non-mental world.

My aim in this essay is to propose a solution to the problem of transparency that speaks to this wider issue. The solution is inspired by Sartre's idea that all consciousness involves a form of 'non-positional' consciousness of our own consciousness. Sartre claimed, in effect, that our capacity to know our own minds is linked to our capacity to know the world because our awareness of the world constitutively involves a kind of implicit self-awareness, and that we draw on this awareness when we reflect. I want to suggest that this idea is the key to resolving the problem of transparency, and that appreciating its relevance to this problem is the key to seeing the truth in Sartre's somewhat darkly-expressed point.

I came to see the importance of Sartre's notion of non-positional self-consciousness while trying to clarify a distinction I had been led to draw, in earlier work (Boyle 2011), between 'tacit' knowledge of one's own mental states and explicit, reflective knowledge of those states. In order to bring out the motivation for Sartre's position, it will help to explain what led me to draw this distinction, and why I now think it must be clarified along Sartrean lines. So I will begin by describing how I arrived at my earlier position, and will situate it relative to three other prominent approaches to the problem of transparency. Seeing the strengths and weaknesses of these approaches will help us to see the point of Sartre's idea.

2. Transparency versus alienation: Moran

The prominence of the term 'transparency' as a label for the relation between questions about one's own mind and questions about the world is primarily due to Richard Moran's work, and his account of why the question whether I believe that p is (normally) transparent to the question whether p (henceforth, 'doxastic transparency') will provide us with a useful starting point, both because it is grounded in certain compelling observations about the character of transparent self-knowledge, and because the other approaches we will consider are framed in part as responses to Moran's position.

Moran famously holds that doxastic transparency is explained by the fact that we normally answer the question whether p by exercising our capacity to determine whether *to* believe that p. It is not the case, he observes, that one can always determine whether one believes p by answering the question whether p: there are occasions on which we can only discover our actual beliefs by observing ourselves, much as a spectator would. These are, however, pathological situations in which we are 'alienated' from our own beliefs, in the sense that we cannot regard these beliefs as governed by our conscious assessment of grounds for taking the relevant propositions to be true. When we are not thus alienated, Moran suggests, we are in a position to know whether we believe p by considering whether p precisely because such consideration settles (i.e., makes it the case) that we believe (or do not believe) p. It is this fact that resolves the puzzle of doxastic transparency:

> What right have I to think that my reflection on the reasons in favor of p (which is one subject-matter) has anything to do with the question of what my actual *belief* about p is (which is quite a different subject-matter)? Without a reply to this challenge, I don't have any right to answer the question that asks what my belief [about, e.g., whether it will rain] is by reflection on the reasons in favor of an answer concerning the state of the weather. And then

my thought at this point is: I *would* have a right to assume that my reflection on the reasons in favor of rain provided me with an answer to the question of what my belief about the rain is, if I could assume that *what* my belief here is was something determined by the conclusion of my reflection on those reasons. (Moran 2003, 405)

Moran summarizes his proposal by saying that I am in a position to have transparent knowledge of my own beliefs just insofar as I am entitled to address the question whether I believe that *p*, not as a 'theoretical' or 'speculative' question about what is (perhaps unbeknownst to me) the case with me, but as a 'deliberative' question about whether *to* believe *p* (cf. Moran 2001, 58, 63). In a slogan, our capacity to have transparent knowledge of our own beliefs rests on our capacity to 'make up our minds'.

It is hard to read Moran's work on doxastic transparency without feeling that he has put his finger on something important, but on closer scrutiny, it is difficult to say just what the insight is and how broadly it applies. For one thing, as a number of critics have pointed out, the phenomenon of transparency is not confined to conditions that can be brought about through deliberation.[7] As we noted earlier, questions about how things perceptually appear also seem to exhibit a kind of transparency to world-directed questions, as for that matter do questions about appetitive desire (e.g., whether I'm hungry can manifest itself in whether a cheeseburger looks delectable). These are not conditions we determine to exist on the basis of reasons: they are conditions to which the question 'What is your reason for X-ing?' does not apply. Whatever explains our entitlement, in these cases, to treat our answer to the relevant psychological question as transparent to a corresponding world-directed question, it surely isn't that we constitute such states by deliberating.

Furthermore, it is not easy to see how Moran's idea can supply a general account even of doxastic transparency. There are, after all, many beliefs of which we have transparent self-knowledge without (it seems) taking a deliberative stance toward them.[8] I believe, for instance, that the former U.S. President William Taft was born in my home state of Ohio, and doubtless I once had some basis for believing this, but I cannot now recall what it was. Did I see it on a plaque, or read it in a history book, or hear it from a teacher? I have no idea: at this point it just stands among the countless things I believe without having specific grounds. Nevertheless, my knowledge that I believe this surely meets the Transparency Condition: I can answer the psychological question whether I believe Taft was born in Ohio simply by deferring it to the factual question whether Taft was born in Ohio. Yet how could the idea that I take a 'deliberative stance' toward the question whether Taft was born in Ohio explain this? It is characteristic of my attitude that I do *not* regard this question as open to deliberation; my view is settled. And while it may be true that I would answer affirmatively to the question whether *to* believe that Taft was born in Ohio, my reason for doing so seems to be precisely my conviction that *Taft was born in Ohio*. So it seems that here, my answer to the question whether to believe this does not determine whether I believe it, but rather the reverse.

Finally, there is a crucial lacuna in Moran's proposal. Consider a case in which I deliberate about whether p and conclude: Yes, p. In so doing, I may in fact make it the case that I believe that p, but even if I do, what puts me in a position to *know* that I believe p? Moran's suggestion seems to be that my warrant for accepting *I believe that p* is connected with the fact that I have effectively concluded that *p is to be believed*, but it is not clear how this is supposed to carry me across the threshold to doxastic self-knowledge. Suppose for the sake of argument that my concluding 'Yes, p' is tantamount to my concluding: p is to be believed. This can surely be the case although I don't believe p. Indeed, as a imperfect being, this is presumably often my situation: there is something it would be right for me to believe, and yet I don't believe it. So it seems that the problem of transparency has not been resolved, just relocated. For what justifies me in answering a question about my own psychology on the basis of a seemingly independent fact about what is 'to be believed'? Moran's explanation of transparency thus does not close the crucial gap.

For all these reasons, Moran's account seems not fully satisfactory as it stands. Nevertheless, I believe it has at its foundation a compelling observation of which we should not lose sight. As we have seen, Moran contrasts the relation in which we stand to our own mental states when we can know them transparently with an alienated, 'spectatorial' relation to those states. He puts this point – focusing, as usual, on the case of belief – by observing that we can have transparent self-knowledge only of our conscious beliefs, and

> to call something a conscious belief says something about the *character* of the belief in question. It is not simply to say that the person stands in some relation of awareness to this belief... I see myself in this belief; my conscious belief forms the basis for my further train of thought about the thing in question. (Moran 1999, 188)

Moran goes on to argue that it is possible to know immediately and without observation that one holds a certain belief, and yet not *consciously* to hold the relevant belief. As an example, he asks us to consider an analysand who has so perfectly internalized the perspective of his psychoanalyst that he knows immediately what beliefs his analyst would attribute to him, and (rightly) ascribes those beliefs to himself, but does not consciously hold the beliefs in question.

I think there is a good point here, though the example is unnecessarily contentious. Whatever we think of the possibility of psychoanalytic knowledge of unconscious beliefs, we should admit that consciously believing p requires more than merely knowing, without observation or inference, that one believes p. To know that one believes (e.g.) that there will be a third world war requires only that one takes *one's own belief-state* to one to be of a certain kind. A person who *consciously* believes that there will be a third world war, by contrast, does not merely know herself to hold this view; she consciously inhabits the relevant viewpoint, in the sense that, when she thinks about the world-oriented question whether there will be a third world war, it seems to her that there will. Moran's insight is that transparent self-knowledge of a mental state is available just when the relevant mental state is conscious in this sense: the point of view one ascribes to oneself is the very one that one consciously inhabits, in such a way that the question of what one believes and the question of what is so fuse into one.

It seems to me that this point embodies an insight that is independent of Moran's more specific claims about the explanation of doxastic transparency. The insight is that transparent self-knowledge is not merely knowledge that can be had immediately and without self-observation; it is knowledge grounded in consciously inhabiting the relevant point of view, and as such contrasts with the knowledge of a spectator. A spectator might know that I believe that p, but it is one thing for her to know this about me and another for *her* consciously to see the world from the perspective of p-believer. If unconscious belief is possible, then it is also possible for me to stand in this sort of spectatorial relation to one of my own beliefs: I can know myself to believe that p, and yet not consciously inhabit the perspective of a p-believer. But at any rate, for a person who consciously believes that p, being aware of her own belief and seeing the world from the perspective of p-believer are two aspects of the same awareness. Such a person does not merely have a point of view on the world, on the one hand, and know of its existence, on the other. She consciously holds the relevant point of view, and can thus express both *belief that p* and *knowledge that she believes that p* in a single act, by saying 'I believe that p'. We can thus say that she knows her own belief from the perspective, not of a spectator, but of an inhabitant of the relevant point of view

This point can be accepted by philosophers who reject Moran's idea that the only alternative to a 'spectatorial stance' toward oneself is a 'deliberative stance'. It may be that Moran overestimates the closeness of the tie between being able to know one's mental states 'transparently' and treating those states as open to deliberation. Perhaps this opposition characterizes only certain kinds of attitudes, if it applies anywhere. Be that as it may, it remains true in general that our relation to mental states we can know transparently is not spectatorial. Perception can again serve as an example. People with normal perceptual awareness can, as Evans observed, have transparent knowledge of their own perceptual appearances. But consider a person with the kind of cerebral damage that produces 'blindsight'.[9] Blindsighted subjects do not consciously see what is presented in the 'blind' region of their visual field, but when prompted, they are able to perform perception-dependent tasks (for instance, making guesses about the features of objects in the blind field) with a better-than-chance rate of success. Such a subject stands in an alienated, spectatorial relation to her own seeing: she can say what she perceives only by drawing inferences from her own behavior (including her dispositions to make guesses about what is present in a certain region). But our normal relation to our visual appearances is not like this: it is not merely that we can know how things visually appear to us with an immediacy that is unavailable to the blindsighted person; it is that we consciously experience *the world* as containing objects with specific features, whereas she does not. Our knowledge of how things perceptually appear to us is thus not spectatorial: we are aware of these states *by inhabiting their perspective*, inasmuch as we consciously perceive the world around us to be a certain way.

At the same time, our knowledge of how things perceptually appear to us is obviously not deliberative: if we could deliberate about whether *to* have specific perceptual appearances, perception would not be the kind of cognitive power that it is. Moran's insight – that the availability of transparent self-knowledge marks a distinctively non-spectatorial mode of awareness of one's own mental states – thus applies more broadly than his emphasis on opposition between spectator and deliberator might lead one to suppose. This insight sets a condition of adequacy on accounts of transparent self-knowledge. I now want to argue that this is a condition some influential accounts of transparency fail to meet.

3. Transparency as inference from world to mind: Byrne

We observed earlier that there is a crucial gap in Moran's account of our warrant for moving from the judgment *p* to the judgment *I believe that p*: how does the former justify the latter? In seeking to fill this gap, there are two natural routes to explore. On the one hand, we might argue that our warrant derives somehow from what we consider: some (seeming) feature of the non-mental world. On the other hand, we might propose that it derives, not from what we consider, but from our consideration itself: some conscious mental state or process that occurs when we take up the relevant world-directed question. Each of these routes has in fact been explored, and I want to examine a prominent example of each approach – not simply for the sake of surveying the literature, but because I think that each approach has significant attractions, but that each also misses something crucial.

The first approach I will consider seeks resolutely to defend the idea that, when one has transparent self-knowledge, the basis on which one ascribes a mental state to oneself is, not any kind of awareness of one's own mind, but a purported awareness of a fact about the non-mental world. As we have noted, this idea is not easy to accept, for it is hard to see how a such a step could be warranted. Nevertheless, if such an approach could be defended, it would provide an elegant solution to the problem of transparency, for it would explain our capacity for non-observational self-knowledge without appealing to any special faculty of introspection or other pre-existing form of self-awareness. It would thus clarify Evans's attractive idea that the relevant knowledge can be acquired simply by looking 'outward', rather than 'inward' toward our own mental states.

An approach of this sort has been forcefully defended by Alex Byrne (2005, 2011, 2018). Byrne's account rests on a simple idea: that we can acquire transparent self-knowledge by making an 'inference from world to mind' (Byrne 2011, 203). In general, Byrne holds, our capacity for inference is a capacity to make rule-governed transitions between acceptance of some set of propositions and acceptance of some further proposition. The problem of transparency is that the relevant inferences – for instance, the *doxastic schema*

BEL: p

_____

I believe that p

look on their face as though they cannot yield knowledge, since their premises neither entail nor evidentially support their conclusions. But, Byrne suggests, this sort of objection to an inference-schema can be overcome if we can show that (1) inferring in accordance with the relevant schema reliably produces true beliefs and (2) such inferences are 'safe' in the technical sense that drawing this conclusion would not have produced false belief in any nearby possible world. If we could show this, and if we had no reason to suppose that BEL is *not* knowledge-conducive, we would, Byrne argues, be entitled to show deference to the view presupposed in our ordinary practice: that making such transitions is a way of coming to know what one believes.[10]

Byrne's project is thus first to identify inference-schemata corresponding to the kinds of mental states we can know transparently, and then to show that these schemata are 'neutral' (i.e., that their premises do not presuppose knowledge of the relevant mental states), reliable, and safe. If this can be shown, he holds, the problem of transparency will be solved, for we will have explained why the relevant inferences are, in spite of appearances, normally knowledge-conducive. Moreover, we will in the process have accounted for the fact that we can speak with special authority about the relevant mental states, and we will have given an attractively economical account of this authority: one that does not appeal to any special introspective faculty, but only to general cognitive capacities required also for other kinds of cognition.

In the case of belief, the relevant inference schema is plainly BEL, and it is easy to show that this schema is safe and reliable. A subject will be in a position to infer according to BEL only if she accepts the premise: p. But this amounts to saying that she will be in a position to apply the rule only if she believes that p, and this ensures that her conclusion will be sound, whether her premise is true or false. In other cases the relevant inference-schema is less obvious, and the argument to its reliability and safety is less direct; but suffice it to say that Byrne makes a forceful case for the claim that, when their application is appropriately restricted, inferences such as the following are neutral, reliable, and safe:

SEE: $\quad$ $[\ldots x \ldots]_V$ & x is an F $\qquad$ INT: $\quad$ I will ϕ

I see an F[11] $\qquad\qquad$ I intend to ϕ[12]

By demonstrating that such analyses can be given in a wide variety of cases, Byrne (2018) seeks to show that the 'inference from world to mind' approach applies wherever transparent self-knowledge is possible.

Although I believe there is a great deal to learn from Byrne's analyses of particular relations of transparency, I think his general account of such transparency implies an unacceptably alienated, spectatorial picture of the subject's relation to her own mental states. To bring this out, I will raise two objections, which highlight different but related aspects this problem.[13]

First, it seems to me that Byrne's approach does not explain the rational intelligibility of these world-to-mind inferences from the subject's own standpoint. Our capacity for (personal level) inference is a capacity to arrive at new beliefs in virtue of seeing one or more (seeming) fact as supplying some sort of *reason* to accept some further proposition as true. The conclusions we reach through inference are not just beliefs that appear unaccountably in our minds; they are convictions for which we take ourselves to have a reason, and this is what makes them sustainable in the face of the capacity for critical scrutiny that belongs to rational subjects as such. What makes Byrne's BEL-inference problematic, it seems to me, is not merely the concern that it would be unreliable or unsafe, but a concern about how a subject who draws such inferences could herself understand them to be reasonable. I cannot see how Byrne's account speaks to this problem.

150 TRANSPARENCY AND APPERCEPTION

Suppose for the sake of argument that a subject concludes that she believes *p* by inferring according to BEL. Let her now ask herself what her grounds are for accepting that she believes *p*. Citing the ostensible fact that *p* sheds no light: this has no tendency to show that that she believes that *p*, as Byrne admits. What would support the subject's conclusion, of course, is the fact that she herself is ready treat *p* as a premise from which to draw inferences. But to represent *this* as her ground for accepting that she believes *p* would be, in effect, to presuppose that she already knows her own mind on the matter, and thus would undermine Byrne's account, which requires the premise of the BEL-inference to be neutral. So Byrne's approach appears to face a dilemma: either it represents the subject as drawing an inference that she should find rationally unintelligible, or else it requires her to have a kind of ground that would undermine the basic idea of the approach.[14]

Moreover – and this is my second objection – reflection on particular cases of transparency suggests that the cognitive transitions we make are not in fact transitions from *sheer* propositions about the world to propositions about the subject's own mental states. To see what I mean by saying that the relevant premises are not 'sheer' propositions about the world, consider the transition from

(1) I will ϕ

to

(2) I intend to ϕ.

I think Byrne is right that if a person judges (1), on a certain sort of basis, this also warrants her in judging (2). This would constitute a vindication for Byrne's approach, however, only if her grounds for so judging were neutral, in the sense that their availability did not presuppose an awareness of her own intentions. Now, (1) is superficially neutral: it does not refer explicitly to the subject's present mental state. But if we think carefully about the kinds of circumstances in which someone might, on the basis of thinking (1), be warranted in thinking (2), we will see that a quite special use of 'will' must be at issue here.

Let us stipulatively define a special 'intention-based' sense of 'will', 'will$_I$', whose use in joining a subject with an action-verb expresses a present intention so to act. We can distinguish 'will$_I$' from a 'will' of blank futurity ('will$_{BF}$'), which merely asserts that the subject will at some future time do something, leaving it open what makes this the case. In the 'will$_I$'-sense, it might be true that *I will walk to work tomorrow* (as I now intend), but false that *I will fall and break my leg tomorrow*, even if of these propositions are both true when 'will' is read in the 'will$_{BF}$'-sense. Now we can ask: in cases where one can move

TRANSPARENCY AND APPERCEPTION 151

transparently from (1) to (2), is the 'will' in (1) 'will$_I$' or 'will$_{BF}$'? Certainly the step is warranted if the 'will' is 'will$_I$': in this case, (2) just unpacks what the subject is already committed to in accepting that she will ϕ. But the step looks much harder to understand if her basis is simply a conviction that she will$_{BF}$ ϕ. Suppose I believe I have been subjected to hypnotic suggestion, and that as a result, when a bell rings, I will$_{BF}$ begin to cluck like a hen. It would be strange to infer from this that I now intend to cluck; and it would be no less strange, perhaps moreso, if my premonition that I will$_{BF}$ do such a thing were ground-less. Yet it looks as though, in such a case, Byrne's INT-schema would encourage me to infer: I intend to cluck like a hen.

The INT-schema thus does not distinguish between convictions about my own future grounded in present intention and convictions about my future that are simply groundless. Once we recognize this, I think the INT-inference looks much less attractive. A plausible hypothesis about what grounds its initial appeal is that we are disposed to read its premise in the charitable way, as

(1a) I will$_I$ ϕ.[15]

But if my normal basis for judging that I intend to ϕ is a conviction that (1a), then although my basis is superficially neutral, it is not genuinely neutral: it presupposes an implicit awareness on my part of what I intend to do. I am, we might say, presupposing that this aspect of my future is mine to decide. Thus my basis for this self-ascription is a judgment about the world, but not a judgment *sheerly* about the world. It is, rather, a judgment about my future that presupposes something about my own cognitive relation to this future.

A plausible story about some of my beliefs about my own future is this: I hold them precisely because I *consciously intend* to make them true. These beliefs express 'practical knowledge' (or at any rate, practical con-viction) about my own future: they do not involve a spectatorial or predictive attitude toward my own future, but a consciousness of this aspect of the future as mine to determine in virtue of my power to choose what I will$_I$ do. Byrne's account, however, posits the contrary order of epistemic dependence: on the basis of a sheer belief about what what I will$_{BF}$ do, I reach a conclusion about what I now intend to do. It seems to me that this would leave me with a knowledge of my own intentions that was palpably self-alienated. For such knowledge would be grounded, not in my seeing a certain act as in my power and regarding it as the thing to do, but simply in my supposing that it will in fact come to pass that I so act. Even if we grant for the sake of argument that an inference to what I intend on this sort of basis could give me knowledge that I intend to ϕ, it seems clear that it would not supply me with me an *agent's perspective* on my future φ-ing: I would not be in a position to see the matter as settled *because* I so settle it.

I believe versions of these problems can be raised in every case to which Byrne applies his account. Both problems arise from the same basic feature of his approach: his resolute insistence that, when we transparently ascribe mental states to ourselves, we do not rely on any awareness of our own minds, but only on a sheer (purported) awareness of facts about the non-mental world. The result of this insistence is, first, that the subject is left without a satisfactory understanding of the rational connection between her self-ascription and its basis; and second, that her relation to the mental state she ascribes is rendered alienated and spectatorial. Even if we grant that she can know *that* she is in the certain state in this way, she does not seem to know it *from a participant's perspective*, as it were: she takes the world to be a certain way and on this basis *supposes* herself to be in a certain mental state, rather than consciously experiencing the state *in* the way she takes the world to be.

To avoid such alienation, it seems that we must reject Byrne's uncompromising insistence on a transition from sheer awareness of the non-mental world to awareness of the subject's own mental state, and allow instead that the subject's basis for her self-ascription draws on some sort of awareness of her own mind. The next view I want to consider seeks to account for transparent self-knowledge in this way.

4. Transparency as inference from judgment to belief: Peacocke

If transparent self-knowledge cannot be satisfactorily explained by an inference from a sheer proposition about the world, it seems that it must draw on some pre-existing awareness of our minds. To focus once again on the case of belief: the idea must be that, although the question on which the subject reflects is whether *p*, her transition to the self-ascription *I believe that p* depends not merely on her (seeming) awareness that *p*, but on some sort of awareness of her own consideration of the question. Christopher Peacocke (1998, 2008) has defended such a view of transparent self-ascriptions of belief. As we will see, however, the way Peacocke conceives of this approach generates a form of alienation no less problematic than the one we found in Byrne's view. Seeing this problem will sharpen our sense of what sort of self-awareness a satisfactory solution must invoke, and how this awareness must relate to the subject's 'outward-looking' awareness of the world.

According to Peacocke, a subject's ability to determine whether she believes that *p* by considering whether *p* rests on her awareness of her own act of *judgment* in response to the latter question. Judgment, Peacocke holds, is a phenomenally conscious act.[16] Hence when a subject judges that *p*, she will be conscious, not merely of the (apparent) fact that *p*, but also of her own act of judging that *p*. This consciousness will in turn warrant her in self-ascribing a belief that *p*, since the act of judging that *p* normally expresses belief that *p* (if such a belief already exists) or produces belief that *p* (if it does not yet exist). Peacocke admits, however, that these connections do not hold universally: sometimes an act of judgment does not express or produce a standing belief. Nevertheless, he maintains, consciousness of judging that *p* is a normally reliable indicator that one believes that *p*, so when a subject has no special reason to doubt that her situation is normal, she may justifiably self-ascribe a belief that *p* on this basis. Moreover, provided her self-ascription is true, she may thereby come to know what she believes.[17]

This seems to me a natural alternative to Byrne's interpretation of doxastic transparency. It rejects the idea that the subject's basis for self-ascribing a belief is sheer awareness that *p*, and holds instead that her basis is awareness of a mental event: *her judging that p*.[18] This is certainly a possible interpretation of the phenomenon Evans described: it might be that I learn what I believe *by* considering a question about the non-mental world, but this 'look outward' warrants me in self-ascribing a belief only because it results in a consciousness of my own act of judgment. This indeed is how Peacocke sees the matter: he holds that his account 'should not be regarded as in competition with' the method described by Evans, since, just as Evans says, it is by 'putting into operation my procedure for answering the question whether *p*' that I come to have a basis for self-ascribing a belief (Peacocke 1998, 72–3).

In spite of its naturalness, I think this account mischaracterizes something crucial about our cognitive relation to our own beliefs. We can see what is odd about it by once again considering the matter from the standpoint of a subject trying to understand her own reason for taking herself to believe that *p*. What can she say to herself?

It is essential to Peacocke's account that the step from consciously judging that *p* to knowing one's own belief that *p* be a step from one item of awareness to another, distinct item of awareness. His view, as we have seen, is that awareness of judging is a normally reliable indicator of belief that *p*, but one that can be present in the absence of such an underlying belief.[19] For my part, I am skeptical of the intelligibility of this notion of conscious judgment. After all, not just any event of consciously entertaining the content that *p* is a case of judging that *p*. If I entertain the notion of *p*'s being the case merely for the sake of argument, or in a counterfactual spirit, I have not thereby expressed conviction in the truth of *p*, and so presumably I have not judged. Judging that *p* requires not merely inwardly affirming that *p* (whatever that might mean), but affirming *p* *in the conviction that p is true*. And it is hard to see how this can mean anything less than: it requires inwardly expressing one's belief that *p*. But then it is hard to see how my consciousness of judging that *p* can provide me with an independently-available ground for believing that I believe that *p*. If I am fallible about whether I believe that *p*, then for the same reason I am fallible about whether I (genuinely) judge that *p*: my warrant for the latter must include my warrant, whatever it may be, for the former

Let us suppose, however, that there is such a thing as the phenomenology of judgment: a phenomenal profile characteristic of judging that *p*, which can be present even when no corresponding belief exists. Could such phenomenology give me a reason to self-ascribe the belief that *p*? My grip on the idea is not firm enough for me to argue with confidence that it could not; but it seems to me clear that, if it did, it would at best put me in a position to have an alienated, spectatorial knowledge of my own belief. To see this, recall that the relevant phenomenal profile is supposed to be one I can be aware of while leaving it open whether I genuinely believe the proposition in question: it is a normally reliable indicator of belief that *p*, but one consistent with its absence. On the basis of this indication, in the absence of a reason to think my situation abnormal, I am supposed to be warranted in self-ascribing the belief that *p*. So do I in fact believe *p*? 'Well,' I really ought to answer, 'it's very likely.' If I assert 'I believe that *p*' on this sort of basis, it is surely a speculation about myself, not a conscious expression of conviction that *p*. In locating my ground for self-ascribing a belief in a fallible indicator of belief, Peacocke's account drives a wedge between my consciously taking *p* to be true (which I express in judging that *p*) and my knowledge that I believe *p* (which I infer from, but am not entitled to identify with, my conscious judgment that *p*). What I can acquire by this method, if anything, is a bit of information about myself, not a consciously held stance on the question whether *p*.

If this is right, then Peacocke's account has failed to meet the constraint we drew from our discussion of Moran. For this reason, I think Peacocke's approach lost hold of the true spirit of Evans's observation, even if it fits the letter of his account. Genuinely transparent self-knowledge is not merely arrived at *by* considering whether *p*; it remains a mode of knowing *in* which I (self-consciously) look outward. This, I believe, is the deeper sense in which our knowledge of our own minds can be transparent: not merely that it can be *based* on a consideration of the world, but that it can *consist* simply in a self-conscious stance toward the world, not an independent knowledge *of* one's holding such a stance.

5. The reflectivist approach

I have objected to Byrne's idea that a subject's basis for transparent self-knowledge is a *sheer* proposition about the world, and also to Peacocke's idea that her basis is a conscious event that serves as an *indicator* of her own belief. For different reasons, I have argued, each of these accounts could at best provide the subject with an alienated knowledge of her own mind. I believe, however, that there is an insight worth preserving in each approach. In effect, Byrne is right in his resolute insistence that transparent self-knowledge must look outward, while Peacocke is right to think that its basis must not be a sheer awareness of the world. But can there be a kind of awareness that satisfies both of these demands?

In earlier work (Boyle 2011), I tried to argue that there can. The interpretation of transparent self-knowledge I proposed, which I called 'reflectivist', holds that we are warranted in self-ascribing mental states on the basis of a consideration of the world because there is already a kind of self-awareness implicit in the relevant ways of representing the world. I put this by saying that the existence of the relevant mental states (perception, belief, intention, etc.) itself involves the subject's 'tacit knowledge' of their existence, so that all the subject needs to do to achieve explicit knowledge of these states is to *reflect* on what she already knows. On this view, the subject's step is not, as Byrne suggests, an inference from a sheer fact about the non-mental world to fact about her own psychology; nor is it, as Peacocke proposes, a transition from consciousness of one mental event to knowledge of another, distinct mental state. It is not an acquisition of new knowledge, but simply a reflective articulation of an awareness that was already involved in the subject's regarding the world in a certain way.

I continue to think that only an approach along these lines can satisfactorily explain transparent self-knowledge, but I am no longer satisfied with the account I gave of reflectivism. The crucial problem lies in making sense of the idea of tacit knowledge. For on the one hand, if a subject already *knows* (e.g.) that she believes that *p*, mustn't this involve her representing herself as believing that *p*? But then in what sense can this knowledge be 'tacit', other than the inconsequential sense that she has not yet verbalized it? And on the other hand, if the subject's knowledge that she believes *p* is truly *tacit*, in what sense can she be said already know this at all? States of knowledge are standardly thought to be individuated by their propositional objects. If a subject does not yet know 'explicitly' that she believes that *p*, what can this mean but that she does not yet possess this particular piece of knowledge? The notion of tacit knowledge thus appears to be in internal tension with itself. Yet appeal to this notion is crucial to the reflectivist position, for only in this way do reflectivists capture the distinction between the cognitive state of a subject who merely has the potential to reflect on a certain belief she holds and the state of a subject who has actually done so.

The reflectivist's claim that belief involves tacit knowledge of belief is also problematic for another reason. Knowledge is commonly assumed to be subject to the following Concept Possession Requirement:

> (CPR) A subject can know that p only if she possesses the concepts necessary for understanding the proposition that p.

If the tacit knowledge invoked by reflectivism were subject to (CPR), then the reflectivist would be committed to holding that a subject can have beliefs only if she possesses the concept of belief. But this is an implausibly strong intellectual requirement on belief. The *concept* of belief seems to be a fairly sophisticated attainment, the first step toward an abstract understanding of what it is to believe, whereas it seems that quite unreflective persons, not to mention young children and nonhuman animals, can have beliefs and act intelligently on the basis of them. So it seems the reflectivist should hold that our 'tacit knowledge' of belief is not subject to (CPR). But if we sever the link between ascribing knowledge that one believes that p and ascribing grasp of the concept *belief*, we make it much less clear what this ascription comes to. Just what does it mean to say that the subject 'tacitly knows' this?

6. Sartre and reflectivism

The reflectivist thus faces formidable challenges, but he is not alone in his predicament. Jean-Paul Sartre's distinction between 'positional' and 'non-positional' self-consciousness grew out of an attempt to respond to a structurally similar set of challenges. Some might doubt whether much help can be expected from this sort of companion, but I want to argue that Sartre's distinction is in fact of great value in responding to the problems noted above.

The positional/non-positional distinction belongs to Sartre's broader enterprise of characterizing 'consciousness', the mode of being characteristic of the entity he calls 'the for-itself'. We can introduce the distinction by explicating four fundamental propositions about consciousness asserted in the Introduction to *Being and Nothingness* (1943):

> (S1) "All consciousness [*conscience*] ... is consciousness *of* something. This means that there is no consciousness that is not a *positing* [*position*] of a transcendent object" (BN li/17).

> (S2) "[A]ll knowing consciousness [*conscience connaissante*] can be knowledge [*connaissance*] of nothing but its object" (BN lii/18).

(S3) "[A]ll positional consciousness of an object is at the same time non-positional consciousness of itself" (BN liii/19).

(S4) "[I]t is the non-reflective consciousness [*conscience non-réflexive*] that makes reflection possible" (BN liii/19).

(S1) is a point that Sartre credits to Husserl: it captures his idea that the defining trait of the psychic aspect of our existence – 'consciousness' being Sartre's generic term for the mode of being of the psychic – is its intentionality, its being *of* or *about* some object distinct from the relevant state consciousness itself.[20] In this sense, consciousness 'transcends' itself to posit a realm of being beyond itself. 'Positing' is Sartre's term for the relation of consciousness to its object (i.e., that which we would specify in specifying what it is a consciousness of: an 'object' in the broadest sense). Consciousness is said to be 'positional' inasmuch as it is of or about an object.

Sartre does not think that all positional consciousness consists in knowing an object – there are other modes of positing, such as imagining, desiring, and so on – but he does regard knowing as a species of positional consciousness: it is a kind of relation in which consciousness can stand to a posited object. That object, and only that object, is what the relevant consciousness is knowledge *of*. This is the thought expressed in (S2).

The crucial point for our purposes is (S3): all positional consciousness of an object involves non-positional consciousness of that very state of consciousness. 'Non-positional' consciousness is supposed to be a mode of awareness that does *not* posit that of which it is aware as its intentional object. This may sound like a paradox: how can there be a consciousness of something that does not posit that thing, if to posit a thing just is to relate to it in such a way that one is conscious *of* it?[21] Sartre argues, however, that there must be such a non-positional awareness of consciousness if there is to be positional consciousness of objects:

> [T]he necessary and sufficient condition for a knowing consciousness to be knowledge *of* its object is that it be consciousness of itself as being this knowing. This is a necessary condition: if my consciousness were not consciousness of being conscious of the table, then it would be consciousness of the table without consciousness of being such, i.e., a consciousness ignorant of itself, an unconscious consciousness – which is absurd. It is a sufficient condition: that I am conscious of being conscious of this table suffices for me in fact to be conscious of it. (BN lii/18)

Sartre thus holds the that to deny the existence of non-positional consciousness of consciousness is absurd: this would be to posit an 'unconscious consciousness', which is a contradiction in terms.

I suspect most contemporary philosophers would not think much of this argument. They would reply that the notion of an 'unconscious consciousness' may sound self-contradictory, but if it just consists in consciousness of an *object* without some sort of consciousness of *that very state of consciousness*, then there is really no contradiction. To insist otherwise is to beg the question. I sympathize with this response, but I think it is possible to make a more forceful case for (S3) than Sartre does here. I will turn to this task shortly. First, however, a brief remark about (S4). We have seen that Sartre holds positional consciousness of an object to depend on non-positional consciousness (of) consciousness. (S4) adds that *reflective* consciousness of our own mental states, in which we 'posit' these states as objects of knowledge in their own right, is made possible by the presence, prior to reflection, of another kind of self-awareness: a non-positional consciousness that belongs intrinsically to the relevant conscious states. Sartre holds that, when we reflect, it is this non-positional consciousness that we draw on and make explicit.

My 'reflectivist' approach resembled Sartre's view in that I also held our capacity for explicit, reflective knowledge of our own mental states to be grounded in another, more basic mode of awareness. I called this more basic awareness 'tacit knowledge', but I have come to think it better to follow Sartre in calling it 'non-positional consciousness', reserving the term 'knowledge' for an awareness that posits its object. To suggest that (e.g.) belief involves *knowledge* of belief raises all the difficulties noted earlier, and adding that the relevant knowledge is 'tacit' does not make clear how to avoid them. Characterizing the relevant awareness as 'non-positional consciousness' does not by itself provide the needed clarification, but it at least marks the spot where clarification is needed. I now want to argue that we can begin to clarify the nature of such non-positional consciousness by connecting it with the problem of transparency.

7. Non-positional consciousness and transparency

As a first illustration of how the notion of non-positional consciousness might bear on the problem of transparency, consider again transparent knowledge of one's own intentions, which we discussed earlier in connection with Byrne.

Byrne plausibly observes that a person can sometimes be warranted in answering a question about whether she intends to ϕ simply by treating it as transparent to a question about her own future: whether she will ϕ. I argued, however, that if such a transition is to give me non-alienated knowledge of my own intention, the 'will' in the question 'Will I ϕ?' must be, not 'will$_{BF}$', but 'will$_I$': a way of thinking of the future that expresses the present intention so to act. My basis for ascribing an intention to ϕ to myself is thus:

TRANSPARENCY AND APPERCEPTION

(1a) I will$_I$ φ.

(1a) is a specific way of thinking that I will φ, namely one that (as we theorists may put it) presents the relevant future action as settled by my present intention to φ. Nevertheless, thinking (1a) is not equivalent to thinking

(1b) I will$_{BF}$ φ in virtue of the fact that I now intend to φ.

If thinking (1a) amounted to thinking (1b), then only subjects who possessed the concept of intention and the concept of whatever relation is signified by 'in virtue of' could think (1a). But this would be an implausible intellectual requirement: surely a person may be capable of thinking about her future in a way informed by her intentions without having mastered special psychological concepts that mark her relation to the relevant future acts. Moreover – and this seems to me the deeper objection – (1b) does not capture the distinctive stance toward my future φ-ing that is expressed in (1a). For (1b) simply asserts a connection between two facts, one about the present (that I intend to φ) and another about the future (that I will$_{BF}$ φ). But it is clearly possible for me to think that such a connection obtains without thereby expressing the intention to *bring it about* that I φ expressed by (1a). (1a) does not merely posit, from a spectatorial standpoint, that a present mental state of mine will cause me to φ; it expresses a practical intent to φ. No mere claim about the relation between my present and my future, however complex, can express this sort of distinctively practical attitude unless it contains some element like 'will$_I$', which expresses the distinctively practical mode of the relevant thought.[22]

Thus, when I think (1a), I do not explicitly ascribe an intention to myself; rather, I think that I will φ in a manner that implicitly presupposes such an intention. The fact that I now intend to do this is, we might say, expressed 'non-positionally' in (1a): it is not made explicit in my thought, but it is also not something to which I am oblivious. My awareness of it will come out in the specific kinds of grounds I consider for propositions like (1a), and the specific kinds of consequences I draw from them. My grounds will speak primarily to the desirability of φ-ing, rather than to the evidential question whether it will be the case that I φ. And I will draw consequences, not about what I am *likely* to do, but about what else I must do in order to φ and how my φ-ing should affect my other plans. I will, in short, treat such propositions in ways which indicate that I understand them to express decisions rather than mere predictions. But this understanding will be expressed, not in my explicitly thinking *I intend to φ*, but in my distinctive way of thinking of my future φ-ing. I hope this example begins to clarify what, concretely, it could mean for positional consciousness of some aspect of the world (in this case, an aspect of my own future) to involve non-positional consciousness of one's present state of consciousness.

Now consider a person who makes the transition from

(1a) I will$_1$ ϕ

to

(2) I intend to ϕ.

The reasonableness of this transition is evident. A person who soundly thinks (1a) already thinks of her future ϕ-ing in a way that implies a present intention to ϕ: her judging (2) just makes this implication explicit. What she must understand in order justifiably to make the transition from (1a) to (2) is simply that the way of thinking of her future involved in (1a) implies a present intention to ϕ. But this is to say that she does not need any further information about her present psychological state beyond what is already contained in (1a). All she needs is a grasp of this condition of application of the concept *intention* itself.

Where this is the case – where a subject's manner of thinking of the world is such that she requires only general competence with a certain psychological concept in order to know, on this basis, that she is in a certain psychological state – I will say that the subject is in a position to know her own psychological state by *reflection*. A reflective transition is not an inference from premises that are 'neutral' in Byrne's sense: accepting the relevant premises presupposes a kind of awareness of one's own psychological state, but this is a *non-positional* awareness, which does not involve application of a psychological concept. Nevertheless, such awareness can warrant a psychological self-ascription, for the application of the relevant concept just makes explicit a consciousness that was already implicit in the corresponding way of thinking of the world.

Turn now to transparent knowledge of one's own perceptual experiences. Consider a subject who makes a transition from the world-oriented observation

(3) This cat is purring.

to the reflective thought

(4) I perceive a purring cat.

How can this be a reasonable transition, given that it is one thing for a cat to be purring and another for me to perceive it? Well, consider the way the cat is represented in (3): it is presented as available for *demonstrative* reference, expressible using a 'this'. Now, an object is available to a given subject for this sort of demonstrative reference only in specific kinds of circumstances. Although a cat may be purring, I cannot successfully think of it as *this cat* when it is miles away, or hidden behind a screen, or known to me only by hearsay. Philosophers commonly call such a 'this' a 'perceptual demonstrative' precisely because it expresses a mode of demonstration that is available just when the relevant object is perceived.

A subject will have the capacity to refer to objects in this way just if she is sensitive to whether she presently perceives the object in question, in a way that enables her to keep track of it and distinguish it from other objects.[23] Nevertheless, a subject who thinks (3) on the basis of perceptual consciousness does not think *that she perceives* the relevant cat: the only object she thinks about is the cat. Nor is her way of thinking of the cat is reducible to a proposition about her own mental state conjoined with a sheer proposition about her environment, as in

(3b) There is a purring cat is here and I perceive it.

(3b) does not capture the distinctively singular mode of presentation of a cat expressed by 'this cat': it represents the subject as having a nonsingular, merely existential thought about a cat that meets a certain description. By contrast, a subject who thinks (3) thinks *de re* about a certain cat, although her manner of thinking about this cat presupposes that she perceives it. We might therefore say that her perceptual relation to the cat is expressed 'non-positionally' in her thought: it is not posited, but it is a presupposition of the soundness of what is posited.

So again, we have a mode of consciousness of the world that is possible only in virtue of non-positional consciousness of one's own consciousness. And if the subject goes on to think the reflective thought

(4) I perceive a purring cat

she will be making explicit a psychological state whose presence was already presupposed in her world-directed representation of the cat.[24] To acquire knowledge of her own perceptual state in this way, a subject need only understand the relationship between this special demonstrative mode of presentation of non-mental objects and her own perceptual state. Such a subject will thus be in a position to achieve *reflective* knowledge of her own perceptual state, provided that she grasps the general relationship between this mode of presentation and her own perceptual state. Provided she grasps this application-condition for the concept *perceives*, she will not need to draw on any further information about her present psychological state beyond what is already contained in (3). What justifies her reflective step is, however, not the sheer fact that a certain cat is purring – supposing that is so – but her *non-positional* consciousness of

162 TRANSPARENCY AND APPERCEPTION

her own manner of apprehending this fact, which is expressed in her manner of thinking of the cat.

Consider finally the case of belief. Suppose I wonder whether there will be a third world war and reach the alarming conclusion that

(5) There will be a third world war.

What I conclude here is a proposition about the non-mental world, but my manner of representing this proposition differs from the way I would represent it if I were merely supposing (5) for the sake of argument, imagining a possible world in which it held true, etc. Moreover, subjects who can deliberate competently about factual questions must have an implicit awareness of their manner of representing such propositions. For such subjects must be able to distinguish between propositions represented in the assertoric mode of belief and those represented in other modes. In particular, they must be able to distinguish between a factual question being open and its being closed: between the attitude toward p involved in considering *whether p* and the attitude involved in settling this question one way or another.

Now consider the kind of openness and closure that are at issue here. Suppose a person regards it as an open question whether there will be a third world war. In what sense does she regard this matter as unsettled? Not in the sense that she must regard the truth of the question as metaphysically indeterminate: she may suppose that there is a perfectly determinate fact of the matter, which she aims to discover. The sense in which she regards the question as open is rather an epistemic one: she regards it as still open *for her*, i.e., a question to which *she* possesses no determinate answer. This is not to say that she must think of herself and her own epistemic situation as such: she need only think of the proposition p in an interrogative mode, as it were. But her manner of thinking of this question distinguishes between a kind of openness which is in fact an openness from her epistemic standpoint and a contrasting form of closure which is in fact closure from her standpoint. When things go well, the latter mode of representation amounts to her knowing whether p; but whether things go well or not, representing the question as closed implies that her own *belief* on the question is settled.

The point here is not merely that the subject's answer to the question whether p expresses a belief she holds, but that she herself already implicitly distinguishes between this mode of representation and a contrasting non-committal mode. She might mark this distinction by using modal verbs in a way that expresses epistemic possibility, so that

(5) There *will be* a third world war

expresses closure of the question from her standpoint while

(6) There *might be* a third world war.

expresses openness. But however she marks it, this is a distinction that she will, as a competent deliberator, implicitly recognize. We might therefore say that in concluding that there will be a third world war, she expresses a *non-positional* consciousness of her own belief: an awareness that figures, not as the object of her thought, but as the necessary background of her thinking of the question of whether there will be a third world war as settled.

If the deliberating subject then goes on to think the reflective thought

(7) I believe that there will be a third world war

she will be making her attitude on the question explicit, but this awareness was already implicit in her world-directed representation of the likelihood of a third world war. To acquire reflective knowledge of her own doxastic state in this way, she need only understand the relationship between a certain mode of presentation of a worldly state of affairs and her own state of belief. And again, what justifies her reflective step will be, not the sheer thought that there will be a third world war, but her non-positional consciousness of her own stance on this question.[25]

8. Conclusion

Let me conclude by noting some advantages of this Sartrean approach to the problem of transparency.

In the first place, this approach allows us to reconcile Byrne's idea that transparent self-knowledge is grounded simply in a consideration of the world with Peacocke's thought that such knowledge must draw on some sort of awareness of our own psychological state. Sartre's idea of non-positional consciousness is the key to this reconciliation: it shows how a look outward can itself presuppose awareness of one's own psychological state without foregrounding this awareness in a way that severs the link between the subject's awareness of her own mental state and her first-order perspective on the world.

By the same token, the Sartrean approach explains why Moran is right to insist that transparent self-ascriptions of mental states express a non-spectatorial knowledge these states. For on the Sartrean view, as we have seen, transparent mental state ascriptions simply make explicit a mode of awareness that is already implicit in the corresponding outward-looking awareness of the world. Hence transparent self-knowledge cannot leave open the question whether the world is as one represents it to be; it can only be a self-conscious look outward.

Finally, the Sartrean approach enables us respond to the concern that reflectivism imposes implausibly strong intellectual requirements on belief, perception, intention, etc. We can admit that a subject might (e.g.) believe that *p* without possessing the concept of belief, for on our Sartrean view, the consciousness of believing involved in belief does not take the form of a *positional* representation of oneself *as* believing, but of a *non-positional* awareness implicit in a certain manner of representing a worldly state of affairs as obtaining. This non-positional self-awareness does not 'posit' the believer herself as a topic of knowledge or represent her condition as being of a certain kind, but provided she possesses the relevant concepts, it enables her to make a warranted self-ascriptive judgment when she reflects. Once we recognize this point, we see the need for a new kind of inquiry into self-knowledge: not an investigation of how we are in a position to know our own minds at all, but an inquiry into the nature of the reflective act by which we transform a necessary non-positional self-awareness into an explicit *knowledge* of ourselves.

Sartre's *Being and Nothingness* is, in effect, an extended investigation of this topic, and it is worth noting how his distinction between non-positional self-consciousness and reflective self-knowledge is connected with another great Sartrean theme, the perpetual threat of self-alienation that characterizes our lives as conscious subjects. A major source of resistance to approaches that represent our minds as essentially self-aware, I think, is the belief that they cannot do justice to the depth and ubiquity of this threat. But precisely because it distinguishes between non-positional self-consciousness and reflective self-knowledge, Sartre's approach can readily acknowledge the many ways in which our reflective self-understanding can distort the reality of our psychic lives, both in the more prosaic sense that it can fail to appreciate the facts, and in the more profound sense that it can involve a kind of 'bad faith' in which there is no stable fact to know. An adequate treatment of this theme would need to consider how our capacity for reflection is the ground both of the possibility of bad faith, and also of the conceivability of a project of authenticity. But these are topics for another essay.[26]

Notes

1. Sartre (1943), 40-41/23-24 I give page references to works by Sartre first in a standard English translation and then, after a slash mark, in a contemporary French edition (Sartre (1943), (1966). I have occasionally modified translations without comment.
2. I will assume that these ways of answering questions about our own mental states are normally ways of coming to *know* our own minds. If there are grounds for denying this, all the substantive points in this essay could be reformulated (more cumbersomely) to accommodate the point. For brevity,

I will sometimes just speak of 'the world' rather than 'the non-mental world'. This is simply an abbreviation: I do not deny that the world broadly conceived includes my present mental states.

3. Cf. Byrne (2011), Setiya (2012).

4. Cf. Moran (2001), Byrne (2012).

5. This question is pressed by Gallois (1996), Moran (2001), and Byrne (2018), among others.

6. The difference between knowing the content of one's attitudes and knowing that one holds the attitudes is forcefully emphasized by Dretske (2003), (2012).

7. Cf. Byrne (2005), 85, Finkelstein (2001), Postscript, and Bar-On (2004), Ch. 4.

8. Cf. Byrne (2005), 84–5 and Shah and Velleman (2005), 205–6.

9. For purposes of making my point, I will rely on the simplified understanding of the blindsight commonly discussed by philosophers. For an account of the phenomenon in its full complexity, see Weiskrantz (1986).

10. Cf. Byrne (2005), 96–8; Byrne (2011), 206–7.

11. Byrne (2012). '[... x ...]$_V$' is supposed to be a 'v-proposition': a proposition ascribing to x only properties characteristically available to vision (shape, orientation, depth, color, shading, movement, etc.).

12. Byrne (2011). The INT-rule is supposed to be defeasible, and the subject must refrain from drawing it if he takes himself to believe that he will ϕ on the basis of good evidence that he will ϕ. For a related proposal, see Setiya (2012).

13. These remarks expand on points made in Boyle (2011).

14. If we grant for the sake of argument that there could be a rational subject who was disposed to make cognitive transitions according to Byrne's BEL-schema, I suppose such a subject could come to appreciate Byrne's arguments for the claim that this inferential disposition is reliable and safe, and then she could have a kind of second-order approval of her disposition to make the BEL inference. But this would be a *post hoc* approval, not an understanding in virtue of which the subject makes the relevant transition itself. The structure of Byrne's account requires that the basic transition be from a proposition sheerly about the world to a proposition about the subject's own mind, and this appears to require that the subject's disposition to make this transition must be automatic, not rational.

15. Note that, although the English verb 'will' is ambiguous between will$_I$ and will$_{BF}$, we do have verbal forms that strongly favor the former reading. If a person declares either 'I shall ϕ' or (more colloquially) 'I am going to ϕ', this normally expresses a present intention to ϕ. I submit that Byrne's INT-schema is initially attractive precisely because we are inclined to read the premise as tantamount to *I shall ϕ*.

16. Peacocke suggests that it is specifically an 'action awareness' (Peacocke 1998, 88, elaborated in Peacocke 2008), but this will not be crucial for the issue that concerns us.

17. Cf. Peacocke (1998), 71–3, 88–90. Peacocke goes on to acknowledge that there may be cases in which a subject self-ascribes a belief without an intervening act of conscious judgment, but he holds that, even in such cases, the subject's warrant will rest, not sheerly on her belief that p, but on the fact that she would have consciously judged that p if she had considered the question (cf. the 'requirement of first-order ratifiability' discussed at Peacocke 1998, 93–4). This complication will not matter for our purposes.

18. Nico Silins has defended a similar view, which he explicitly contrasts with Byrne's approach in this respect. Cf. Silins (2012), 304, fn. 12 and 306, fn. 17.
19. Cf. Silins (2012), 309, fn. 20.
20. I will follow the common practice of speaking of 'states' of consciousness, though Sartre himself would reject this mode of expression as implying a kind of passivity that is foreign to consciousness (cf. Sartre (1962), 61–8/45–51 and 109n/15n). It will be useful to have some common noun designating the sort of thing exemplified when a subject is conscious of something, and I think the term 'state' is innocuous once its potentially misleading connotations have been flagged.
21. To avoid outright paradox, Sartre places the 'of' in parentheses when he speaks of non-positional consciousness (of) consciousness (cf. Sartre (1956) liv/20). But this maneuver is obviously of no help without an explanation of this other mode of aboutness.
22. This is true even if we add a self-referential device to the reformulation, as in

(1c) I will$_{BF}$ hereby ϕ because I now intend to ϕ. (cf. Setiya 2012)

Adding 'hereby' marks the fact that my now representing this causal connection will contribute to making the relevant connection to obtain, but it is clear that even this more complex thought might express a disengaged observation about the causal relationship between various facts, rather than an intent to make things so. (On another reading, perhaps, the 'hereby' itself expresses what we have been using 'will$_i$' to express: that I resolve to make things so. But if this is what 'hereby' expresses, then it does not contribute to an account of the intention-expressing 'will$_i$' in terms of independently-intelligible materials; it is simply an alternative marker of the relevant mode of representation.)
23. Cf. Evans (1982), Ch. 6, esp. 170–176 and 192–196.
24. The presupposition of her thought may of course be false: her representation *this cat* may express a merely apparent awareness of a cat. More would need to be said in a full account of our warrant for self-ascriptions of factive and non-factive perceptual states. More would also need to be said to account for the ways in which we can acquire reflective knowledge of the specific sensory modality involved in a given perception, of which properties are perceived, etc. I believe all this can be done. Here I am just trying to illustrate the basic Sartrean strategy in accounting for transparent knowledge of one's own perceiving.
25. Note that, although we have developed this point with reference to an example in which a subject deliberates, the occurrence of deliberation is not essential to our account. What is crucial is that the subject's believing involves non-positional awareness of her holding a question to be closed. In a subject capable of considering propositional questions, such awareness will characterize all beliefs, even those about which the subject does not deliberate.
26. This essay was originally written for the 2013 SPAWN Conference on "Transparency of Mind" at SyracuseUniversity. I am very grateful to André Gallois for inviting me to this event and to Amy Kind for her insightful comments on the paper. The paper has remained in gestation for so long that I fear I'm not able to recall all the people who have helped me with it, but I recall particular debts to Dorit Bar-On, Alex Byrne, Matthias Haase, David Hunter, Béatrice Longuenesse, John McDowell, Dick Moran, Sarah Paul, and Kieran Setiya.

References

Bar-On, D. 2004. *Speaking My Mind*. Oxford: Oxford University Press.

Boyle, M. 2011. "Transparent Self-Knowledge." *Proceedings of the Aristotelian Society* Supplementary Volume LXXXV, 223–240. doi:10.1186/1556-276X-6-223

Byrne, A. 2005. "Introspection." *Philosophical Topics* 33 (1): 79–104. doi:10.5840/philtopics20053312.

Byrne, A. 2011. "Transparency, Belief, Intention." *Proceedings of the Aristotelian Society* Supplementary Volume LXXXV, 201–221.

Byrne, A. 2012. "Knowing What I See." In *Introspection and Consciousness*, edited by D. Smithies and D. Stoljar, 183–210. New York: Oxford University Press.

Byrne, A. 2018. *Transparency and Self-Knowledge*. Oxford: Oxford University Press.

Dretske, F. 2003. "How Do You Know You are Not a Zombie?." In *Privileged Access: Philosophical Accounts of Self-Knowledge*, edited by B. Gertler. Aldershot: Ashgate 1–13.

Dretske, F. 2012. "Awareness and Authority: Skeptical Doubts about Self-Knowledge." In *Introspection and Consciousness*, edited by D. Smithies and D. Stoljar, 49–64.New York: Oxford University Press.

Evans, G. 1982. *The Varieties of Reference*. Oxford: Oxford University Press.

Finkelstein, D. 2001. *Expression and the Inner*. Cambridge, Mass: Harvard University Press.

Gallois, A. 1996. *The World Without, the Mind Within*. Cambridge: Cambridge University Press.

Moran, R. 1999. "The Authority of Self-Consciousness." *Philosophical Topics* 26 (1–2): 179–200. doi:10.5840/philtopics1999261/242.

Moran, R. 2001. *Authority and Estrangement*. Princeton: Princeton University Press.

Peacocke, C. 2008. *Truly Understood*. Oxford: Oxford University Press.

Peacocke, C. 1998. "Conscious Attitudes, Attention, and Self-Knowledge." In *Knowing Our Own Minds*, edited by C. Wright, B. Smith, and C. MacDonald. Oxford: Oxford University Press.

Sartre, J. P. 1943. *L'Être et le Néant*. Paris: Éditions Gallimard.

Sartre, J. P. 1956. *Being and Nothingness*. Trans. H. Barnes. New York: Philosophical Library.

Sartre, J. P. 1962. *The Transcendence of the Ego*. New York: Farrar: Straus and Giroux.

Sartre, J. P. 1966. *La Transcendence De l'Ego*. Paris: Librairie Philosophique J. Vrin.

Setiya, K. 2012. "Knowledge of Intention." In *Essays on Anscombe's Intention*, edited by A. Ford, J. Hornsby, and F. Stoutland, 64–97. Cambridge, Mass: Harvard University Press.

Shah, N., and J. D. Velleman. 2005. "Doxastic Deliberation." *Philosophical Review* 114 (4): 497–534. doi:10.1215/00318108-114-4-497.

Silins, N. 2012. "Judgment as a Guide to Belief." *In Smithies and Stoljar* 2012.

Weiskrantz, L. 1986. *Blindsight: A Case Study and Its Implications*. Oxford: Oxford University Press.

Index

Achtung 98
act-independent contents 27, 29
active self 94, 98–99
agential approach to self-knowledge
85–86, 108–109, 135n1; Kant on
111–113, 131; and transparency
110–111
Allison, Henry 40n39, 79n3, 79n5,
80n8, 102n13
Ameriks, Karl 65–66, 81n15
analytic cognition 118, 123
analytic principle 75–76, 81–82n20
analytic unity: of apperception 28, 30,
81n19; of the 'I think' 75, 89; of pure
apperception 89
a posteriori principle 118–119
appearance 41n45, 71–73, 94–95, 99;
and existence 31, 33, 41n42, 71; of
intelligence 71, 77–78; of ourselves
30, 69, 74, 93, 97, 98; perceptual
appearances 140–141, 147; and
sensations 115, 119, 125, 128–129;
and things in themselves, distinction
between 95
apperception: analytic unity 28, 30,
81n19, 89; empirical apperception
18–19, 21, 29–34, 31, 32; original
apperception 25, 74, 125; original-
synthetic unity of 41n44, 76–77, 82n22,
87–89, 92, 109, 113–114, 118, 121, 124,
127–129, 128, 131–132, 133–134; pure
apperception *see* pure apperception;
synthetic unity of 89; transcendental
apperception *see* transcendental
apperception; transcendental unity of
103n17, 112–114; unity of 77
a priori: efficient cause a priori 68, 71–72;
and existence 96
a priori concepts 122, 127
a priori consciousness 117

a priori entitlements 110–111, 127, 135n2
a priori principles 118–119, 120, 124,
126; purely intellectual a priori
principles 127
a priori warrant 108–109, 134–135; for
principles of thinking 132–133
Aristotle 34, 39n31
Armstrong, D.M. 14–15n2
assertion 1–2; and belief 4, 7, 8, 9, 10–11,
162; deliberate assertions 15n9; and
doxastic justification 10; elements 53;
honest assertions 2–14, 15n13; and
judgment 39n25, 39n26, 52–53; and
mental utterance 53; by mistake 8–9;
norms for 2–4, 7–8; as rules 3; sincere
assertion 53–55, 58–59, 61n12; and
truth 9–10
assertoric force 53
a-temporal mental act 125, 126, 132
attitudes 1, 6, 14, 15n4, 108, 112, 146;
doxastic attitudes 3; practical attitude
159; propositional attitudes 45, 48;
on questions 162–163; and self-
knowledge 85, 112, 136n10; *see also*
belief; desires
autonomy 67, 72

Barz, Wolfgang 60n1
Beck, J.S. 137n16
being in the world 20, 21, 22, 23, 36n5,
36n7, 37n12; identifying oneself
with 36n7
belief(s) 1–2, 45–47, 56, 108, 142, 143–146,
145, 148–149, 162–163; acting from the
point of view of 5–6, 7, 8, 11, 13, 52; and
assertion 2–4, 7, 8, 9, 10–11, 162; about
belief 5; belief-forming method 56–58;
clairvoyant's beliefs 50–51; consciously
believing 113, 131, 146; about external
world 52; first-person belief ascriptions

140; first-person knowledge 12; about future 151; grasp of 12; and honest assertion 3–7; and judgment 48–49, 59–60; and knowledge 15n4; non-empirical knowledge of 13–14; from the point of view of 5–7; rationally permissible beliefs 50–51; second-order belief 4, 6; self-ascriptions of 12, 14, 112, 113, 131, 140, 153–154, 165n17; and self-knowledge 85, 135n1; tacit knowledge of 156; third-personal beliefs 6; as third-personally known 12; transparency as inference from judgment to belief 152–154; transparency of 110–111, 136n7; and truth 8–9

Boghossian, P. 49

BonJour, Laurence 50–51

Boyle, Matthew 38n19, 41n41, 51–52, 60, 61n8, 85, 88, 101–102n8, 136n7, 136n10

Burge, Tyler 110–111, 112, 135n2, 136n10

Byrne, Alex, on transparency 50–51, 58, 60, 155, 158, 163, 165n11, 165n12, 165n14; Boyle's criticism of 51, 60; doxastic transparency 153; as inference from world to mind 147–152

Campbell, L. 61n8

Carruthers, Peter 15n2

Cassam, Quassim 15n2, 93

closed question 162–163

cognition 73, 95, 100n2, 109, 112, 113, 122–123, 130, 136n9, 136n11, 149; analytic cognition 118, 123; capacity of 119, 120–121, 122, 123, 135n4; empirical cognition 67; higher capacity of 119, 122–123, 135–136n4; intellectual form of 120, 126, 127; and 'I think' 137n15; lower capacity of 123; moral cognition 67, 72; objective validity of 26, 27–28, 75; practical cognition 96–97, 105n27, 105n29; and principles 118–119, 120, 126, 134; pure apperception as 100n2, 102n13, 130, 132; rational cognition 112–113; relation to an object 25–26, 27–28, 75, 87, 128–129, 137n17; and representation 135–136n4; and self-knowledge 84–85, 86, 88, 90–92, 100, 113, 131; spontaneity of 133; theoretical cognition 39n21, 84–85, 96–97, 105n29, 132, 133; and transcendental apperception 91–92; see also concepts; intuitions

combination of manifold 115, 117–118; concept of 117–118; in general 115, 116, 117, 119, 121–124, 131, 132; of intuition 117; of representations 117, 119; see also syntheses

Concept Possession Requirement 156

concepts 90, 112, 117–118, 122, 136n9, 136n11

conceptualism/non-conceptualism debate 82n22

conclusion 1, 13, 47–48, 55, 57–58, 61n12, 62n15, 145, 149–150, 162

consciously believing 113, 131, 146

consciousness 22–23, 28, 30–31, 35, 37n14, 112, 130–131; of being in the sense of being true 27; de se consciousness 113, 117, 120, 127–128, 129, 130, 131, 136n12, 137n15; determinate consciousness 98; double consciousness 93, 104n23; of the 'I' 88, 90; individual consciousness 36n5; intellectual consciousness 126, 127, 131; and judgments 26; Kant on 81n18; logical consciousness 120, 131; of myself 75–76; non-positional consciousness see non-positional consciousness; non-thetic consciousness 22–23; nothingness of 23; of objective unity 28; positional self-consciousness 32, 156–158; a prior de se consciousness 113; a priori consciousness 117; Sartre on 32, 37n14, 142–143; and sensibility 90; states of 166n20; temporal consciousness 32; thetic consciousness 20; of thinking 27; transcendental consciousness 94, 130; unity of 104n24; see also self-consciousness

constitutivism 13–14

contents 26–27, 101n8, 142

critical reasoner 108, 110–111, 112, 135n2, 136n7, 136n10

Critique of Practical Reason 65, 68–69, 70, 71, 72, 78–79, 79–80n5, 81n16, 97

Critique of Pure Reason: A-*Critique* 65, 66, 74; B-*Critique* 65, 66, 67, 73–74, 78, 87, 111

Dancy, Jonathan 5

deliberate assertion 15n9

deliberation 47, 56, 101n6, 144, 146, 147, 163, 166n25; doxastic deliberation 45, 46; process of 47, 48, 53

deliberative stance 101n6, 144–145, 146

demonstrative reference 160–161

Descartes, René 114, 121
de se: consciousness 113, 117, 120, 127–128, 129, 130, 131, 136n12, 137n15; a priori warrant 109, 133; representation 128
desires 45, 77, 85, 141, 144
determinability 33–34
determinable self 93, 94
determinate consciousness 98
determination 32–33, 38n19, 41n42, 67, 103n19, 120–121, 137n15; of beliefs 141, 143–145, 152; of existence 31, 34, 90–91, 96, 99; of self-attitude 85; self-determination 34, 42n51, 92; of self-knowledge 101n6; and time 31; by transcendental I 34
determined thinking 116–117, 119–120, 124–127, 129, 131, 133
determining self 93, 94
determinism 11, 73, 98–99
dignity 67, 79
discursive understanding 119, 120–121, 126, 135
double consciousness 93, 104n23
doxastic attitudes 3
doxastic deliberation 45–46
doxastic justification 10, 11
doxastic self-attribution 14
doxastic self-knowledge 1–2, 6, 46, 58, 145; achievement process 48–49, 50, 52, 57–58, 59; and empirical conception 9–10, 12–13, 14–15n2; and evidence 9; and honesty 3; role of seeming-truth in 12; self-conscious conception of 14; transparency of 12–13
doxastic transparency 12–13, 143–144, 146, 153

Edgley, Roy 136n5
efficient cause a priori 68, 71–72
empirical apperception 18–19, 21, 29–34
empirical awareness 10n10, 25
empirical conception, of doxastic self-knowledge 8, 9–10, 12–13, 14–15n2
empirical ego 20, 23
empirical I 19, 21, 22, 30, 32–33, 35, 36n7; emptiness of 32, 41n44; identification with spatio-temporal perspective 32–33; intelligibility 19; of 'I think' 21; as object of experience 30; and pure apperception 20; of theoretical cognition 39n21; and thinking 34; and transcendental I 24, 30, 35; transparency of 33

empirical intuition 33–34, 41n44, 96, 115, 129
empirical knowledge 1–2, 14n2, 94
empirical self 19, 35, 97–99
empirical self-awareness 32, 42n50
empirical self-consciousness 99
Engstrom, Stephen 39n22
Enoch, D. 56, 57, 58, 61–62n15
epistemic rule 50
Erkenntnis 86, 90, 100n2
Evans, Gareth 32–33, 136n12, 147, 148, 153; on bodily self-awareness in inner sense 36n6; on self-ascription 110, 113, 140–141, 142; on self-identification 37n11; on self-locating thoughts 36n7; on transparency approach to self-knowledge 46, 47; on transparency of doxic self-knowledge 12–13, 14; on transparency of empirical apperception 32; on transparency of pure apperception 20–22, 23
evidence: -based account of outward-oriented mental activity 46–47; -based judgment 48–49; and doxastic self-knowledge 9; first-personal evidence 6, 7; knowledge grounded in 1–2, 6
existence 33–34, 102n15; and appearance 31, 33, 41n42, 71; determination of 31, 34, 90–91, 96, 99; intuition of 42n51; Kantian category of 33; metaphysical ground of 71; and a priori 96; sensible existence 71, 75, 77, 78, 79
experiences 24, 31, 45, 74, 119, 122, 125; of moral obligations 71–72, 81n13; perceptual experience 142, 160; and pure apperception 87, 88; of thinking 103n18
externalism 57, 61n15, 142
extrospection 46

false judgment 26, 39n23
Fichte, J.G. 95–96, 104–105n25, 105n27
first-order judgment 49, 51, 60; transition to second-order judgment, inherent rationality of 51–52, 53, 62n15
first-personal evidence 6, 7
first-person ascriptions, of perceptual appearances 140–141
first-person authority 2, 14n2
first-person belief ascriptions 140
first-person knowledge: authority of 84, 85–86, 87, 142; of beliefs 12; immediacy and authority of 85

INDEX

first-person perspective 20
first-person plurality 35
first-person self-awareness 31
first-person standpoint 22, 26, 36n5, 37n12
freedom 24, 68, 70, 73, 78, 81n13, 81n16; and autonomy 67; concept of 67–68; and determinism 73; positive and negative 79n4
free will 11, 75, 105n32

Gertler, B. 14n1
Ginsborg, H. 103–104n21
Goldberg, S. 15n3
Groundwork of the Metaphysics of Morals 65–66, 74, 78, 79n3, 79n5, 80–81n13, 80n6, 80n12, 81n15, 97, 99
Groundwork of the Metaphysics of Morals II 81n14
Groundwork of the Metaphysics of Morals III 66–67, 75; problem of 67–68, 72–73; solution to problem of 68–72
Guyer, Paul 79n4

Hegel, Georg Wilhelm Friedrich 105n32
Heidegger, M. 41n48
Henrich, Dieter 137n20, 137n21
honest assertion 2–3, 15n13; and articulation 8; and beliefs 3–6; phenomenal seeming 10–11; from the point of view of a belief 6–7; speaker-world relation 7–8; and truth 8–9
Hornsby, Jennifer 39n28

'I' 19, 21, 58, 75–76, 86, 89–90, 93–94, 94–95, 97, 102n9; accessibility 97; characteristics of 91; consciousness of 87, 88, 90, 93; doubling of 24, 93–94; of empirical apperception 34; empirical I *see* empirical I; of inner sense 94; as intelligence 95; of non-thetic self-consciousness 23; as object of awareness 20–22, 93; of pure apperception 94; pure self-activity of 95, 97–98; subject 22–23; transcendental I *see* transcendental I
'Ich denke' 121
indeterminate intuition 33–34, 42n51
individual consciousness 36n5
inference 51, 56, 57–58, 109, 113, 131, 146; from judgment to belief, transparency as 152–154; from world to mind, transparency as 147–152
inferential justification 59, 62n17
inferential knowledge 15n2

inner perception model 84, 87, 88, 101n4
inner sense 18–19, 29, 31–32, 40n39, 41n45, 74, 98, 102n9, 104n22, 126, 133; bodily self-awareness in 36n6; 'I' of 94, 95, 97; and judgment 49–50, 77; Kant on 29, 30–31, 33, 41n42, 101n8, 102n9, 103n18, 104n22; ourselves as objects of 39n40, 41n41, 87, 89–90, 93, 94; and outer sense 25, 30; and pure apperception 86, 88, 92, 93, 94, 100, 130; and representations 113, 126–127, 131, 133, 137; and self-consciousness 74, 87, 88; and self-knowledge 85, 86; spatial perspective 42n50; and time 76; in Transcendental Aesthetic context 87; and transcendental apperception 21; *see also* self-consciousness
intellectual consciousness 126, 127, 131
intellectual form 114, 119–120; of act of thinking 121, 124, 126, 132, 133; of cognition 120; of pure thinking of thing 120
intellectual intuition 70, 95–96, 104–105n25, 105n27
intellectual synthesis 127
intelligence 71–72, 73, 75, 77–78, 91–92, 95, 97
intelligible cause 70
intelligible world 69–72, 75–77, 80n8, 81n14
intention/intentionality 24, 38n19, 85, 150, 157, 158–160; sense of 'will' based on 150; and thinking 25
introspection 6–7, 8–9, 12, 13, 14, 46, 148
intuitions 31, 88, 112, 136n9, 136n11; indeterminate intuition 33–34, 42n51
'I think' 18, 20–21, 23, 40n38, 75, 81n19, 89, 103n17, 110, 137n15; accompanying representations 75, 89, 109, 111–112, 114, 121–124, 127, 129; analytic unity of 89; empty forms 28, 39–40n33; empty representation 23; formal concept 28, 30; I of 28; objective unity 28; objects of 30; in Transcendental Deduction 74–75

judgments 75, 88, 92–93, 115, 131, 150, 152–153; act of judging and content judged, distinction between 27; and assertion 39n25, 39n26, 52–53; and beliefs 48–49, 59–60, 152–154; and consciousness 26; copula 'is' in 25, 27–28; emptiness of logical functions of judging 40n33; evidence-based and spontaneous, differences between 48–49; about external world and one's own mind 49; false judgment 26, 39n23; first-order judgment 49, 51, 60; first- to second-order judgment transition 51–52, 53, 62n15; inner sense 49–50, 77; Kant on 18, 27, 39n26; as mental analog to making an assertion 52–53; about mental states 49; objective validity 25–26; phenomenology of 154; problematic judgments 39n26; second-order judgments 49, 50–52, 53, 57, 58, 59–60, 61–62n15; and self-ascriptions 151, 152, 164; spontaneous judgment 47–48; transparency as inference from judgment to belief 152–154; true judgment 26, 27, 50

Kant, Immanuel 19, 36n7, 39–40n33, 39n21, 41n41, 41n44, 65, 68; on agential approach to self-knowledge 111–113, 131; analytic claim 75; B-Transcendental Deduction 25, 66, 73, 74–78, 111, 134; on category of existence 33; claim that there is no 'doubling' of I's 24; on cognitive role of self-consciousness 66–67; on consciousness 81n18; *Critique of Practical Reason* 65, 68–69, 70, 71, 72, 78–79, 79–80n5, 81n16, 97; *Critique of Pure Reason,* first edition 65, 66, 74; *Critique of Pure Reason,* second editing 65, 66, 67, 73–74, 78, 87, 111; on empirical apperception 19; on existence category of 33; on freedom 67–68; on inner sense 29, 30–31, 33, 41n42, 101n8, 102n9, 103n18, 104n22; on 'I think' 18, 20–21, 23, 30; on judgments 18, 27, 39n26; on outer sense 29, 31; *Paralogisms* 28, 66–67, 74, 87, 91; practical philosophy of 97–98; on problematic judgments 39n26; on pure apperception 18, 19, 20; and Sartre, comparison of approaches 22–23; on self-consciousness 18, 66–67; on self-determination 42n51; on sensations 114, 128; on soul 65–66; on syntheses 75–77, 82n22, 114; on temporally extended acts of the mind 32; on transcendental apperception 18, 22, 25–29, 88, 99; Transcendental Deduction 66–67, 74, 135; Transcendental Deduction, B-edition 25, 66, 73, 74–78, 111, 134;

on truth 25; world of understanding and intelligible world, distinguishing between 80n8
Khurana, Thomas 105n30
Kitcher, Patricia 41n47, 112–114, 131, 136n6, 136n11, 136n12
knowledge norm 2, 7–8
Korsgaard, Christine 37n12

Leibnizian identity 137n20, 137n21
logical consciousness 120, 131
Longuenesse, Béatrice 36n4, 41n47, 47n41, 102n10
luminosity 45

Marcus, Eric 61n8
McDowell, John 26, 27, 37n11
meaning 54
mental analog 52–53, 54
mental noticing 54
mental representations 50, 77
mental sentences 53, 56, 61n9
mental states 1, 44, 45, 51–52, 145, 148–150, 158–159, 164–165n2; inferences from 131; judgment about 49; knowledge of 141; self-ascriptions of 20, 38n19, 41n47, 148, 152, 155, 163; and transcendental unity of apperception 112–113; and transparent self-knowledge 145, 146–147
mental utterances 53–60; authorship 56–57, 61n11
mental words 53, 61n9
Metaphysics of Morals 78
mind-independent world-fact 21, 29
misinterpretation 2, 13
moral constraint 72
morality 65, 67, 69
moral laws 65, 68, 72, 75, 76, 77, 81n13, 98
moral obligations 71–72, 78, 81n13
moral principle 67
moral self-assessment 68
Moran, Richard 12, 37n12, 37n18, 38n19, 46, 48, 84, 101n6, 110, 112, 136n7, 136n10; on transparency versus alienation 143–147

Narboux, Jean-Philippe 37n17
necessary relation (*Beziehung*) 75, 76, 77, 121, 124–125, 130
non-empirical self-knowledge 9, 13–14
non-mental world 141–142, 147–148, 153, 155, 161–162

INDEX

non-positional consciousness 157,
161–162; of self-consciousness
142, 156–158; and transparency
158–163
non-positional self-awareness 164
non-thetic consciousness 22–23
non-thetic I 24, 34
non-thetic self-awareness 38n19
non-thetic self-consciousness 23,
37n15, 38
nothingness 34; of consciousness 23; of
empirical I 32, 41n44; of 'I think' 23,
28, 39–40n33; of logical functions of
judging 40n33; of representation 23;
of transcendental I 32, 41n44

object-ego 24
objective knowledge 22, 87, 88
objective sensation 114–115, 129
objective validity 25, 26, 27, 39n30,
40n34, 87, 101n5; of cognition 26,
27–28; non-accidental truth 27; of
principle of contradiction 137n17;
a priori 135
objective world 20, 21, 22, 30
object of thought 20, 30, 34, 38n19
obligation 71–72, 78, 81n13, 105n31
O'Neill, Onora 80n10
open question 162–163
original apperception 25, 74, 125
original-synthetic unity: of apperception
41n44, 76–77, 82n22, 87–89, 92, 109,
113–114, 118, 121, 124, 127–129,
131–132, 133–134; of representations
29; *see also* syntheses
outer sense 19, 25, 29, 31–32, 34, 36n6,
77, 104n22
outward-oriented mental activity 46, 47

Paralogisms 28, 66–67, 74, 87, 91
Peacocke, Christopher 60n4, 155, 165n16,
165n17; on transparency as inference
from judgment to belief 152–154
perceptions 24, 31, 33, 41n47, 58, 112,
147, 155, 160–161, 164, 166n24;
agent's perspective on future 152; 'I'
as object of 19, 88, 94, 103n19; inner
perception model 84, 87, 88, 101n4;
and inner sense 29; and judgment 142;
participant's perspective 152; sensory
perceptions 24, 46, 129
perceptual appearances 144, 147;
first-person ascriptions of 140–141
perceptual experiences 45, 142, 160–162
perceptual judgments 111, 115

person, concept of 36n5
phenomenal seeming 10
phenomenal transparency 45–46
Pippin, Robert 102n13
Plato 29
Pollok, K. 81–82n20
positional self-consciousness 32,
156–158; and non-positional self-
consciousness, distinction between
156–158
practical cognition 39n21, 96–97,
105n27, 105n29
practical philosophy 97–98, 99, 100
practical reason 68, 86
practical self-consciousness 86, 105n32
practical self-relation 85
pragmatic indispensability 56–57
primary truth-bearers 27, 40n37
principles 118; of contradiction 118, 119,
122, 123, 137n17; of thinking 116, 118,
119, 120, 122, 125, 128
privileged self-knowledge 141
proper self 97–99
propositional attitudes 45–46
psychological knowledge 142
public utterances 54–55
pure apperception 19, 35, 74, 87, 100n2,
101n6, 102n13, 114, 116–117, 118, 124,
125–126, 130; agential aspect in 97,
101n6; agential self-relation of 101n6;
analytic unity of 89; as cognition
100n2, 102n13, 130, 132; and empirical
I 20; and experiences 87, 88; human
being cognizing itself through 102n14;
and inner sense 86, 88, 92, 93, 94, 100,
130; 'I' of 94; obscurity of 129–131; and
self-cognition 92; synthetic activity
89–90; in Transcendental Analytic
context 87; and transparency 87;
transparency of 19, 20–24, 25, 35
pure intuitions 104–105n25, 125
purely intellectual concept 122–123
purely intellectual principles 126,
131, 133
purely intellectual self-consciousness 127
purely logical conditions 124
pure practical self 99
pure self-activity 69, 97
pure understanding 109, 119,
121–122, 123

rational cognition 112–113
rational intelligibility 149
rationality 51, 56, 57
rationally permissible beliefs 50–51

reasons 29, 35, 67–68, 79–80n5, 80n6, 98, 144
reflection/reflective approach 51–52, 61n8, 119–120; to transparent self-knowledge 155–156
reflective knowledge 143, 158, 161, 163, 166n24
representations 31, 50, 75, 77, 111–112, 114–115, 117, 122, 128; and cognition 135–136n4; combination of manifold of 117, 119; de se representation 128; empty representation 23; and inner sense 113, 126–127, 131, 133, 137; 'I think' accompanying 75, 89, 109, 111–112, 114, 121–124, 127, 129; original-synthetic unity 29; self-ascriptions of 111–112, 113, 131; and transcendental synthesis 90
respect 67, 105n30
Rödl, Sebastian 40n36, 41n43
rules 3, 109, 118, 120
Ryle, Gilbert 14–15n2, 45

sameness 24, 41n46; of the I with anything it thinks 30, 35; of the transcendental and empirical I's 30–31, 35, 39n21
Sartre, Jean-Paul 19, 22–24, 32, 33, 37n14, 37n15, 37n18, 38n19, 142–143, 163–164, 166n20; on consciousness 37n14; and Kant, comparison of approaches 22–23; on non-positional consciousness 142–143; on non-thetic I 24, 34; on non-thetic self-consciousness 37n15; on positional consciousness 32; and reflectivism 156–158; on transcendental apperception 22–23; on transparency of pure apperception 20; on transparency of the empirical I 33
Schechter, J. 56, 57, 58, 61–62n15
second-order belief 4, 6
second-order judgments 49, 50–52, 53, 57, 58, 59, 61–62n15; and permanent inferential justification 60
seeming contradiction 72–73
seeming-to-be-true 10
seeming-truth in doxastic self-knowledge 12, 15n13
self-affection 30, 31–32, 41n43, 77
self-ascriptions 21, 23, 34, 152, 166n24; of belief 12, 14, 112, 113, 131, 140, 153–154, 165n17; and judgment 151, 152, 164; of mental states 20, 38n19, 41n47, 155, 163; of representation

111–112, 113, 131; see also 'I think'
self-awareness 93–94, 101n8, 152, 164; bodily self-awareness in inner sense 36n6; empirical 31–32, 42n50; first-personal self-awareness 31; non-positional 158, 164; non-thetic self-awareness 38; tacit self-awareness 52; thetic self-awareness 38; and time 33; virtual self-awareness 52
self-consciousness 21, 66, 74, 78, 79, 81n16, 88, 104, 113, 130; doxastic self-knowledge conception 14; empirical self-consciousness 99; formal self-consciousness 21; and inner sense 74, 87, 88; Kant on 18, 66–67; non-positional consciousness of 142, 156–158; non-thetic self-consciousness 23, 37n15, 38; positional self-consciousness 32, 156–158; practical self-consciousness 86, 105n32; of pure apperception 91; purely intellectual self-consciousness 127; Sartre on non-thetic self-consciousness 37n15; thetic self-consciousness 38n19; transparency 23; without self-reference 20; see also inner sense; pure apperception
self-determination 34, 78; and intuition of existence 42n51
self-identification 24
self-intimation 45
self-knowledge 1–2, 7, 14–15n2, 49, 51, 100n2, 101n6, 103n17, 108, 110; agential approach to 85–86, 108–109, 110–113, 131, 135n1; and attitudes 85, 112, 136n10; and beliefs 85, 135n1; cognition 84–85, 86, 88, 90–92, 100, 113, 131; determination of 101n6; doxastic self-knowledge see doxastic self-knowledge; epistemic entitlement to 135n2; and honest assertion 9; as inferential knowledge 15n2; and inner sense 85, 86; interpretive account of 15n2; kinds of 85; and mental states 145, 146–147; non-empirical self-knowledge 9, 13–14; practical stance 85; privileged self-knowledge 141; theoretical cognition 84–85; transparency approach to 8–9, 15n9, 46–40, 52, 54, 58, 110–111; transparent self-knowledge 13, 14, 141, 143–149, 152, 154, 155–156, 163; unity of 99
self-locating thought 21, 36n6, 36n7
self-reference 20, 21, 36n7

self-relation 88, 92, 93, 96; agential 86, 101n6; practical 85, 86; theoretical 99
self-thought 120, 126, 129
sensations 31, 101n8, 112, 122, 123, 124; Kant on 114, 128; objective sensation 114–115, 129; self-knowledge of 85, 86, 88, 92–93, 136n10; subjective perceptions 129
sensibility 69, 74, 90, 101, 123, 125, 129; and consciousness 90; fundamental form of 76; and synthesis 77
sensible existence 71, 75, 77, 78, 79
sensible intuitions 77, 95, 102n13, 104n24, 109, 122, 123
Shah, Nishi 46, 47
Silins, Nico 166n18
sincere assertion 53–55, 58–59, 61n12
Smith, Norman Kemp 100n2
soul 65–66
spatio-temporal framework 20, 21, 32–33, 34, 40n35, 41n45, 76, 82n22, 104n21
spectatorial stance 84, 143, 145, 146–147, 149, 151, 152, 154, 159
spontaneity 65–66, 86, 87, 91, 98, 101n8, 124–125; and apperception 74; of cognition 109, 132, 133; and pure apperception 118, 127, 128, 129, 130; of understanding 74, 77
spontaneous judgment 47–48, 59
spontaneous knowledge 41n43
Strawson, P. 21, 36n5, 37n9
syntheses 75–76, 101n5, 104n24, 115–116, 121; and cognition 39n29; of imagination 34, 41n45, 42n50, 77, 123; and judgment 27, 28; Kant on 75–77, 82n22, 114; of representations 27, 90, 117–118, 124; self-conscious synthesis 89; of understanding 82n22, 88–89, 90; see also combination of manifold; original-synthetic unity

tacit awareness 60
tacit knowledge 143, 155–156, 158
tacit self-awareness 51–52, 60
temporal consciousness 32
temporal intuition 32, 34
temporally extended acts 25, 31–32
theoretical cognition 39n2, 84, 96–97, 105n29, 132, 133
thetic consciousness 20
thetic self-consciousness 38n19
third-personal beliefs 6
time: and inner sense 76; and intuition 76–77; and space see spatio-temporal

framework; time-determinations 31, 40n35
Timmermann, Jens 79n3
transcendental apperception 18–19, 20, 22–23, 32, 35, 41n47, 91–92; and empirical apperception 21; Kant on 25–29, 88, 99
transcendental consciousness 94, 130
Transcendental Deduction 66–67, 74, 135; B-edition 25, 66, 73, 74–78, 111, 134
transcendental I 21, 24, 29, 30, 34, 35, 38n19, 39–40n33, 40; emptiness of 32, 41n44
transcendental idealism 22, 94
transcendental logic 23, 26, 103n17, 120, 131
transcendental subject 29, 123, 125, 130, 133, 137n20, 137n21
transcendental synthesis: of the imagination 77; of manifold of the representations 90
transcendental unity of apperception 103n17, 112–114
transparency 18, 44–45, 101n6, 136n7; of beliefs 110–111; and agential approach to self-knowledge 110–111; versus alienation 143–147; Byrne on 50–51, 58, 60, 147–152, 153, 155, 158, 163, 165n11, 165n12, 165n14; of doxastic deliberation 46; of doxastic self-knowledge 12–13; doxastic transparency 12–13, 143–144, 146, 153; of empirical I 12–13, 14, 20–22, 23, 32, 33, 46, 47, 136n12; as inference from judgment to belief 152–154; as inference from world to mind 147–152; Moran on 143–147; and non-positional consciousness 158–163; notion of 45–48; Peacocke on 152–154; phenomenal transparency 45–46; as phenomenon and as problem 140–143; problem of 142; and pure apperception 19, 20–24, 25, 35, 87; of pure apperception 19, 20–24, 25, 35; Sartre on 20, 33; self-consciousness 23
transparency, puzzle of 48–50; solution to 52–60
transparency approach to self-knowledge (TA) 8–9, 15n9, 46–40, 52, 54, 58, 110–111
transparent I 20, 21, 24
transparent self-knowledge 13, 14, 141, 143–149, 152, 154, 155–156, 163
truth 7–8, 40n35, 54–55, 58, 69, 110, 150–151, 153–154; and assertion

9–10, 11; and beliefs 7, 8–9, 51, 148; consciousness of 28; contexts of 40n35; empirical truths 28; and honest assertion 8–9; Kant on 25; non-accidental truth 27; objective validity 28, 39n30; primary truth-bearers 27, 40n37; seeming-truth 9–10, 12, 15n13; true judgment 10, 25, 26–27, 29, 50
truth-bearers 27, 28, 40n37
Tye, M. 45

understanding 25, 56, 77, 78, 88, 90, 98, 135–136n4; capacity of 59, 108, 109, 114, 116, 124, 126–128, 130, 132–133, 134; discursive understanding 119, 120–121, 126, 135; pure synthesis of 82n22; pure understanding 109, 119, 121–122, 123; self-understanding 6; spontaneity of 74, 77; syntheses of 82n22, 88–89, 90; world of 69–72, 75, 78, 80n8

uniformity assumption 85

Valaris, Markos 32–33, 40n40, 42n50
Velleman, David 46, 47
virtual self-awareness 52

Ware, Owen 79n1
'will' 150, 165n15; of blank futurity 150–151, 158–159; intuition-based sense of 150–151, 158–159, 166n22
Williamson, T. 45
Wittgenstein, L. 19, 31
Wood, Allen 79n3, 79n5
world-directed question 136n7, 136n12, 142, 144, 147, 161, 163
world of sense 69–75, 78, 105n31
world of understanding 69–72, 75, 78, 80n8

Zimmerman, Aaron 136n10